The Roger Caras Dog Book

ROGER CARAS

The Roger Caras Dog Book

THIRD EDITION

Principal Photography by
ALTON ANDERSON

Other photographs by
Amber Alliger, Jane B. Donahue, and Bette Isacoff

M. EVANS AND COMPANY, INC.
New York

For
Yankee, Penny, "T", Nel, Jeremy, Oomiac, Bridgitte, Tigger,
Ludo, Libby, Winnie, Peter, Tutu,
and lots of other friends standing square on four legs.

M. Evans and Company, Inc.
216 East 49th Street
New York, New York 10017

Library of Congress Cataloging-in-Publication Data
Caras, Roger A.
    [Dog book]
    The Roger Caras dog book : a complete guide to every AKC
breed / Roger Caras ; photographs by Alton Anderson. — 3rd ed.,
new & rev.
        p.   cm.
    Includes index.
    ISBN 0-87131-799-0
    I. Anderson, Alton.   II. Title.
SF426.C34   1996
636.7′1—dc20   95-52784
                                                            CIP

Typeset by Classic Type, Inc.

Manufactured in the United States of America

9 8 7 6 5 4 3 2 1

Contents

Author's Note

The descriptions that follow have been written to help potential but relatively inexperienced dog owners make breed selections best suited to their own life-styles. All the information in this book should be viewed in that light.

There are very few absolutes in this world, at least in my experience, and much of what follows is admittedly opinion. It is not my opinion alone, however. There has been input from dog handlers, judges, and breeders. John Mandeville, assistant to the president of the American Kennel Club, has read the manuscript and made valuable suggestions. Violent disagreements, though, should be directed to me alone. The final choice of language and each individual statement or assessment was mine alone to make.

Check the scaled characteristics. They are relative, of course, but again they are opinion *after* consultation. They suggest the amount of exercise and coat care a breed is likely to require and how well suited it is likely to be to an urban environment. Inevitably there will be readers whose personal experience with a representative of a breed will differ from that suggested by the scale. This is the old problem of absolutes again. The scales indicate the general rule one is likely to encounter when dealing with a breed.

A popularity ranking is listed for each breed. This number is derived from the population of dogs of that breed registered with the American Kennel Club in 1994. Again, it is not necessarily an absolute, but it is indicative.

A point of clarification: the word *dog* is used indiscriminately, both in these opening remarks and in other places in this book. In true canine parlance *dog* means male alone and *bitch* means female, just as *drake* is the male and *duck* is the female of the species. As used here, though, the generic *dog* means canine friend of either sex.

The superb photographs in this book are largely the work of one man, Alton Anderson. He has been called the Karsh of Canines. I rather think of Karsh as the Anderson of People. His work is representative of some of the finest dog photography ever done, and I am honored to share this volume with him. Unfortunately, Alton died before this new edition appeared. He is missed. To the other photographers who have added to Alton's work since the first edition, my gratitude.

The use of *Ch* before a dog's name means that he or she was a champion when the photograph was taken. If no *Ch* appears, the dog was probably on the way to becoming a champion. A champion is a dog who has won fifteen points in recognized shows. There are also stipulations about major shows—a major show is one in which a given minimum number does vary from breed to breed, and a show may well be a major for one breed but not for another.

Under most breeds there will be entered a breed club with an address. This address is almost invariably the home of an officer of the club and it can change as elections are held. You can check with the American Kennel Club at 51 Madison Avenue, New York City, NY 10038 for an update on a club's address.

Well over half the homes in the country have dogs as members of the family. Man has been keeping dogs for over twenty-five centuries, since well back into the time of the cave dwellers. There must be something to the idea, to the dog itself, and what it does to our hearts and our sense of belonging. My family owns nine dogs at the moment, and although I expect few of my readers to be mad enough to try that many companion animals at one time, I do hope many of you will find the help you need in the pages that follow, enough to select the one or two or three dogs best suited to you and best able to share a life-style with you. Happy reading but, above all, happy dog.

Introduction:
Owning a Dog

The most important aspect of dog ownership is original selection. Everything starts with your choice—all that is good and all that might turn out badly.

What then are the considerations? What is important for the prospective dog owner to know? Given an individual or a family on the one hand and the whole vast world of dogs on the other, the only way to proceed is by process of elimination. Let's see what you should consider, and how you should honestly assess your answers.

Point One: Should you own a dog at all? Not everyone should own a dog. Not even everyone who thinks they should! Dogs are meant for certain kinds of people. Before committing yourself, make certain you are one of them.

This is not to suggest that people who aren't right for dogs are themselves bad or deficient. It is essentially a matter of life-style. Does your life style allow you to accept the responsibility for another very dependent life? Dogs, unlike children, are never independent. From the day a dog enters your life until the day he leaves (and that can be fifteen years or even longer), he will be wholly dependent on you for all the essentials of canine treatment. As one who has owned not one but several dogs all his life, I do not see these matters as problems. They all are attended to without a second thought. But that is not necessarily the way it will be for everyone.

This is a book on dog selection, not a book on dog care or training. We must, though, touch on those matters briefly in this discussion of whether you as an individual should consider adding a dog to your life. Are you active physically? If you are, then there is an endless variety of dogs for you to select from—*if* you are willing to share your active physical time with your pet. If you are sedentary by nature or restricted in your activities, then you are either not a dog-owning candidate or a person who should choose from a smaller range of breeds.

Do you travel a great deal? If you do, who will care for your pet while you are away? Is your home empty all day and sometimes into the evening? Who will be a companion for your pet during those long hours? A dog is not a fixture, he is a companion, and only with companionship will your dog keep the promise of his breeding.

Are you the kind of person who will control your temper when a puppy breaks the rules? For all puppies do break all rules. They wet and mess in the house, they chew shoes, and they cry in the middle of the night. None of this need be a problem for the dog lover, because the dog can be trained away from each bad habit as it is revealed, just as children are trained. But as it is with children, you must be gentle and understanding, though firm. Is that you?

New dogs must be licensed and must get shots. All dogs must be fed every day (some more often than once). They must have clean water at all times, they must be given heartworm medicine during the mosquito season, they must be wormed periodically. They must also be checked for ticks in the summer, be exercised under control, have coats seen to, and be loved. Is all of that your thing?

I purposely have tried to stress the negatives here because to understate them would be a disservice to the people who are thinking of getting their first dog, and to the dog they might buy or adopt. None of these things need be problems or hardships when seen in the balance of pro and con, but they can be of considerable importance to some people.

What of that balance? What are the positive elements of dog ownership? Love and companionship head the list. Your dog will give you both without limit or qualification. No dog ever accused his owner of doing something wrong, of forgetting something, or complained of his mood. A dog just loves, no questions asked. In a world full of pressures, that is worth a great deal.

Dogs help children grow up into healthy adults. Dogs teach children a kind of love and responsibility that they can get nowhere else. We learn all kinds of love in this world from all kinds of sources: siblings, parents, grandparents, teachers, friends, playthings—and pets. Dogs have a brand of love all their own, and demonstrably children benefit from it.

Dogs are objects of pride. People talk about their dogs and show them off. You have seen that yourself, surely. Pride is worth something in hours of doubt. Your dog can be an "up" factor when everything else is "down."

I have known people so roughly treated by time and fate that a dog was all they had left in the world. I remember a very old man, a widower whose only child was either deceased or living on the other side of the world, I have forgotten which. The man was restricted in his physical abilities by poor health. His seventeen-year-old Boston Terrier was literally all that was left to him on this earth. The love that man knew for and from that dog was remarkable. I truly believe he would have gone quite mad without it. When the veterinarian finally convinced the old man that his dog had aged beyond help and really had to be put to sleep, the man stuffed papers under the kitchen door, turned on the gas from his range, and sat down with his friend in his arms. They went to sleep together.

I know a certain home for severely alienated alcoholics of the skid-row type. At the time these men (and sometimes boys) are admitted, they rarely are able to talk to each other, much less anyone who doesn't share their bitterness. They have hit bottom. As an initial phase of their treatment, they are given Labrador Retrievers to care for. It has been found that the dogs enable the men to bridge over into normal give-and-take relationships that they otherwise might find impossible to achieve. One man in that home told me that *his* dog was the first responsibility he ever had been able to accept without panicking. He also pointed out that *his* dog never asked him why he was a drunk and a "bum."

I visited a school for PINS (people in need of supervision). We used to call them juvenile delinquents. The boys live in cottages, twenty-four to a unit, and each unit raises a breed of dog. The boys do a fine job of it and learn not only how to trust something that loves them but how to accept the responsibility for caring for something that needs their love in return. The authorities at this school believe that the program has helped immeasurably in the effort to save boys on their way to permanent trouble.

There are scores of stories like these, all examples of how man can benefit from owning a dog. On the other side of the ledger stand such nuisances as housebreaking, rabies shots, and chewed shoes. Now you decide whether you should have a dog. At this point, the choice is a matter of human consideration. Only later will it involve a dog.

Point Two: Do you want a purebred or a random-bred dog? There has been so much nonsense written on this subject that some clarification is needed. All dogs, purebred and random-bred (I prefer *random-bred* to *mongrel*, *mutt*, or *mixed breed*), are members of one species. It may seem hard to believe that the Chihuahua, the Saint Bernard, and the Old English Sheepdog are all one species along with the nondescript random-bred in the local pound, yet it is true. Purebred dogs, all former random-breds themselves, have been refined by continuous breeding in order to obtain certain characteristics. By breeding generation after generation with a goal in mind, a dog is evolved that "breeds true." As long as he is henceforth bred to his own kind, he will produce his own kind. At some point (and that point for many breeds has been vague, indeed), the dog is said to be purebred.

Because all dogs belong to one species, they all have approximately the same needs. It is simply not true that a random-bred dog makes a better pet or is more intelligent than a purebred dog. A single random-bred dog *may* be more intelligent that some individual purebreds, but he almost certainly will be less intelligent than others. Certain breeds have been bred for intelligence, but we will get to that matter shortly.

Well, then, what is it to be—purebred or random-bred? There are pluses in obtaining a random-bred from a pound or humane shelter. The cost is negligible, and you will have the satisfaction of saving that dog from the gas chamber or worse. But there are also decided advantages to the purebred dog. You will have some idea of what you are getting. By knowing the breed and its characteristics, you at least can make a reasonable assessment of your puppy as a mature animal. That is rarely true with a random-bred pup. You can show a purebred dog, while you cannot show a random-bred. And some people just like the feeling of having a superb example of anything around them. Although either kind of dog can make a loving pet, some people just like that added feeling of style and perfection. I feel my family has the solution. We always have both around, and we love them equally.

If you do opt for a random-bred dog, there are two things you must remember. He will require exactly the same food, veterinary care, and love that the finest purebred dog would need, and you *must* have the females spayed and the males altered. *No random-bred dog should ever be permitted to reproduce.* Millions must be destroyed every year for the want of homes.

Point Three: Should you choose a dog or a bitch? Which makes the best pet? There is no definite answer. Bitches do *tend* to be a little softer, and this is more true of some breeds than others. Even there, though, it is a matter of opinion and experience. I honestly can't say which is best, and in our house we always have both.

Are there any clear-cut advantages or disadvantages? Some. It is more expensive to spay a bitch than it is to alter a male. (Spayed and altered dogs cannot be shown, but if dogs are not intended for the show-ring, then your life and theirs will be much improved by a little surgery.) Bitches that have not been spayed can be messy when they come into heat twice a year, and they tend to attract a lot of stray males to your front yard.

Many people will disagree with my next statement, but I think it is easier to find a splendid male example of most breeds than it is to find a superb female. Many females tend to have a "bitchy look," and that is often less attractive than the broader, heavier, "doggy" or masculine, look. That is *not* a rule, however, and some of the most magnificent show dogs seen every year are bitches. You may have to look a little longer, that's all.

Males tend to wander and fight more than females, but that is a tendency, not an inevitable fact of life. There is also the fact that mature males lift their legs, and if you have a lot of expensive shrubs in your yard, that can be bad. Dog urine can burn and eventually kill even hardy evergreens. Bitches do not have this problem, and since they generally don't go around marking territory as dogs do, they can be taught to use a special place in the corner of the yard.

Once again, when it comes to male versus female, it is a matter of personal choice. Of course, if you are getting a superlative example of a breed and you wish to do further breeding, it is the bitch that has the puppies—an incontrovertible fact of life.

Point Four: What age should the puppy be?   Only under the most extraordinary circumstances should you consider a puppy under ten weeks of age. A puppy needs that time with his mother and to some extent with his litter mates. After the age of ten to twelve weeks, though, it becomes a matter of options that have more to do with your ambitions than with the dog himself. A young pup will be *likely* (not certain) to settle into a new home and become imprinted with his new family quickly. Older dogs may be slower to do so, but often that is not the case.

If you are seeking an example of the breed for showing or breeding (more likely, both), you will do well to wait a little longer than three months, because the older the pup gets, the more you will be able to tell what he will be like at maturity.

These factors must be weighed in each individual case, and no declarations of absolute certainty can be made. I have seen four- and five-year-old dogs come into a household, settle down immediately, and be the best of all possible pets, and I have seen young puppies simply not make it at all. I have owned two Poodles in my life. The first one was obtained as a puppy of twelve weeks. After biting everything and everybody in sight from the beginning, he had to be given up on. He was the only dog I have ever failed with. The other Poodle came to us at the age of four and was probably the nicest little dog I have ever known. She came from a home where there were no children and no other pets into a new home literally exploding with kids and animals. She adapted instantly.

Point Five: Should you get a coated or noncoated dog?   Whether you have settled on a purebred or a random-bred dog, you can pretty well divide either field into dogs with coats that need care and dogs with coats that do not. Eventually, whatever else you do by way of selection, you will have to choose between the two. With purebred dogs it can be more important because there is a standard you are trying to maintain, although coated random-bred dogs also should be kept neat and clean and free from nasty mats and tangles.

As to which you select, it is a very personal choice. Do you want to fuss? No one knows but you. In the breed descriptions that constitute the bulk of this book, the amount of coat care each breed needs is indicated. The rest is a matter of taste and how much time or money you want to invest. You do have that choice—if you don't like caring for a dog's coat or if you haven't the time, you can have it done by a service, which will even pick up and deliver. All you have to do is pay. But do not select a coated breed unless you are going to see to the job one way or the other. A coated dog is a commitment, but as the descriptions that follow show, it is a matter of degree.

Point Six: Do you want a large or small dog? If you have, let us say, decided on a purebred dog and have chosen between a male and a female (although you should not do that until you find what the breeder has available) and between a coated and a noncoated dog, you have gone a long way toward eliminating a fair percentage of the dog world. The next major determination should be size. How big a dog should you get?

The factors here are many and often complicated because they involve you and your life-style, your immediate neighbors, the place where you live, and not least of all, the welfare of the dog you select.

Large dogs produce more fecal matter than small dogs and are messier to that degree. Large dogs, generally, are more intimidating and make people who are not dog fanciers uncomfortable in elevators and apartment-house lobbies. A very large dog who is not obedience-trained or is ill-behaved in any way is more of a menace than a small dog in direct proportion to the size difference. Also, of course, a large dog who tends to be nervous or even hostile with strangers is a very heavy responsibility.

Throughout the breed descriptions in this book it will be noted that I generally am opposed to large dogs in the urban setting, as well as in some suburban settings. It is not just that large dogs need a great deal of exercise, and they do; it is the life-style in a crowded environment that militates against them. Many small dogs require even more exercise than some large breeds, so exercise isn't so much the problem as how your neighbors will react to your dog. That must be taken into account if future unpleasantness is to be avoided. Few spectacles are as disheartening as fights and lawsuits between neighbors because one of them has gotten the wrong dog or has failed to train him properly. It is a bad situation, and often the dog is the victim. Either he is poisoned or shot by someone whose senses have left him altogether, or he is passed along from home to home. It is much wiser to get the right dog in the first place.

There are easy-to-train and very difficult-to-train large and small dogs, so the division cannot be made along those lines. There are lethargic and very active large and small dogs, so the division does not lie there either. The main factors governing size are: How much house room do you have, assuming your dog will be an inside animal? Will you or your guests be constantly tripping over your pet, and will you have to drive him from room to room because his size is oppressive? How much outside room do you have? Will your dog get regular exercise? Remember, the shorter a dog's legs are, the less ground he has to cover to be exercised. A Corgi walking one mile is like a Great Dane walking five or six. Big dogs need big areas at least part of the time. How close are you to your neighbors? Will you be going through an apartment-house lobby, or up and down in a public elevator? Will your neighbors react to a Bull Mastiff or a Rottweiler the way they will to a Corgi or a Boston Terrier? That, surely, must be taken into account.

Some people favor large dogs in any setting because they are afraid of intruders and see their pet as a deterrent. There is no doubt that some people with criminal potential will to a degree be deterred by a large, formidable dog, and there is no doubt whatsoever that some dogs make better watch-dogs than others (this is all discussed in the breed sections that follow). But deterrence is not reason enough. There are some things you should know about so-called guard and attack dogs before making any decision based on safety precautions.

Professional criminals rarely are bothered by guard dogs. Any dog who is close enough to bite is close enough to be put out of action. A man with a gun can shoot a dog as easily as he can shoot you. A professional "casing" a home or business can easily poison a dog in advance. Poisoned bait tossed into a yard or pen or slipped through a mail slot or window that has been jimmied open an inch or two is all that is needed. A five-dollar tear-gas pen or a can of Mace ordered through the mail will also wipe out any dog for several minutes at least. Anyone wanting to enter a fenced yard simply has to climb the fence and wait for the infuriated guard dog to start leaping up at him. A cinder block dropped from six or eight feet settles things down very quickly. It is not the professional criminal who gets hurt; it is the innocent bystander or the crazy kid who decides on impulse to break in. The punishment for teen-age burglary and vandalism in this country is not death, and that should be taken into account when considering the need for guard or attack dogs.

Five out of the six breeds now in the Caras household are large dogs. We have Bloodhounds, a Golden Retriever, a Siberian Husky, an English Bulldog, a random-bred something-or-other Shepherd, a Yorkshire Terrier, and a Papillon. Past dogs have included the two Poodles, a Pug, and other random-breds; as a boy I had an English Cocker Spaniel, a Collie, a Wire-haired Fox Terrier, a Boston Terrier, and other assorted canines of less than clear-cut origin. I point this all out to show that I am not personally preju-diced. We have nine dogs today, five of them large, because we live in a country house and have land and our own beach, a large fenced area, and enough people always on hand to care for our pets. We also have five cats, a horse, and other sundry creatures. I have no prejudices against any animal, but I have a great many against a person who will buy the wrong animal for the wrong reason in the wrong place. Not only will that animal suffer, but discontentment grows and feeds upon itself. In time, poorly chosen animals brought into urban and suburban settings result in ever stricter rules and regulations affecting all pet owners. The wise choice of a pet is the most important step any pet owner ever takes.

Point Seven: Where do you get your pet?   The obvious answer is that you get your pet wherever you can find a fine, healthy puppy who is what you want him to be. A friend may give him to you; you may discover perfectly fine, pet-quality, purebred as well as random-bred pups in pounds and shelters waiting for adoption; or you may buy through an ad in the local newspaper. There are some *best* places, however.

If you are looking for a random-bred pup, then you should adopt him. There are hundreds of pounds and shelters in this country and they all have puppies, all the time. You gain a double blessing when you adopt a pet from them. You gain your friend and companion, and you save a life. Millions of these animals are destroyed every year for the want of a home.

If you are seeking a purebred dog, however, you should seek the specialty breeder. Perhaps a point of clarification is in order here. By definition, anyone who breeds a dog is a breeder. Simple as that. If I take two dogs of any kind and put them together and they mate and have puppies, I am a breeder. The differences among *kinds* of breeders, however, are profound and should be of interest to every prospective dog owner.

In the American Midwest principally, but in other parts of the country as well, a number of people (many of whom seem to be hog farmers) supplement their income by mass-producing puppies for the pet trade. The wholesale trade journals carry ads, and one farmer advertises that he has sixty-four breeds of dogs in stock!

A professional breeder who devotes his or her life to perfecting a line of one breed (rarely two) finds it a full-time occupation. One does not develop outstanding examples of Cocker Spaniels, or Basset Hounds, by tossing two similar dogs in a pen. It is a long, arduous job that takes years of development and consultation, heartbreak, investment, and ultimately triumph. No hog farmer can do that properly with sixty-four breeds in his spare time.

Repeatedly, these backyard breeding operations are raided by local law enforcement authorities and humane organizations, and the conditions they find in many cases are appalling. I have gone through the files of the ASPCA in New York City, and the photographs in those files defy description. I have personally visited a number of "puppy-mill" breeders in Kansas and Missouri. It is hog-farm operations like these that produce many of the puppies we see in pet shops. Other sources of "puppy-mill" dogs are incidental local breeders, regular breeders who want to dispose of what they consider substandard puppies, and anyone else, really, who walks off the street with a basket of salable puppies. Most, I would venture to say, come from the mass-producers.

You are not going to get a show-quality puppy from a mass-producer or a pet shop except by accident. You may not even get the full-blooded dog you are paying for.

There is no possible way that the American Kennel Club, the principal dog-registration agency in the United States, can check on the hundreds of thousands of dogs that are registered every year. Let us say that I own a registered Beagle dog and a registered Beagle bitch. I breed them, register the litter, and ship the puppies to a pet shop along with copies of their pedigree. Fair enough. Then either my bitch or my dog dies or grows too old to breed. I happen to have a Foxhound or even a mixed-blood Beagle that looks pretty good. The A.K.C. has no way of knowing that my dog has died or that he or she is no longer breeding, and so I produce another litter using the mixed-blood Beagle or the Foxhound and record the same sire and dam names I did on the previous registration and in the previous pedigree. Only I know the true facts, and the pet shops and their customers cannot be the wiser. There is no way that this can be controlled, and a pedigree and registration papers are only as good as the honesty of the people who file them. The pet shop and the pet-shop customer never really know who these people are, much less can they vouch for their honesty. Such practices go on all the time.

The biggest problem in buying from a puppy mill is the fact that they deal in puppies and not dogs. You, as an inexperienced customer, see some puppies playing on shredded newspaper in the shop window, or you walk in and have a puppy thrust at you, and you are overwhelmed. All puppies are undeniably cute. You don't happen to know much about this breed, and you ask a few questions. The clerk, who is likely to be a high school or college kid working part time, gives you all the usual assurances. You do not know anything about that particular puppy's background, and the clerk may never even have seen a mature specimen of the breed, much less handled or attempted to train one. But you make your purchase. Many thousands of times a year the result is total disenchantment.

As a rule of thumb, "Never buy the puppy." Buy the dog the puppy one day will be. That means, simply, look ahead. Know all you have to know about the breed, and about the background of the puppy you are taking under consideration.

The best way to go about selecting and buying a purebred dog is hardly a mystery. It does require that you do your homework, however. Here are the steps in logical sequence:

Step 1:   Go to one or more all-breed dog shows. You may think you know the breed you want, but take a last look around. Spend a pleasant day or two with your family at a couple of shows. Watch the judging, wander around the bench or exercise areas, and talk to people. Ask them about their dogs. Meet mature specimens of the breeds that seem to interest you. Get to know some people and some dogs. Then, when you find yourself homing in on one or more breeds, start doing your real spadework.

Step 2: Read. Carefully check the breeds that interest you in the breed descriptions of this book. Read about your breed. You may want to consult a veterinarian for an opinion. Check with a dog trainer at an obedience school, and by all means go back to a dog show and get to know some breeders of that breed. Get involved with it, ask a lot of questions, and know what you are thinking of getting into for the next ten to fifteen years. A dog should be a carefully considered addition to your family, not an impulse purchase.

Step 3: Visit the breeders you have gotten to know. Meet the adult dogs they are using for parent stock if you have not already done so and then, and only then, make your purchase.

The satisfaction you are likely to gain over the years may be directly proportionate to the amount of care you take at the beginning. Surely, if you want a show dog, this is the way to go about it. When you do visit a dog show, keep in mind that those superb examples you see of each breed generally were obtained with at least this much care and caution. They were not impulse purchases except in the rarest of circumstances.

Point Eight: What do you pay for your puppy? Here, clearly, there is no single answer. Larger, rarer breeds usually cost more than common breeds and very often cost more than smaller breeds. That rules flies into a cocked hat, however, once you start dealing with fine examples of any breed. Irish Wolfhounds and Scottish Deerhounds, for instance, may generally be more expensive than Beagles or Cocker Spaniels. But then a superb Beagle or Cocker, as an individual animal, may cost many times what even a very good Irish Wolfhound might command. It depends on the individual animal, his lineage, and most of all his potential.

Many breeds start at between $75 and $100 for pet-quality animals. For that price you are not going to get a show specimen. Difficult-to-breed and extremely small toys are going to start at a much higher figure (from $250 or $300 and up), and so will the larger, rarer breeds. Show-quality animals of any breed are going to start at $400 and go straight up from there. We once paid $600 for a five-month-old show-quality dog, and by the time he was a year old and a champion, he was worth $3,500 had we been willing to sell him, which we most certainly were not.

The selection of a breed and the selection of an individual puppy are both personal and involve taste, living style, ambition, and self-image (and not just that of one person, very often, but that of an entire family). Purebred dogs are best purchased only after great care and consideration and then only from breeders who can be met face to face and whose dogs also can be met and known. As for the random-bred dogs, they make super pets in millions of homes (there are over forty-seven million dogs in American homes today), and they are free and literally dying for love and care. It is my own opinion that every dog-owning home should have both if possible.

{Group 1}

The Sporting Dogs

Pointer
German Shorthaired Pointer
German Wirehaired Pointer
Chesapeake Bay Retriever
Curly-Coated Retriever
Flat-Coated Retriever
Golden Retriever
Labrador Retriever
English Setter
Gordon Setter
Irish Setter
American Water Spaniel

Brittany
Clumber Spaniel
Cocker Spaniel
English Cocker Spaniel
English Springer Spaniel
Field Spaniel
Irish Water Spaniel
Sussex Spaniel
Welsh Springer Spaniel
Vizsla
Weimaraner
Wirehaired Pointing Griffon

The Pointer was developed in Europe during the Middle Ages, but no one is certain just where. One hears, from various supposed authorities, that France, Belgium, Germany, Spain, and Portugal were all the original home of this breed. We simply aren't sure, but we do know that from the mid-1600s on, England is where this breed flourished. ¶Originally Pointers were used in conjunction with Greyhounds. The Pointer found the hare, and the Greyhound ran it to ground. Later, when ballistics made wing-shooting possible, the Pointer became exclusively a bird dog. He is considered to be the ultimate dog in this field today. ¶Pointers are pow-

Pointer

Land of origin: MAINLAND EUROPE, then ENGLAND

Original purpose: Pointing hare and later wing shooting

Recent popularity ranking by A.K.C. registration: 90th

American Pointer Club, Inc.
Lee Ann Stagg, Secretary
7094 Branch Hwy.
Branch, LA 70516

HEIGHT: Dogs to 28 inches   Bitches to 26 inches

WEIGHT: Dogs to 75 pounds   Bitches to 65 pounds

COAT
Smooth and short but dense and with a very definite sheen.

COLOR
Liver, lemon, black, or orange—solid colored or any one in combination with white.
Great variety seen.

Amount of care coat requires: 1 2 3 4 5 6 7 8 9 10

Amount of exercise required: 1 2 3 4 5 6 7 8 9 10

Suitability for urban/apartment life: 1 2 3 4 5 6 7 8 9 10
WHOLLY UNSUITED

erful, durable, clean-lined dogs of great poise and character. They do well in bench shows and excel in field trials. They are better suited to kennel life than are most large sporting dogs, for they require somewhat less human attention. Pointers will work well for a stranger more readily than will most other field dogs. The Pointer has one thing on his mind: Find that bird. ¶This breed is packed with nervous energy and requires an enormous amount of exercise. A Pointer that is cooped up is ready to explode when finally brought out into the open. There are exceptions, of course, but the Pointer is generally not as ideal a pet as are some of the other large sporting dogs. Pointers have quick tempers and really would rather be working than wasting their time on other things. Some have made excellent pets, but usually with a family that works the dog in the field. How good they are in the average household is questionable. For a nonsporting family, one that cannot build a bond with the dog in the area the dog knows and loves best—field work—the Pointer may be less than ideal. ¶Pointer owners are, of course, devoted to their splendid breed. Because Pointers are so energetic and intent on their profession, they are not good city dogs—certainly not apartment dogs. It has taken hundreds of years to perfect this masterpiece of upland wing shooting, and it is a rare Pointer indeed who will respond well to any other life-style. None of this is to say that the Pointer is not an affectionate pet. He can be, but he is best suited to a master of a special type.

German Shorthaired Pointer

Land of origin: GERMANY

Original purpose: All-purpose hunting

Recent popularity ranking by A.K.C. registration: 29th

German Shorthaired Pointer Club of America
MaryBeth Kirkland, Secretary
130 Gallop Ln.
Maidens, VA 23102

HEIGHT: Dogs to 25 inches   Bitches to 23 inches

WEIGHT: Dogs to 70 pounds   Bitches to 60 pounds

COAT
Short and thick, tough and hard.

COLOR
Important: solid liver or liver and white (gray) only.

Amount of care coat requires: 1 2 3 4 5 6 7 8 9 10

Amount of exercise required: 1 2 3 4 5 6 7 8 9 10

Suitability for urban/apartment life: 1 2 3 4 5 6 7 8 9 10
                                          UNSUITED

The handsome German Shorthaired Pointer carries a number of blood lines, only a few of which we know about with certainty. An old German bird dog is there, a Spanish Pointer and a scent hound, perhaps even the great Bloodhound himself. There is terrier there, too. The Germans who bred this animal up from obscurity, drawing on dog from all over Europe, outdid themselves. This is one of the better pets among the heavy field dogs. ¶The German Shorthaired Pointer is a supremely active animal and generally is unsuited to apartment or city life. He is full of energy and always ready to go—and *go* does not mean simply to the curb and back. This is an animal that has to move! ¶The German Shorthaired Pointer is a loving companion and constant friend. He is not petty or mean, ill-tempered or moody, and he gets along with his master's family. If cooped up, however, his whole manner can change; in the city he can become crazed and act beyond control. He becomes yappy and foolish and seems to lose his intelligence along with his dignity. The German Shorthaired should always be dignified—and will be if trained and worked. You certainly don't have to be a hunter to use this combination upland-lowland dog—this trailer, pointer, and retriever in one package—but you have to like long walks in the clean, crisp air. Don't expect a German Shorthaired Pointer to display all of his original characteristics and quality on hard pavement and in crowded living conditions.

When the Germans decided they wanted the perfect all-purpose hunting dog, they took their justifiably famous Shorthaired Pointer and combined him with Terrier, Poodle, and other bloodlines to evolve the striking German Wirehaired Pointer, one of the finest hunting dogs in the world today. ¶The German Wirehaired Pointer is everything you could desire in a field dog—a flawless retriever, a pointer, a steady, solid, and determined friend and companion animal. His coat, one of the breed's most striking and important features, provides protection against all weather; it is virtually water-repellent, so there need be no hesita-

German Wirehaired Pointer

Land of origin: GERMANY

Original purpose: Rugged, all-purpose hunting

Recent popularity ranking by A.K.C. registration: 70th

German Wirehaired Pointer Club of America, Inc.
Ms. Barbara Hein, Corres. Secretary
3838 Davison Lake Rd.
Ortonville, MI 48462

HEIGHT: Dogs to 26 inches   Bitches to 24 inches

WEIGHT: Dogs to 70 pounds   Bitches to 60 pounds

COAT
Extremely important feature: protective undercoat, full and dense in winter and all but invisible in summer. Outer coat straight, harsh, wiry, rather close lying; 1½ to 2 inches in length.

COLOR
Liver or liver and white. Nose dark brown. Head brown, occasionally with white blaze. Ears brown. Any black is a serious fault.

Amount of care coat requires: 1 2 3 4 5 6 7 8 9 10

Amount of exercise required: 1 2 3 4 5 6 7 8 9 10

Suitability for urban/apartment life: 1 2 3 4 5 6 7 8 9 10
UNSUITED

tion about using the dog to retrieve in icy waters. The coat also protects against briers and thorns in the roughest terrain. There is even a bushy mass to protect the eyes. In winter the coat is thick, but it thins considerably by summer. It is easy to care for and naturally clean—the dog shakes dirt off the way he does water. Coat condition is obviously an important factor and is carefully considered by all judges. ¶The German Wirehaired Pointer is one of those dogs really not at all suited to city life. He was bred for the field, and only in the open will he display his exceptional qualities. ¶This breed makes almost ideal companion animals for their owners, though cross or ill-tempered examples should not be tolerated. While not unfriendly or aggressive, the dog is aloof and slow to accept strangers. ¶The German Wirehaired is an exceptional breed when living in special, planned-for circumstances. In other situations—if forced to fit into an inappropriate lifestyle—the good qualities he is known for may vanish. Some people try to take outstanding working or sporting dogs and remold them. It usually does not work, and only rarely will the family be satisfied. In a country setting, of course, dogs like the German Wirehaired Pointer make fine family pets. ¶This special and highly developed breed should never be obtained from anyone but a specialty breeder who can show you not only the parents' conformation show ribbons but their field-trial awards as well. Although handsome, rugged, and even noble in his canine way, the German Wirehaired Pointer was made to perform, and that should be clearly evident when you examine a prospective puppy's background.

The Chesapeake Bay Retriever is descended from two dogs rescued from a sinking British brig off the coast of Maryland in 1807. The dogs are believed to have been Newfoundland puppies named Sailor and Canton, and there are many guesses as to what was bred to these two dogs, or possibly to their offspring. Approximately eighty years later a definite type emerged—the dog we today call the Chesapeake Bay Retriever. ¶The Chesapeake is by all standards a superior dog. He is one of the greatest of all water retrievers and one of the hardiest. No weather will deter this dog from doing what he was born to do: go into the water

Chesapeake Bay Retriever

Land of origin: UNITED STATES

Original purpose: Water retrieving

Recent popularity ranking by A.K.C. registration: 42nd

American Chesapeake Club, Inc.
Maggie Hoagland, Secretary
455 Greenwood Rd.
Kennet Square, PA 19348

HEIGHT: Dogs to 26 inches   Bitches to 24 inches

WEIGHT: Dogs to 80 pounds   Bitches to 70 pounds

COAT
Thick and short, up to 1½ inches long only, with a fine, dense, and woolly undercoat. Coat is wavy in places but never curly.

COLOR
From dark brown to "deadgrass." Solid color preferred, but very small white spots on chest and/or toes allowed.

Amount of care coat requires: 1 2 3 4 5 6 7 8 9 10

Amount of exercise required: 1 2 3 4 5 6 7 8 9 10

Suitability for urban/apartment life: 1 2 3 4 5 6 7 8 9 10

and retrieve fallen game. Not only is he peerless with waterfowl, he is also a consummate companion. ¶The Chesapeake is a good watchdog and a responsive pet. He is fine when obedience-trained, since he is one of the most intelligent dogs and one of the most willing. Put him to any task and he will do it. Disposition is an extremely important factor in judging, for this is one breed of dog that is expected to be even-tempered, sensible, and nonaggressive. Anything less than that is considered unworthy. ¶All of this is not to say that the Chesapeake is wishy-washy or without strong character. Just the opposite. This is a dog of great purpose and highly developed skill. He is aloof to yapping nonsense but fine with other animals who show an appropriate amount of respect. ¶The Chesapeake Bay Retriever, one of the few American breeds, has been used successfully as a guide dog for the blind. He can survive in an apartment as long as he is surrounded by people who care about him and as long as he gets sufficient exercise. It is not fair nor is it even humane to have an active sporting dog like this living the life of a toy. The Chesapeake thrives on work, on being needed for a tough and demanding job. Above all, the Chesapeake wants and needs open water. If one of these splendid dogs is kept in the city, it should be by people who will exercise him every day and from time to time get him out to some river, lake, or shoreline where he can retrieve sticks and display his real nature.

The arguments among dog people as to the real origin of the Curly-Coated Retriever will go on as long as there are dog people to argue. It usually is stated that the breed comes down from the English Water Spaniel popular in the 1500s. To that line is said to have been added a form of setting retriever. The Irish Water Spaniel is also said to be a foundation breed to which everything from Poodle to Newfoundland is supposed to have been added. However it may have come about, several hundred years ago the base was laid down, and by 1803 a breed could be described. Its first appearance in shows came in 1859. ¶The Curly-Coated Retriever is a special-pur-

Curly-Coated Retriever

Land of origin: ENGLAND

Original purpose: Water retrieving

Recent popularity ranking by A.K.C. registration: 123rd

Curly-Coated Retriever Club of America
Beth Ellen Roop, Corres. Secretary
P.O. Box 12
Dover, DE 19903-0012

HEIGHT: Dogs to 24 inches   Bitches to 23 inches

WEIGHT: Dogs to 70 pounds   Bitches to 65 pounds

COAT
Crisp curls all over the body, the tighter the better. Saddle or area of uncurled coat seriously faulted in judging.

COLOR
Black or liver; sparse white hairs on chest allowed.

Amount of care coat requires: 1 2 3 4 5 6 7 8 9 10

Amount of exercise required: 1 2 3 4 5 6 7 8 9 10

Suitability for urban/apartment life: 1 2 3 4 5 6 7 8 9 10
UNSUITED

pose dog with incredible stamina and skill. As a water retriever he is surpassed by few breeds. Popular with duck hunters in Australia and New Zealand, the breed hardly is known here. Most people have never seen an example, and he can be confused with the Irish Water Spaniel by those who have seen only one or two of that breed. The Irish Water Spaniel has a distinctly rat-like tail, while the breed we're discussing has a tail covered with ringlets. Actually there is little difference in popularity—the Irish dog rates 130th in this country and the Curly-Coated 123rd. ¶The Curly-Coated Retriever is not suited to apartment or urban life. He is an action dog for foul weather and water. He needs and wants to swim, to know the wind and the feel of freshly forming ice on salty marshes under a gray and threatening sky. It is not easy to re-create those conditions in the living room. People who try to take this breed into an apartment and reshape the dog will be dissatisfied. Walks along city streets simply are not enough. The Curly-Coated is a good companion for his owner and even for his family, but demands should not be made upon him by strangers. They should be quite satisfied with him when he is aloof. ¶Training should start early with this breed and continue over a long period of time. It is a serious matter for dog and master. This dog is smart, very smart, and will take over if allowed. Because he is a big animal, such assertiveness is intolerable, and snapping should be severely curtailed. Like many other really fine hunting breeds, the Curly-Coated Retriever can be stubborn, or, rather, single-minded. Without that quality he would not be the great field performer he is. ¶You will not find it easy to locate an outstanding specimen of this breed.

It is ironic that the Flat-Coated Retriever should rank down near the very bottom of the popularity poll in America. Not only is he an exceptional dog, but also he is one of the few truly American breeds. He was derived from the Newfoundland and the Labrador Retriever. His main development, however, took place in England during the reign of Queen Victoria. ¶The solid, sturdy, and well-muscled Flat-Coated Retriever is a field dog first and foremost, but he also can be an ideal family pet. Marvelous with children, he is loving and gentle with the whole family. He holds his peace with strangers, though he wants to know a lot about someone coming

Flat-Coated Retriever

Land of origin: AMERICA

Original purpose: Water and upland retrieving

Recent popularity ranking by A.K.C. registration: 100th

Flat-Coated Retriever Society of America, Inc.
Miriam Krum, Secretary
16705 W. 327th St.
Paola, KS 66071

HEIGHT: Dogs to 23 inches   Bitches to 22 inches

WEIGHT: Dogs to 70 pounds   Bitches to 65 pounds

COAT
Dense, fine, and flat.

COLOR
Black or liver.

Amount of care coat requires: 1 2 3 4 5 6 7 8 9 10

Amount of exercise required: 1 2 3 4 5 6 7 8 9 10

Suitability for urban/apartment life: 1 2 3 4 5 6 7 8 9 10
UNSUITED

through the door before he offers friendship. Once one of these fine dogs does offer it, the arrangement is permanent. They are loyal and outgoing, stable and intelligent. ¶The Flat-Coated Retriever lives for his master and takes training very well. He wants to learn and to please, and he loves being congratulated and rewarded. In this he is like a child, once his interest in a project is aroused. More cheerful than some of the other gundogs of his general size and configuration, he resembles the Golden Retriever and Labrador Retriever in his attitude toward human beings. Though not exactly a jolly clown, he is a pet and he does need attention. ¶A Flat-Coated Retriever should be taken regularly to an open area where he can run and retrieve. He is particularly fond of water and should be allowed to swim—in any weather. His coat is easy to maintain, and he is easily kept. ¶Considering the popularity that the Golden and Labrador Retrievers enjoy, it just might be that the Flat-Coated Retriever will have his day. The breed is now obviously only on the first rung of the popularity ladder. For comparison it should be noted that in 1974 the American Kennel Club reported registering 36,689 new Labradors and 20,933 Goldens; the number of Flat-Coated Retrievers registered was a mere 90. ¶People wanting a dog of the retriever style, but also wanting something different, might think about starting the long, hard hunt to find a really good example of this rare breed. They could be getting in on the start of a whole new thing.

It was in early nineteenth-century England that the retrievers first came into prominence. Four main types were developed almost simultaneously—the Curly-Coated, the Flat-Coated, the Labrador, and the Golden. Setters, water spaniels, and other sporting dogs were crossed with a light retrieving dog known as St. John's Newfoundland to achieve these ends. ¶From the beginning the extraordinary qualities of the Golden Retriever were recognized. He is a truly superior hunting dog with a soft mouth and great intelligence. The Golden is hardy and can thrive in almost any weather. He will never shy from leaping into icy

Golden Retriever

Land of origin: ENGLAND

Original purpose: Water retrieving

Recent popularity ranking by A.K.C. registration: 4th

Golden Retriever Club of America
Ms. Catherine E. Bird, Secretary
9900 Broadway, Ste. 102
Oklahoma City, OK 73114

HEIGHT: Dogs to 24 inches   Bitches to 22½ inches

WEIGHT: Dogs to 75 pounds   Bitches to 70 pounds

COAT
Dense and water-repellent. Good undercoat. Flat against body with some wave.

COLOR
Lustrous gold of different shades. Solid. No white markings allowed.

Amount of care coat requires: 1 2 3 4 5 6 7 8 9 10

Amount of exercise required: 1 2 3 4 5 6 7 8 9 10

*Suitability for urban/apartment life:**   1 2 3 4 5 6 7 8 9 10

---

*But *only* if exercised, or at least walked, no less than two hours every day in all kinds of weather.

water to please his master and do the job he was bred to do. He is hurt and seemingly embarrassed when denied the opportunity to help, to carry, to bring you something in order to show his affection. His need to retrieve is legendary—he is never as happy as when he is fetching and carrying. ¶The Golden is never mean or petty. He naturally loves children and other animals, cats and kittens included. He is loyal, almost unbelievably affectionate, and so intelligent that he is becoming one of the most popular of all guide dogs for the blind. All these qualities make him an ideal family dog and pet. ¶It is difficult to discuss this breed without allowing a distinct prejudice to creep in. The author believes that the Golden Retriever comes very close to being the greatest of all breeds. Although other people may have different favorite breeds, almost no one has anything bad to say about this one. ¶The Golden Retriever is so much the perfect companion and fam-ily dog that there is very naturally a tendency to think of him as perfect for every set of circumstances. This is not quite true. The Golden Retriever is an outdoor animal, and although he will adapt to city life (he will adapt to *anything* as long as he has his family nearby), he requires exercise—lots and lots of exercise. No one should think of owning a Golden unless he is willing to walk the dog at least two hours every day, no matter what the weather. It isn't fair to treat this superb dog otherwise. He also should have frequent opportunities to retrieve, especially from water. He loves to swim all year round. The Golden isn't a terribly expensive dog to buy; $250 should fetch a good example of the breed. Since retrievers are prone to a congenital malformation known as hip dysplasia, they should be obtained only from reputable breeders. Animals that show any signs of dysplasia should not be bred, for there is a 65 percent heritability factor.

It is no accident that the Labrador Retriever has become one of the most popular dogs in America, now consistently ranked among the top ten. He is a peerless pet as well as a superlative performer in the field, under the gun or in field trials. He can be used as a guide dog for the blind or as a general watchdog. There are people who insist that the Labrador Retriever is the most even-tempered of all dog breeds. ¶The Labrador can be owned under almost any circumstances because he is so sensible, so steady, and so adaptable. It is up to the owner, however, to be fair and give the dog a chance to be himself. There is no doubt that this splendid animal needs

Labrador Retriever

Land of origin: NEWFOUNDLAND and ENGLAND

Original purpose: Water retrieving

Recent popularity ranking by A.K.C. registration: 1st

Labrador Retriever Club, Inc.
Mr. Christopher G. Wincek, Corres. Secretary
9690 Wilson Mills Rd.
Chardon, OH 44024

HEIGHT: Dogs to 24¹/₂ inches   Bitches to 23¹/₂ inches

WEIGHT: Dogs to 75 pounds   Bitches to 70 pounds

COAT
Short, very dense, and not wavy. Feels hard to the hand, and there are no feathers.

COLOR
All black, yellow, or chocolate. Very small white spot on chest allowed. Eyes black to pale yellow; brown or hazel generally preferred.

Amount of care coat requires: 1 2 3 4 5 6 7 8 9 10

Amount of exercise required: 1 2 3 4 5 6 7 8 9 10

Suitability for urban/apartment life:*   1 2 3 4 5 6 7 8 9 10

*But *only* if given a great deal of exercise every day plus opportunities for periodic workouts in the open.

exercise, and it is unkind to keep one locked away all day and night without an opportunity to get out and go. It is also less than kind to maintain a Labrador in a city apartment or a suburban house without a place to swim. Labradors were made for the water, and diving in after a stick is their greatest joy—whatever the weather. The coat does not require a lot of care, but daily brushing for a few minutes will help keep it glistening and healthy. ¶Labrador Retrievers are legendary with children as responsible baby-sitters and faithful guards. They are fine with strangers who do not appear dangerous to the household, and they are perfect with other animals. ¶Labradors will fight, of course, but only if pressed into it. They are never petty or mean, rarely sulky or moody. They are not as demonstrative or openly affectionate as Golden Retrievers, but their love of master, family, and home is quite genuine. The very slight reserve does not suggest less love or less reliability. The Golden and Labrador Retrievers stand side by side as two of the most desirable dogs in the world. ¶Because "Labs" are so popular, it is extremely important that they be obtained only from the best professional specialty breeders. There has been too much mass production, which is to be discouraged. ¶Because the Labrador Retriever can be trained to do anything, or *almost* anything, that any other dog can do, some have been trained as attack dogs. This is nothing less than criminal, and a dog so trained should not be looked upon as a Labrador Retriever at all. He is no more reliable than any other potential killer. The prospective owner concerned about the safety of his or her home should not think an attack-trained Labrador is safer around a family than any other dog in that lamentable condition.

Very few dog fanciers would disagree with the claim that the English Setter not only is one of the handsomest dogs but also has one of the sweetest dispositions of all dogs and is a splendid performer in the field. No wonder that he has always had a loyal following. ¶No one knows all the steps that had to be taken to create the English Setter, but we believe he was derived several hundred years ago from Spanish land dogs—dogs that came to be called *spaniels* after their place of origin. The English Setter has done nothing but improve, until today his beauty and dignity symbolize the striving for perfection in the dog world. ¶English Setters have few peers

English Setter

Land of origin: SPAIN and ENGLAND

Original purpose: Hunting

Recent popularity ranking by A.K.C. registration: 83rd

English Setter Association of America, Inc.
Mrs. Dawn S. Ronyak, Secretary
114 S. Burlington Oval Dr.
Chardon, OH 44024

HEIGHT: Dogs to 25 inches   Bitches to 24 inches

WEIGHT: Dogs to 70 pounds   Bitches to 60 pounds

COAT
Flat, without curl, not soft or woolly, and of medium length. Thin, regular feathers on legs
and tail.

COLOR
Black, white, and tan; black and white; blue belton; lemon and white; lemon belton; orange and
white; orange belton; liver and white; liver belton; or solid white. Heavy patches of color not as
desirable as flecking all over.

Amount of care coat requires: 1 2 3 4 5 6 7 8 9 10

Amount of exercise required: 1 2 3 4 5 6 7 8 9 10

Suitability for urban/apartment life: 1 2 3 4 5 6 7 8 9 10
                                                    UNSUITED

as family dogs. They are affectionate and loyal and are exceptional all-around companions. They love children and demand a great deal of affection in return. They are fine, smooth-working bird dogs that work and play well with other animals. ¶The Setter's coat requires some brushing every day to keep its fine appearance; this is an easy task and need not take more than a few minutes. It is shameful to let the coat go, since it is such an important element of the dog's appearance. English Setters are hams when it comes to showing, and when they set up they are breathtaking. For this reason, and because they are so easy to manage, they have long been favorites in the show-ring. Few dogs have been painted as often or by so many different artists. ¶There is one catch that the prospective owner should take into account. The English Setter needs an enormous amount of exercise, and he does not thrive in the city. He really should be exercised or allowed to exercise for hours every day, and that is usually not practical in an urban setting. Even the mild, sweet disposition of the Setter can fray and show signs of going sour if he is held in the city and denied his true nature. This should be considered very seriously, because a lot of people do find Setters stylish, and some pet shops will sell them with the assurance that they are ideal apartment dogs. They distinctly are not.

This exceptionally handsome field dog dates from the early 1600s in Scotland, but it wasn't until the fourth Duke of Gordon took the breed under his guidance a century and a half later that it really came into prominence. It has been admired and praised by dog fanciers ever since. Daniel Webster was the first American to import examples of the breed into the United States. ¶It is hard to tell why the English and Irish Setters have been more popular in this country than the Gordon, unless it is because they are both a little faster in the open. That is the only advantage they have over the Gordon though, for this is a nearly perfect companion animal for the man afield. ¶A Gordon in good condition is one of the handsomest of dogs, silky and shiny with the distinctive pattern of black and red that sets it apart from all other sporting breeds. This breed tends to be more stable than the Irish Setter—rather more like the English Setter in temperament. ¶There is a saying that no one ever knew a Gordon Setter who would bite a child, and that is a lot closer to fact than fiction. Although

Gordon Setter

Land of origin: SCOTLAND

Original purpose: As upland game gundog

Recent popularity ranking by A.K.C. registration: 61st

Gordon Setter Club of America, Inc.
Ms. L. Alison Rosskamp, Corres. Secretary
945 Font Rd.
Glenmoore, PA 19343

HEIGHT: Dogs to 27 inches   Bitches to 26 inches

WEIGHT: Dogs to 80 pounds   Bitches to 70 pounds

COAT
Shiny, soft, slightly waved or straight, but not curly. Long hair on ears, under the stomach, and on chest, tail, and legs.

COLOR
Black with tan to red mahogany or chestnut markings. There may be black "pencil lines" on the toes. Lighter markings are important; they should appear over the eyes, on the muzzle and throat, on the chest and inside of the hind legs, under the tail, and on the feet. No red or tan hairs should be mixed in with the black. A *little* white is allowed on the chest.

Amount of care coat requires: 1 2 3 4 5 6 7 8 9 10

Amount of exercise required: 1 2 3 4 5 6 7 8 9 10

Suitability for urban/apartment life: 1 2 3 4 5 6 7 8 9 10
UNSUITED

active, Gordons are sensible, even-tempered, and affectionate. They don't usually throw themselves at strangers and are happier with their own human family. They demand a great deal of attention, which can be a problem when there is more than one dog. Gordons can be jealous; this is often the cause of dogfights in which the Gordon participates. In fact, Gordons apparently would like it very much if all other dogs and people just vanished and left them alone with their immediate family, which is not to say that Gordons are unfriendly or quarrelsome, just that they have a preferred way of living: privately and stage center within their household. ¶Because of the breed's high style, some people do make city dogs out of Gordons. The dog can adapt because of his great affection for people, but the City Gordon Setter just isn't the same animal as the country Gordon. City life can make him tense, silly, and sometimes hard to control. The smooth, natural world of open field and cool, clean air is the ideal setting for an animal who wants to please, responds easily to training, and provides nearly perfect canine companionship. The dog held in the city will require intensive obedience training and a great deal of walking. The Gordon Setter is not a dog just to be led from apartment door to curb and back; less than two miles a day may not be cruel, but it certainly is unkind. This is an animal who was bred to move, and only in movement can one appreciate the bold, strong driving quality of his gait and character.

Once a red and white dog (and still seen that way in England), the Irish Setter is now a rich red mahogany animal of great and enduring beauty. Certainly one of the handsomest dogs, the red Irishman may have been in part undone by his splendor. He was originally a field dog, a bird dog, and there was none better. But in recent years, at least in the United States, he has been a show animal, and many people familiar with the breed think this is a sad waste of talent. ¶We are not sure where the Irish Setter came from. It seems certain that some spaniel and English Setter, perhaps some Gordon Setter and some Pointer were involved. Any trace of black

Irish Setter

Land of origin: IRELAND

Original purpose: As bird dog

Recent popularity ranking by A.K.C. registration: 51st

Irish Setter Club of America, Inc.
Mrs. Marion Pahy, Corres. Secretary
16717 Ledge Falls
San Antonio, TX 78232-1808

HEIGHT: Dogs to 27 inches   Bitches to 25 inches

WEIGHT: Dogs to 70 pounds   Bitches to 60 pounds

COAT
Of moderate length and flat. Feathering long and silky on ears and forelegs. Ideal is free from wave or curl.

COLOR
Mahogany or rich chestnut red. *Any* trace of black is a serious fault. Very small amount of white allowed on chest, throat, or toes.

Amount of care coat requires: 1 2 3 4 5 6 7 8 9 10
•••••••••••••

Amount of exercise required: 1 2 3 4 5 6 7 8 9 10
••••••••••••••••••••••••

Suitability for urban/apartment life: 1 2 3 4 5 6 7 8 9 10
UNSUITED

today (which would go back to the Gordon) is considered a grievous fault. ¶Wherever he came from and however he is used, the Irish Setter is a stunning animal and a terrible clown. A pet dog through and through, he is affectionate and extremely demonstrative. But he can be a first-class pain when he is not obedience-trained. He is capable of taking over a household where there is not a firm and knowing hand, but he is equally capable of learning anything that reasonably can be expected of an upland dog. He is one or the other, a model of decorum, or a dunce and a nuisance—it will depend on the owner. ¶There is a difference of opinion as to where and how the Irish Setter is best maintained. In my own opinion, the red Setter, although adaptable and loving under any circumstances, is far too active for apartment life. He needs an enormous amount of exercise, and he needs it every day. In an apartment there is no way in which this can be achieved. A walk is not the same as a run. I have seen some perfectly splendid examples of the breed as "flaky" as a dog can be from overconfinement. It is sad to see one of these splendid field dogs leaping and lunging in an apartment-house elevator for want of proper exercise. ¶Irish Setters tend to stray, and in the suburban setting they should be carefully supervised. They are also terrible thieves, so don't be surprised if you wake up some morning to find that your Irish Setter has brought home an Oriental carpet or a family Bible. They are also born clowns and will never leave you short of stories to tell. Endearingly beautiful, active, and affectionate, in the right setting and in the hands of the right owner, the Irish Setter cannot be beat.

This hunting dog originated in the American Midwest, but not much more is known about its early history. The Irish Water Spaniel, the Curly-Coated Retriever, and the old English Water Spaniel are all suggested forebears, and other spaniel blood may have figured in as well. It is not a matter that is likely to be settled. ¶From whatever stock he came, the American Water Spaniel is a splendid hunter. He is a superb water retriever, serves as well on land, and has an excellent nose. No weather or water temperature will deter this dog, and he will work upland game as readily as he will seek out injured waterfowl. Although not a pointer, he is

American Water Spaniel

Land of origin: UNITED STATES

Original purpose: Water retrieving and other hunting

Recent popularity ranking by A.K.C. registration: 108th

American Water Spaniel Club
Patricia A. St. Onge, Secretary
4835 S. Mill Loop Rd.
Maple, WI 54854-9011

HEIGHT: Dogs to 18 inches   Bitches to 18 inches

WEIGHT: Dogs to 45 pounds   Bitches to 40 pounds

COAT
Closely curled or with marcel effect. Dense enough to protect against water and weather. Not straight, kinked, soft, or fine.

COLOR
Solid liver or dark chocolate. No white except on toes and chest; as little as possible is desired.

Amount of care coat requires: 1 2 3 4 5 6 7 8 9 10

Amount of exercise required: 1 2 3 4 5 6 7 8 9 10

Suitability for urban/apartment life:*   1 2 3 4 5 6 7 8 9 10

*If exercised properly every day without fail.

hard to beat in any other category of field sport. ¶Except for the fact that he is not quite as lovely to look at as some of the other spaniels, the curly American Water Spaniel is almost everything anyone could want in a dog. He is, in most respects, an easy dog to keep. Unlike a good many other sporting breeds, he is a good, solid watchdog; although not testy with strangers, he will let you know when one approaches. This is an intelligent dog who is very willing to learn. He is extremely affectionate, something not necessarily true of all sporting dogs. He should be handled with care, for he thrives on praise and takes scolding to heart. He is splendid in the family setting and seems especially drawn to children. He is sensible and will fit in with other family pets. His disposition is flawless, and he takes to training as well as he does to water. He is not strenu-ous to deal with or difficult in any way. ¶This is one sporting breed that will adapt to a city apartment; as a matter of fact, this dog will adjust to virtually any situation as long as his family is nearby. It is not fair to keep this loving animal purely as a kennel dog. If kept in the suburbs, he should not be allowed to roam, for he just might be enticed to wander off too far. When kept in the suburbs or the city, he should be given a great deal of exercise on a regular basis. It is only right to give him a workout in the water as often as possible. Retrieving a stick from the water is fine exercise and will allow him to fulfill his natural original mission. ¶Not very well known in most parts of the country, the American Water Spaniel is one of those special treats awaiting the potential dog owner willing to do a little research.

The Brittany is actually too leggy to be called a spaniel, or at least he is one of the least spaniel-like of all spaniels. He is as high in the withers as he is long. He comes from ancient Spanish stock carried across Europe so long ago we can't even fix the period. While most spaniels developed in the British Isles, this breed was developed in France and has been known to European sportsmen for centuries. He shares common ancestry with all the other spaniels, the setters, and the pointers. In size and appearance he may be close to those ancestral dogs from which all three groups arose. ¶The Brittany is never shown with a tail substantially longer than four inches. The

Brittany

Land of origin: FRANCE, from ancient Spanish stock

Original purpose: Hunting

Recent popularity ranking by A.K.C. registration: 31st

American Brittany Club, Inc.
Joy Searey, Corres. Secretary
800 Hillmont Ranch Rd.
Aledo, TX 76008

HEIGHT: Dogs to 20¹/₂ inches   Bitches to 19¹/₂ inches

WEIGHT: Dogs to 40 pounds   Bitches to 37 pounds

COAT
Dense and flat, wavy but not curly. Skin loose but not so loose as to form pouches.

COLOR
Dark, rich orange and white or liver and white. Never to be tricolored or to show any black at all. Colors should be strong and not faded.

Amount of care coat requires: 1 2 3 4 5 6 7 8 9 10

Amount of exercise required: 1 2 3 4 5 6 7 8 9 10

Suitability for urban/apartment life:* 1 2 3 4 5 6 7 8 9 10

*But *only* if properly exercised on a regular basis.

tail is sometimes docked, but many Brittanies are born with mere stubs, and some are born without tails at all. The first tailless specimens we know of appeared about a century ago in the Douron Valley in France. ¶The Brittany is an excellent field dog, and as such his true qualities show best. The breed is by nature aggressive and loyal. Since Brittanies are not keen on strangers, they are natural watchdogs and are quite fearless. They should, though, be watched around strangers, for they can become a little too tough and may be quite intimidating. They tend to be one-personish but will live with a family most amicably. They can be raised with other animals. ¶The Brittany is not as elegant as some of the other spaniels, although he has a certain keeness about him that is attractive. His coat can be handsome although it is not as fine as those of other spaniels.

Brittanies are sturdy, well boned, strong, and driving. Never clumsy or awkward, they move fast, their long legs serving them well. They have minimum feathering and their ears are not long, so coat care is less than for the other spaniels. ¶The Brittany needs a great deal of exercise, and if one is brought into a confined suburban home or a city dwelling, that should be kept in mind. All the wonderful drive and energy that make this breed so desirable in the field *can* degenerate into plain silliness and hyperactivity. The splendid field dog improperly cared for can become a pest. If you keep a Brittany, long walks on a regular basis are a must. ¶Beware of poor breeders and mass-producers. There are a lot of Brittanies around. You should know the original source well, and buy only after careful consideration. The range in looks, and especially in behavior, is great.

One of the least spaniel-like of all span-iels, the Clumber has a mysterious background. The long, low, and rather heavyset body suggests Basset Hound blood (and many people insist this is true), and the heavy, Saint Bernard-like head suggests an old Alpine spaniel we may no longer know. It is a matter that will never be resolved, as is true for many breeds. Animals were bred for a need of the time, and apparently no one felt that anyone in the future would be interested in how shapes and forms were arrived at. ¶The name of this breed is derived, it is believed, from Clumber Park, the seat of the Dukes of Newcastle in Nottingham. The records

Clumber Spaniel

Land of origin: ENGLAND and FRANCE

Original purpose: Flushing game and retrieving

Recent popularity ranking by A.K.C. registration: 124th

Clumber Spaniel Club of America, Inc.
Ms. Barbara Stebbins, Secretary
9 Cedar St.
Selden, NY 11784

HEIGHT: Dogs to 18 inches   Bitches to 16 inches

WEIGHT: Dogs to 65 pounds   Bitches to 50 pounds

COAT
Straight, silky, very dense, but not too long. Feathers long and abundant.

COLOR
Lemon and white or orange and white. Better if there are fewer markings on body. Ideal has lemon or orange ears, even head and face markings, and ticked legs.

Amount of care coat requires: 1 2 3 4 5 6 7 8 9 10

Amount of exercise required: 1 2 3 4 5 6 7 8 9 10

Suitability for urban/apartment life: 1 2 3 4 5 6 7 8 9 10

indicate that the Duc de Noailles sent several dogs over from France in the nineteenth century, dogs of a type he had been perfecting for years. No doubt they figured heavily in the development of the breed, so the listing of England as the home of the breed may be only partly true. ¶The Clumber is a large, slow, and very deliberate worker in the field. He has enormous strength and is hardy enough to withstand almost any weather and almost any work regimen. He is a great retriever and very willing. ¶The Clumber is, or at least can be, devoted to his master, but once again we encounter a breed that may not be everybody's ideal pet. He prefers one master and can be temperamental—some people even say sullen—when placed in a position of working with other people or animals. He is a highly polished professional at his work and goes about it in a stolid, purposeful, nononsense way. He does not readily express great joy and does not want to bother with anyone but his master—that is, after his master has established his right to that position. The Clumber wants to be trained early and well, and only then will that excellence in performance be evident. ¶People selecting a fine, steady field dog without enormous social grace may want to consider this somewhat dour character. Those wanting the excitement of a canine pal and fellow socializer may find this breed less than ideal.

The Cocker Spaniel is not only one of the handsomest dogs ever bred, he also has a long record as a fine sporting animal. He is a true gentleman of the field. Without doubt the Cocker Spaniel comes down from a Spanish dog and has the same ancestry as the setters and larger spaniels of our time. Long ago, he was reduced in size, with one branch going off into the toy spaniels—strictly companion animals—and one branch developing toward the smallest of the true sporting dogs. The Cocker as we know him got his name from "cocking" dog, being especially adept with woodcocks. ¶Over the years the great beauty of this little gem of a dog began taking prece-

Cocker Spaniel

Land of origin: ENGLAND

Original purpose: Hunting

Recent popularity ranking by A.K.C. registration: 6th

American Spaniel Club, Inc.
Margaret M. Ciezkowski, Corres. Secretary
846 Old Stevens Creek Rd.
Martinez, GA 30907-9227

HEIGHT: Dogs to 15 inches   Bitches to 14 inches

WEIGHT: Dogs to 28 pounds   Bitches to 26 pounds

COAT
Flat or slightly wavy but *never* curly. Silky in texture and of medium length. Good undercoating. Well feathered on ears, chest, abdomen, and legs, but never to be excessive or deny sporting-dog character of breed.

COLOR
Black, white, tan, liver, and other solids with white on chest only—no white is better on colored dogs. Parti-colors definite and primary color to be less than 90 percent. The Cocker is shown in three varieties; black, parti- and ASCOB, any-solid-color-other-(than)-black.

Amount of care coat requires: 1 2 3 4 5 6 7 8 9 10

Amount of exercise required:* 1 2 3 4 5 6 7 8 9 10

Suitability for urban/apartment life: 1 2 3 4 5 6 7 8 9 10

*Varies greatly among animals.

dence over his ability in the field. More and more he was bred for the bench, while his intelligence was ignored or subordinated. Breeders strove to outdo each other in the feathery glory of their champions. When several truly magnificent Cockers began chalking up spectacular show careers, the fad was on, and everybody on the block had to own one of these dogs. The mass-producers had their day, and the Cocker Spaniel as a field dog all but disappeared. Here is a classic example of the fate that awaits the fad dog who is turned out by the basketload. ¶Through it all, however, much of the true character of the original Cocker Spaniel has remained. It wants only for enough breeders to show enthusiasm for this breed's intelligence: It will not necessarily require breeders to sacrifice much of the animal's admitted beauty to resume breeding for character, sense, and intelligence. ¶Anyone availing themselves of a Cocker Spaniel today is getting a dog not only of enormous style and class but also of noble field lineage. If they intend to breed, they are also investing in an opportunity to help reconstruct one of the truly great breeds. The true Cocker Spaniel is a steady, even dog, affectionate and fine with children. He is also a dog who should be able to accept training. Unfortunately, there is a better than even chance that a careless buyer will get a snappy, yappy brat without the strength of canine character to do anything but pose, if even that. The prospective owner should buy with care and only from breeders of reputation. It is time for the Cocker Spaniel to make his comeback.

English Cocker Spaniel

Land of origin: ENGLAND

Original purpose: Hunting

Recent popularity ranking by A.K.C. registration: 71st

English Cocker Spaniel Club of America, Inc.
Kate D. Romanski, Secretary
P.O. Box 252
Hales Corners, WI 53130

HEIGHT: Dogs to 17 inches   Bitches to 16 inches

WEIGHT: Dogs to 34 pounds   Bitches to 32 pounds

COAT
Medium length with good undercoating. Hair flat or slightly wavy and silky in texture. Well feathered but not too profuse.

COLOR
Broken and evenly distributed—white, roan, blue, liver, red, orange, lemon, black, tan, and others; should be attractive in balance and placement.

Amount of care coat requires: 1 2 3 4 5 6 7 8 9 10

Amount of exercise required:* 1 2 3 4 5 6 7 8 9 10

Suitability for urban/apartment life:† 1 2 3 4 5 6 7 8 9 10

*Varies greatly among animals.
†Only if appropriately exercised.

The English Cocker Spaniel is a perfectly splendid-looking dog with the same background as the American Cocker Spaniel. He is, though, a little larger. Note these comparisons:

	WEIGHT RANGE	HEIGHT RANGE
Cocker	22–28 lbs.	14–15 in.
English Cocker	26–34 lbs.	15–17 in.

It wasn't until 1892 that the Kennel Club in England recognized that the English Cocker Spaniel and the English Springer Spaniel were different breeds. Up to that time they appeared in the same litter, separated only by size. ¶There is no doubt that the Sussex, Cocker, Field, and Springer Spaniels have been closely associated and that all manner of interbreeding occurred even after they were acknowledged as different breeds and set upon their own courses of development. Interbreeding is no longer permitted. Fanciers of these handsome breeds feel each spaniel has its own character and desirable qualities. ¶The English Cocker Spaniel is one of the finest of the small field dogs and is both intelligent and responsive. If kept in the city or suburbs, he should be exercised regularly; the more often he is taken into the country, the better. His coat does need care, but it is not a long and arduous task if the dog receives proper attention. In show specimens we often see an exaggeration of the elaborate feathering on the legs and ears. This can be overdone, and the feathering should not be so profuse as to hide the true field-dog character of this breed.

English Springer Spaniel

Land of origin: ENGLAND

Original purpose: Hunting

Recent popularity ranking by A.K.C. registration: 21st

English Springer Spaniel Field Trial Association, Inc.
Ms. Marie L. Andersen, Corres. Secretary
29512 47th Ave. S.
Auburn, WA 98001

HEIGHT: Dogs to 20 inches   Bitches to 19 inches

WEIGHT: Dogs to 55 pounds   Bitches to 46 pounds

COAT
Flat or wavy, medium length. Waterproof, weatherproof, and thornproof. Fine and glossy. Never rough or curly.

COLOR
Liver or black with white markings, liver or black and white with tan markings. No lemon, red, or orange.

Amount of care coat requires: 1 2 3 4 5 6 7 8 9 10

Amount of exercise required: 1 2 3 4 5 6 7 8 9 10

Suitability for urban/apartment life:*   1 2 3 4 5 6 7 8 9 10

---

*Must be appropriately exercised.

The English Springer Spaniel carries in him all the best qualities of the English land spaniels. As a breed, he was separated from the English Cocker Spaniel at the turn of the century and is considerably larger. ¶The English Springer by nature is affectionate and loyal. This is a wonderful breed for children. He may be slow to take up with strangers, but he is not snappy or silly about it. He just likes to be sure of his ground. He therefore can make a first-rate watchdog. ¶The English Springer Spaniel is still a splendid field dog, although he will take well to a quieter and less active life. In city and suburban settings he should be given very long walks. It is a great kindness to get him out into the country as often as possible. He loves water and loves to retrieve. Most of all he loves to belong to a family and will return affection pound for pound. ¶The Springer coat, like that of all well-furnished spaniels, must be seen to if the dog is to remain handsome and regal. That does require some care, although the task need not be difficult. It is quite different, however, if a Springer is allowed to go long periods without attention. The feathering on the ears, chest, and legs will become matted, and he becomes a case for a professional. Things should not be allowed to go that far. ¶The English Springer Spaniel is one of those dogs who is as nice in character as he looks. The standards call for him to be friendly, eager to please, quick to learn, and willing to obey. One cannot ask for much more than that in a dog who already has refined beauty going for him plus a fine tradition of service and companionship!

Field Spaniel

Land of origin: ENGLAND

Original purpose: Hunting

Recent popularity ranking by A.K.C. registration: 128th

Field Spaniel Society of America
Sally Herweyer, Corres. Secretary
11197 Keystone
Lowell, MI 49331

HEIGHT: Dogs to 18 inches   Bitches to 17 inches

WEIGHT: Dogs to 50 pounds   Bitches to 45 pounds

COAT
Flat or slightly wavy. Never curly. Dense, silky, glossy. Feathering setterlike.

COLOR
Usually black but also liver, golden liver, mahogany red, roan—or any of these with tan markings. Should not be so colored and marked as to resemble a Springer Spaniel.

Amount of care coat requires: 1 2 3 4 5 6 7 8 9 10

Amount of exercise required: 1 2 3 4 5 6 7 8 9 10

Suitability for urban/apartment life:*   1 2 3 4 5 6 7 8 9 10

*If properly exercised.

The Field Spaniel, the least-known spaniel in this country, was badly hurt by some rather bizarre breeding experiments that for a long time kept this dog from being as appealing as his spaniel kin. He is thought to have been derived from the Cocker and Sussex Spaniels, with the Cocker strain being largely Welsh. Much of that may be conjecture. ¶In an effort to improve the look of the breed, both Cocker and Springer Spaniels were bred in, and eventually the present-day Field Spaniel emerged. There are very few in this country (only thirty-nine specimens were registered with the American Kennel Club in 1978), but interest in this breed could increase. ¶By nature the Field Spaniel is steady and determined although essentially good-natured. He is not fast and flashy, but he's reliable. He will probably never be a popular gundog in this country but will make it, if he does in fact become popular in the future, as a pet. ¶The Field Spaniel is fine in the suburbs and even in apartments if properly exercised he is, after all, a sporting dog designed for the field—and his coat, although rather more setter-like than exaggerated as in some Cockers, does require a reasonable amount of attention. It is not the sort of task that need be oppressive, just acknowledged and taken care of regularly. ¶Anyone seriously interested in this potentially very fine breed of companion animal may want to think about importing specimens to combine with the finest available examples here. It would be a kind of "ground-floor" venture that could pay off in satisfaction not generally available from coming into a breed after it has already become a fad. The Field Spaniel may be a dog of the future.

The Irish Water Spaniel is not everybody's dog. This is a special-purpose breed with excellent qualities and a superb record of performance. He is so ancient that we have no real information about his origin. He may go back six thousand years to Asia Minor, he may have inhabited the Iberian Peninsula when the Romans were there, and he may have arrived in Ireland with the earliest settlers of that land. All maybe, but we do know that he reached his present state of excellence in Ireland and that even Shakespeare wrote of his outstanding characteristics. ¶The excellence of this dog lies in his devotion to his master and his tolerance of his family. The

Irish Water Spaniel

Land of origin: IRELAND, but possibly far back in ancient Asia Minor

Original purpose: Water retrieving and other hunting uses

Recent popularity ranking by A.K.C. registration: 130th

Irish Water Spaniel Club of America
Renae Peterson, Secretary
24712 SE 380th St.
Enumclaw, WA 98022-8833

HEIGHT: Dogs to 24 inches   Bitches to 23 inches

WEIGHT: Dogs to 65 pounds   Bitches to 58 pounds

COAT
Extremely important point. Dense, tight ringlets without any woolliness. Longer on legs, wavy and abundant.

COLOR
Solid liver. No white markings.

Amount of care coat requires: 1 2 3 4 5 6 7 8 9 10
             •••••••••••

Amount of exercise required: 1 2 3 4 5 6 7 8 9 10
             •••••••••••••••••••••••

Suitability for urban/apartment life: 1 2 3 4 5 6 7 8 9 10
                                      UNSUITED

Irish Water Spaniel is a great water dog of endurance and skill. He is obedient, if well trained early in life, and is a top-level performer in any field for which he is suited. He is not necessarily the best of general pets, since he is tricky with strangers. For that reason he makes a better watchdog than most sporting dogs, but he does have to be guided since his natural suspiciousness tends to be nonselective. He also must be well controlled when around other animals. He can be a scrapper. ¶None of this is to say that the Irish Water Spaniel is a vicious dog (that word does not properly apply to dogs unless they have been made that way by ill treatment or disease), but rather that he is an assertive, hardheaded animal who is not approving of people he does not know well or see regularly. This can be a problem, particularly in an urban environment. ¶The distinctive ringleted coat of the Irish Water Spaniel does not require much heavy grooming unless it is badly neglected, and there's the rub. The coat does tend to mat and retain dirt unless it is brushed every three or four days at least. Although not a long or arduous process, it is an essential one that should be infallibly performed. ¶The Irish Water Spaniel is a breed with staunch devotees. They like the look of the animal, including the distinctly ratlike tail; they like the purposeful gait and stance and fiery willingness of the animal to work, to perform, to please. This, the tallest of the spaniels, despite his somewhat clownish appearance, is a special dog for special owners. Casual dog owners who are not accomplished at the art of being a master may be disappointed. Real dog people who are attracted to the dog for his antiquity, his skill in the field, and his aloof independence will be delighted.

Sussex Spaniel

Land of origin: ENGLAND

Original purpose: Hunting

Recent popularity ranking by A.K.C. registration: 136th

Sussex Spaniel Club of America
Ms. Barbara Barnard, Corres. Secretary
908 Cowan Dr.
Columbia, MO 65203

HEIGHT: Dogs to 16 inches   Bitches to 15 inches

WEIGHT: Dogs to 45 pounds   Bitches to 40 pounds

COAT
Abundant and either flat or slightly waved. No curl allowed. Moderate feathering on legs and stern.

COLOR
Rich golden liver.

Amount of care coat requires: 1 2 3 4 5 6 7 8 9 10

Amount of exercise required: 1 2 3 4 5 6 7 8 9 10

*Suitability for urban/apartment life:**   1 2 3 4 5 6 7 8 9 10

*If properly exercised.

The Sussex Spaniel is one of the least-known dogs in this country, and during 1975 only thirty-three new specimens were registered with the American Kennel Club. The breed apparently originated—or at least was perfected—in the county of Sussex, England. When it was developed, hunting was still done on foot, and there was plenty of game around. What was needed was a slow and steady dog who was at the same time companionable. These developments all took place in an area and a period of what was called rough shooting. ¶The Sussex Spaniel is a slow, not terribly elegant animal who is intelligent and deliberate in everything he does. He has a *massive* appearance, although even a big male will be under fifty pounds. He makes a good pet and will do well in any normal family situation. He has not caught on in this country because he is not stylish looking enough to fascinate the show enthusiast, and he is really not well suited to modern American hunting needs and habits.

¶Because he is slow and steady, neither mean nor silly, and because he is loyal and eminently trainable, the Sussex Spaniel holds real promise as a companion animal in this country. It is moot as to whether the breed will ever be given an opportunity to show its worth. All it takes, really, is a few determined enthusiasts to take the breed on. ¶The Sussex Spaniel is a reasonably good watchdog; he is usually calm and gentle, has very little odor, and gets along well with other animals. ¶Anyone seriously interested in this breed will probably find it difficult to locate puppies for sale. After checking with whatever breeders can be located, the potential enthusiast might want to think about importing specimens from England. Anyone looking for a cause as well as a pet might want to think about this gentleman from Sussex. There is a lot of quality built into the breed, and a little public relations could launch it on a whole new and unexpected American career.

The Welsh Springer is not anywhere near as well known in this country as its cousin the English Springer Spaniel. They are different breeds with very similar qualities. The Welsh Springer developed in Wales over four centuries ago and has always been quite distinctive. Here are some major differences between the breeds:

	HEIGHT RANGE	WEIGHT RANGE
Welsh Springer	15½–17 in.	32–40 lbs.
English Springer	17–20 in.	35–55 lbs.

	COLORS	COAT
Welsh Springer	Red and white	Not wavy
English Springer	Liver, black, tan, white, blue, roan in many combinations	Often wavy

The main differences to the eye are color and length of back. The English is the larger dog. ¶The Welsh Springer Spaniel is a tireless hunting dog and is easily trained for a variety of tasks. The breed is intelligent,

Welsh Springer Spaniel

Land of origin: WALES

Original purpose: Hunting

Recent popularity ranking by A.K.C. registration: 110th

Welsh Springer Spaniel Club of America, Inc.
Karen Lyle, Corres. Secretary
4425 N. 147th St.
Brookfield, WI 53005-1608

HEIGHT: Dogs to 17 inches   Bitches to 16$1/2$ inches

WEIGHT: Dogs to 45 pounds   Bitches to 38 pounds

COAT
Straight, flat, thick, and silky. Not wiry or wavy; curliness considered especially bad.

COLOR
Red and white; colors clear, strong, and rich.

Amount of care coat requires: 1 2 3 4 5 6 7 8 9 10

Amount of exercise required: 1 2 3 4 5 6 7 8 9 10

Suitability for urban/apartment life:*   1 2 3 4 5 6 7 8 9 10

*If very well exercised regularly.

steady, and responsive to approval. It is as fine a companion as it is a hunting breed. ¶In the home the Welsh Springer shows his other and equally desirable side. He is sensible and steady and not quarrelsome or foolish. He loves to play and will be the wise old dog or the clown, depending on age and the demands of the moment. He loves to participate in all group activities and does not take well to being left behind. He is naturally fine with children and will adjust to any reasonable family situation. He needs a lot of exercise, though, as might be expected of a sporting animal, and no one should attempt to maintain one in the suburbs or the city unless a good exercise regimen can be developed and adhered to. No weather is too tough for this Welshman, and he will not understand why you find any condition not perfect for a long walk or a romp. He needs that exercise not only for his peace of canine mind but also for body conditioning. ¶A certain amount of brushing is required if that fine and elegant spaniel look is to be maintained. It isn't much of a chore if it is performed faithfully as part of a regular weekly schedule.

The Magyar hordes swarming into central Europe ten centuries ago brought with them a hunting dog that was probably already an old breed. We believe that dog gave rise to the hunting dog of Hungary known today as the Vizsla. This is a fast, tensely mounted animal of boundless energy and willingness. He wants to work, he wants to please, and he wants reward in the form of praise. ¶This graceful animal is an aristocrat, not unlike a thoroughbred horse with its neat, perfected conformation and smooth, even power. The Vizsla is also extremely headstrong and determined to have it out once and for all with his master. Someone, man or dog, is going to be boss.

Vizsla

Land of origin: HUNGARY

Original purpose: All-purpose hunting

Recent popularity ranking by A.K.C. registration: 54th

Vizsla Club of America, Inc.
Patricia Carnes, Corres. Secretary
P.O. Box 1755
Stevensville, MD 21666

HEIGHT: Dogs to 24 inches   Bitches to 23 inches

WEIGHT: Dogs to 60 pounds   Bitches to 55 pounds

COAT
Short, dense, and smooth. Lies flat, no undercoat.

COLOR
Solid rusty gold or dark sandy yellow. Dark brown and pale yellow not desirable.

Amount of care coat requires: 1 2 3 4 5 6 7 8 9 10

Amount of exercise required: 1 2 3 4 5 6 7 8 9 10

Suitability for urban/apartment life: 1 2 3 4 5 6 7 8 9 10
UNSUITED

Sanity with a Vizsla in the home requires that this issue be settled early on. A Vizsla who has not been properly trained for life in a home is a monumental pest. Left alone he just might decide to go sailing through a plate-glass window in order to have some fun outside. He'll keep on running your glazier's bill up, too, until the rules are outlined for him and his stay-at-home manners learned. ¶The Vizsla can be fine with his master's family, though he may be very slow to take to strangers, and he can be aloof, to say the least. Shyness, however, would be considered a fault. ¶As is often the case with large, smooth-coated field dogs, the Vizsla is a poor choice for urban or even suburban living and not really the dog for people who are sedentary in habit. One way or another, the Vizsla is going to get the workout he needs to stay in shape and burn up his endless energy reserve. If you don't work him in the field, then he is going to be bumptious and a nuisance. Of course, you don't have to be a hunter, but you do have to like very long walks. A Vizsla needs to run and explore and respond to cool, even, but very forceful commands. ¶You cannot fault the Vizsla on his qualities as a field dog. He is intelligent, responsive, perfected for the job he was designed to do. The Vizsla is one of the special-purpose dogs for special kinds of committed dog owners.

The Weimaraner is an all-purpose hunting dog developed in Germany from the Bloodhound. He is a large, assertive, intelligent animal of unmistakable quality. He is also a dog who requires special qualities in his master. ¶The Weimaraner makes a better watchdog than almost any other breed of sporting dog because he is aggressive and quite fearless. He is a dog of great character, and he spends much of his time telling everyone about it. If allowed to have the upper hand, there is no worse pest than this breed. He should not be a person's first dog. ¶This is a breed that simply must be given a full course of obedience training at the professional level. If the owner is

Weimaraner

Land of origin: GERMANY

Original purpose: Big-game hunting

Recent popularity ranking by A.K.C. registration: 41st

Weimaraner Club of America
Mrs. Dorothy Derr, Corres. Secretary
P.O. Box 110708
Nashville, TN 37222-0708

HEIGHT: Dogs to 27 inches   Bitches to 25 inches

WEIGHT: Dogs to 85 pounds   Bitches to 70 pounds

COAT
Short, smooth, sleek.

COLOR
Solid—shades of mouse gray to silver gray. Small white spot on chest alone allowed. A distinctly blue or black coat is grounds for disqualification.

Amount of care coat requires: 1 2 3 4 5 6 7 8 9 10

Amount of exercise required: 1 2 3 4 5 6 7 8 9 10

Suitability for urban/apartment life: 1 2 3 4 5 6 7 8 9 10
UNSUITED

competent, that is fine; if not, then the cost of taking your Weimaraner to a top obedience school should be considered a part of the acquisition price. An untrained Weimaraner is going to walk all over his owner, his family, and their friends. While not dangerous, he can be pushy and extremely unpleasant to have around. Conversely, a well-trained Weimaraner is one of the most splendid-looking and gentlemanly of all breeds, sporting or otherwise. ¶The Germans were almost neurotic in the severity with which they governed the breeding of Weimaraners. Poor specimens were destroyed, and good specimens were only bred after the most careful consideration. Predictably, when the breed became known here around 1929, it caught on. Equally predictable was the slippage in breeding standards. Weimaraners bred in this country range from the really excellent to the utterly hopeless. Retail all-breed puppy outlets often feature these dogs, but they should never be obtained from this source. Be suspicious of the inexpensive Weimaraner: only the finest show and field-trial stock should be accepted, and only after a visit with the breeder and a chance to see and meet the puppy's parents. ¶The only real problem with the Weimaraner as a breed is that he is often more intelligent than the person who owns him. When this happens, it is not the happiest of man dog relationships. The owner should always be smarter and should always be in command. Any person smart enough and strong willed enough to properly select, train, and manage a Weimaraner is in for an unparalleled dog-owning experience. The owner who overrates himself or underrates his Weimaraner is in for an ordeal.

This seldom-seen hunting dog began his career in Holland late in the nineteenth century. One man, really, was responsible for developing the breed from a mixture of spaniels, setters, hounds, and mixed-breed dogs. Because of a family quarrel the man, E. K. Korthals, eventually left Holland for Germany and then moved on to France. He took his dogs with him and kept up the breeding experiments for the rest of his life. In France they will refer to this dog as the Korthals Griffon. ¶The Wirehaired Pointing Griffon is a somewhat slow, very deliberate, and skillful multipurpose hunting dog. He is a pointer, as well as a retriever. His harsh, rough coat

Wirehaired Pointing Griffon

Land of origin: HOLLAND

Original purpose: All-purpose hunting

Recent popularity ranking by A.K.C. registration: 113th

American Wirehaired Pointing Griffon Association
Kathryn Haberkorn, Corres. Secretary
36340 Hillside Ln.
Lebanon, OR 97355-9224

HEIGHT: Dogs to 23½ inches   Bitches to 21½ inches

WEIGHT: Dogs to 60 pounds   Bitches to 55 pounds

COAT
Unique in sporting dogs—downy undercoat and hard, dry, stiff outer coat like bristles on a wild boar.

COLOR
Steel gray, white with chestnut splashes, all chestnut, or dirty white and chestnut. Black a serious fault.

Amount of care coat requires: 1 2 3 4 5 6 7 8 9 10
                • • • • • •

Amount of exercise required: 1 2 3 4 5 6 7 8 9 10
                • • • • • • • • • • • •

Suitability for urban/apartment life: 1 2 3 4 5 6 7 8 9 10
                           UNSUITED

makes him an ideal dog for cold climates, miserable weather, and tough terrain like saltwater marshes. This is a steady, positive, and intelligent breed of dog. He is also a particularly pleasant companion breed. ¶The Wirehaired Pointing Griffon is loyal to his master and good with children. He is calm and reasonable with strangers, although he can be slow to offer affection or to show enthusiasm. He is detached and perhaps cautious by nature when he is unsure of newcomers. ¶The Wirehaired Pointing Griffon, a very rare dog in America, is not an apartment or city dog. Confined, he cannot be relied upon to retain his naturally calm, intelligent way of dealing with life. He needs enormous amounts of exercise to stay well and happy, and the more exposure he gets to rough terrain and hard living, the happier he seems to be. People attempting to remold Korthals's many years of hard work and skillful breeding in a single generation are in for a disappointment. This is one breed that will not be recast easily. This is a dog for an active family—perhaps ideally an active single person. He thrives on miserable weather, rough water, and long days that begin before sunrise. If you have that kind of abuse and misery to offer, you are going to have a happy dog. He will curl up by the fire at night and kick his legs in dreams that re-create the day, but he wants that day to be rough enough to try him. ¶A Wirehaired Pointing Griffon should not be difficult or ill-tempered. There is a solid, workaday look about him, a pragmatic Dutch way of going about the day's labors.

{Group 2}

The Hounds

Afghan Hound
Basenji
Basset Hound
Beagle
Black and Tan Coonhound
Bloodhound
Borzoi
Dachshund
American Foxhound
English Foxhound
Greyhound

Harrier
Ibizan Hound
Irish Wolfhound
Norwegian Elkhound
Otter Hound
Petit Basset Griffon Vendéen
Pharoah Hound
Rhodesian Ridgeback
Saluki
Scottish Deerhound
Whippet

The handsome Afghan Hound is an aristocrat. The breed goes back almost six thousand years, and he was no doubt the companion of kings. He is also a clown, for he loves to play and romp and is almost never mean or petty. ¶The Afghan Hound is one of the few large active dogs who can make it in the city. Although this dog requires a great deal of exercise and should be taken on long, fast walks several times a day, he can adapt to apartment life. Despite the "klutzy" act he puts on and the general prejudice that the coursing, or sight, hounds aren't always the brightest dogs on the block, the Afghan is a willing dog who is anxious to please. Because of the Afghan's size and his occasional good-natured bumptiousness, it is a good idea for a new owner and his dog to take obedience classes together. ¶The Afghan is a stun-

Afghan Hound

Land of origin: SINAI PENINSULA, then AFGHANISTAN

Original purpose: Hunting, including leopard

Recent popularity ranking by A.K.C. registration: 72nd

Afghan Hound Club of America, Inc.
Norma Cozzoni, Corres. Secretary
43 W. 612 Tall Oaks Trl.
Elburn, IL 60119

HEIGHT: Dogs to 27 inches   Bitches to 25 inches

WEIGHT: Dogs to 60 pounds   Bitches to 50 pounds

COAT
Thick, silky, very fine in texture. Not clipped or trimmed. Long hair except on back in mature dogs, where saddle is short.

COLOR
All colors are seen, but white markings, especially on the head, are not desirable.

Amount of care coat requires: 1 2 3 4 5 6 7 8 9 10

Amount of exercise required: 1 2 3 4 5 6 7 8 9 10

*Suitability for urban/apartment life:**   1 2 3 4 5 6 7 8 9 10

*Assuming that the dog will be taken on long walks several times a day and at least occasionally be taken someplace where he will be able to run.

ning-looking dog, and the coat should be well brushed to enhance the liquid motion that is so characteristic of this animal of style and beauty. Ropy or matted Afghans are unforgivable and tell one a great deal about the owners who bought a dog they were not prepared to properly keep. ¶Afghans are fine with children, although there is the problem of small toddlers being bowled over by a great galumping hound bounding to the door to see who is there. ¶This ancient hound does well with other animals and usually will not fight. Of course, *two* mature males always can be a problem, but perhaps less so with this breed than with a good many others. ¶There is no doubt that many people like the idea of high style in a dog, and one would have to go far to find a breed better suited to that ego need than this one. And this is not to be condemned. It is just as easy to love a dog who gives an added aesthetic satisfaction as it is to adore one who doesn't. The potential Afghan owner should, however, be certain that it isn't *just* style he wants. This breed is sensitive, constantly in need of affection and a sense of participation; although splendid-looking in a fashion layout, the Afghan is not merely an ornament. ¶Any dog, once purchased, becomes a long-term commitment. It is no more true of any other breed than it is of this ancient hound. He once shared the tents of sheikhs in the Sinai wilderness and later coursed the rugged mountains of Afghanistan for leopard and gazelle in blistering summer heat and bone-cracking winter cold. Despite his picturesque and seemingly delicate beauty, the Afghan remains a hunting hound—hardy, tough, and willing.

There aren't many animals from Africa on the European and American scene, and for that reason alone the Basenji began catching on almost as soon as he was first seen in America in 1937. He was a curiosity with a fascinating history. This dog was brought to Egypt for the pleasure of the pharaohs thousands of years ago. With the fall of that ancient civilization, the breed was able to hang on in its native central Africa, where it was used for hunting. ¶The Basenji is a swift, silent dog with a remarkable nose and great determination. He is an active animal and should be given a great deal of exercise every day. He has a lovely, high-stepping gait and is great fun

Basenji

Land of origin: CENTRAL AFRICA

Original purpose: Hunting

Recent popularity ranking by A.K.C. registration: 65th

Basenji Club of America, Inc.
Susan Patterson Wilson, Secretary
P.O. Box 1076
South Bend, IN 46624-1076

HEIGHT: Dogs to 17 inches   Bitches to 16 inches

WEIGHT: Dogs to 24 pounds   Bitches to 22 pounds

COAT
Short and silky. Coat very pliant.

COLOR
Chestnut red, pure black, black and tan—always with white feet, chest, and tail tip. White legs, blaze, and collar allowed as optional.

Amount of care coat requires: 1 2 3 4 5 6 7 8 9 10

Amount of exercise required: 1 2 3 4 5 6 7 8 9 10

Suitability for urban/apartment life: 1 2 3 4 5 6 7 8 9 10

---

to watch. When happy, he bounds and leaps and is like a little deer with glistening coat. ¶It is not true that the Basenji is mute. He does not bark like other dogs, but he does make a giggling, yodeling sound that is impossible to describe or imitate. It is a happy sound, generally reserved for close friends. ¶The Basenji is one of the cleanest dogs. His coat needs almost no care, and he rarely if ever needs bathing—certainly not more than a couple times a year. Almost unique in the dog world is his habit of washing himself all over, just like a cat. The result is a perfect pleasure of a dog for the fastidious homeowner. ¶Naturally well-behaved and intelligent, the Basenji will take training easily, especially if he is included within the family circle. He is a calm dog, surprisingly so for one so active. He seems to have everything under control, however, and to know instinctively how to please. ¶Basenjis can be good with children—in almost any family situation—but they do insist on being a part of the action and are often suspicious of strangers. A Basenji who is left out, even inadvertently, is an unhappy dog. ¶In play and pleasure, in the show-ring and on the street, the handsome, sprightly little fox-terrier-sized hound called the Basenji never fails to attract attention. One can predict with fair certainty that the breed will only increase in popularity as time passes.

The Basset Hound is an old breed developed in France and Belgium mostly from the Bloodhound, whose saint-like disposition it shares. ¶The Basset has been popular in Europe for centuries and has always been highly regarded for his many fine qualities. He is a slow trailing dog but one with tremendous stamina and deliberateness. He is said to have a nose second only to that of the Bloodhound, that grandfather of all scent-hounds. The ears of the Basset, designed to swirl up stale scent particles into the ever-receptive nose, also point to the undoubted Bloodhound ancestry of the breed. Because of a naturally oily skin, he does have a pleasant, some-

Basset Hound

Land of origin: FRANCE

Original purpose: All-purpose hunting

Recent popularity ranking by A.K.C. registration: 20th

Basset Hound Club of America, Inc.
Marian "Mimi" Brandolino, Secretary
6414 E. Corrine Dr.
Scottsdale, AZ 85254

HEIGHT: Dogs to 15 inches   Bitches to 14 inches

WEIGHT: Dogs to 45 pounds   Bitches to 35 pounds

COAT
Hard, smooth, short, and quite dense. Skin loose and elastic.

COLOR
Any recognized hound color. Distribution of markings of no importance in judging.

Amount of care coat requires: 1 2 3 4 5 6 7 8 9 10

Amount of exercise required: 1 2 3 4 5 6 7 8 9 10

Suitability for urban/apartment life.* 1 2 3 4 5 6 7 8 9 10

*But plenty of exercise *is* required—preferably three or four long walks a day.

what musky, "doggy" odor. ¶The Basset is one of the most pleasant and adaptable of dogs. Almost never snappy or aggressive, he gets along well with his master (whom he adores), family, and friends (whether two- or four-legged) and he should always be included in family activities. He is peaceful, sensible, affectionate, and simply marvelous with children. As a puppy he is an engaging as an animal can be, and his cheery outlook remains with him all his life. He can be serious, of course, and when charged with a job the Basset goes about it with almost comic intensity. ¶More agile than he appears, the Basset requires a great deal of exercise. It would be unfair to keep a Basset Hound shut in week and week out. This is an active field animal, and he has been bred for that purpose for hundreds of canine generations. He should not be penalized just because he also happens to be almost unbelievably pleasant. The Basset Hound should be walked several times a day—long, well-paced walks—and taken to the country for an open-air run as often as possible. Because family is far more important to a Basset than anything else, he will adapt to apartment life and is quiet and reasonable when inside. ¶Bassets are fairly long-lived, are generally strong and healthy, and can be good watchdogs. They have very loud voices. Naturally obedient and easy to train, they are good natured about taking orders. A large, fine hound of many exceptional qualities, the Basset deserves all the favor he is experiencing. Very few hounds outrank him in popularity.

The Beagle is one of the oldest of the scent hounds, probably dating back to pre-Roman times. It is believed that the breed formed in England and possibly in Wales, although we can never know for sure. Beagles have been evident all through recorded history in that part of the British Isles. ¶The Beagle is a hunting hound who works well alone or in small groups or large packs. He has been used on rabbit and hare and other game as well. The ancestry of some packs in England is very old, and their bloodlines are jealously guarded. The breed is by nature loyal, very easily trained, and courageous. For his size this tough little dog will take almost anything that any other dog can handle. No weather bothers him, no terrain—no matter how rough

Beagle

Land of origin: Probably WALES and ENGLAND

Original purpose: Hunting rabbits

Recent popularity ranking by A.K.C. registration: 7th

National Beagle Club
Susan Mills Stoue, Secretary
2555 Pennsylvania NW
Washington, DC 20037

HEIGHT: Variety 1—Dogs to 13 inches   Bitches to 13 inches
             Variety 2—Dogs 13 to 15 inches   Bitches 13 to 15 inches

WEIGHT: Under 13 inches—to 18 pounds
             Over 13 inches—to 20 pounds

COAT
Close, hard, typical hound; medium length.

COLOR
Any true hound color—white, tan, black in different combinations and markings.

Amount of care coat requires: 1 2 3 4 5 6 7 8 9 10

Amount of exercise required: 1 2 3 4 5 6 7 8 9 10

*Suitability for urban/apartment life:** 1 2 3 4 5 6 7 8 9 10

*But only if properly exercised.

and broken—is too hard, and no amount of running will wear him down. For endurance and courage this dog is not to be beat. ¶All of that, though, has to do with the dog in the field. Most Beagles in America today are house pets, and they excel at that assignment as well. Beagles and children are a natural mix, and the dog gets along splendidly with other animals. Beagles are often good little watchdogs, although they are fine with strangers once they have been introduced. They are affectionate and outgoing, and they have a lovely hound voice. In the city young Beagles need to be trained not to overdo the vocalizing. A Beagle loves a good howling session and may tend to do a solo when left alone. That can be a bit tiresome for the neighbors. ¶It is no accident that the Beagle is in seventh place among American Kennel Club regis-trations today. He has been on top for years and probably always will be there. Beagles are splendid country dogs, fine in the suburban home and in the apartment as well—as long as they get exercise. They are not silly or ever ugly; they are calm, gentle, and loving. They are also clean and quite easy to train ¶There are so many Beagles produced in this country each year—fifty-nine thousand new Beagles were registered with the A.K.C. in 1994; and that is only a fraction of those born—that great care must be taken to obtain a really good example of the breed. It is wise to bypass the mass-producers and seek out the specialist. There are two distinct sizes of Beagle—up to thirteen inches and from thirteen to fifteen inches. Over fifteen inches is outsized and not to be encouraged. No sense in trying to turn a Beagle into a Foxhound.

Black and Tan Coonhound

Land of origin: UNITED STATES

Original purpose: Hunting, especially raccoon and opossum

Recent popularity ranking by A.K.C. registration: 114th

American Black & Tan Coonhound Club, Inc.
Victoria Blackburn, Corres. Secretary
700 Grand Ave.
Elgin, IL 60120

HEIGHT: Dogs to 27 inches   Bitches to 25 inches

WEIGHT: Dogs to 85 pounds   Bitches to 80 pounds

COAT
Short, dense, and able to withstand rough country.

COLOR
Coal black with rich tan above eyes, on sides of muzzle, chest, legs, and breeching.
Black penciling on toes.

Amount of care coat requires: 1 2 3 4 5 6 7 8 9 10

Amount of exercise required: 1 2 3 4 5 6 7 8 9 10

Suitability for urban/apartment life: 1 2 3 4 5 6 7 8 9 10
UNSUITED

The handsome Black and Tan Coonhound apparently is descended from the English Talbot Hound, the Bloodhound, and the English Foxhound. In this country the American Foxhound was crossed in, and the breed emerged as we know it today. It shares many skills and characteristics with other Southern hound breeds not recognized by the American Kennel Club. It has been bred not only for field performance but also for its distinctive colors. ¶The Black and Tan Coonhound is a large, active, working hound. He has a magnificent voice, which he uses when he picks up a trail. He trails like a Bloodhound, seeking microscopic particles of scent material. He is all but impossible to shake off once he latches on. ¶The Black and Tan shares other characteristics with the Bloodhound: the elements of personality. Like the more ancient breed, the Black and Tan is a big, delightful slob. Although massive and powerful and without limit in his energy and endurance, he is delightful as a companion animal. There is the almost inevitable tendency to think of the Black and Tan as a ferocious dog looking for people and things to tear apart. Such is not the case at all. What the Black and Tan likes above everything else is attention, affection, and approbation. He is the near perfect dog in a give-and-take situation. Black and Tans are seldom quarrelsome with other animals, although adult males or adult females can vie with others of their own sex until a suitable pecking order has been established. In all other situations they are generally gentle and playful despite their great power and original use. ¶The Black and Tan Coonhound can be kept in the suburban home, but plenty of exercise is needed and should be an original element in the decision to own this breed. Only the most reliable specialty breeders should be consulted, and adults in the dog's line ought to be carefully examined. The Black and Tan Coonhound is a handsome, splendid breed of dog, and only breeders devoted to the maintenance of their high standards should be trusted.

The Bloodhound often is referred to as the grandfather of all scent hounds. His origins go back to ancient times, and he probably has been known in something like his present form for two thousand years. The modern scent hounds (as distinct from sight hounds such as the Greyhound and Borzoi)—the Beagles, Bassets, and Foxhounds, for example—all carry the blood of the Bloodhound. ¶Interestingly, Bloodhounds probably got their name from the fact that in the Middle Ages in England it was only the people of blue blood—aristocrats, that is—who owned this animal. To suggest that the name *Bloodhound* comes from any

Bloodhound

Land of origin: Probably ancient GREECE or ROME

Original purpose: Hunting, then man trailing

Recent popularity ranking by A.K.C. registration: 67th

American Bloodhound Club
Ed Kilby, Secretary
1914 Berry Ln.
Daytona Beach, FL 32124

HEIGHT: Dogs to 27 inches   Bitches to 25 inches

WEIGHT: Dogs to 110 pounds   Bitches to 100 pounds

COAT
Short, dense, and able to withstand rough country.

COLOR
Coal black with rich tan above eyes, on sides of muzzle, chest, legs, and breeching.
Black penciling on toes.

Amount of care coat requires: 1 2 3 4 5 6 7 8 9 10

Amount of exercise required: 1 2 3 4 5 6 7 8 9 10

Suitability for urban/apartment life: 1 2 3 4 5 6 7 8 9 10
                                    UNSUITED

sanguinary propensity is just plain silly. Bloodhounds are lovers. They do not *hunt* men; they follow trails, and that is their game. The Bloodhound's almost unimaginably keen nose enables him to follow trails no other dog could detect. When he gets to his quarry, be it a child or an escaped convict, he does not attack but wags his tail and often tries to kiss. ¶Apart from the nonsense myth of the attacking, bloodthirsty hound, there are other nonsense tales. Bloodhounds normally are used alone, not in packs. Occasionally a brace (pair) may be used, but no more than that. They do not barrel along a trail yowling—almost all Bloodhounds trail silently. A Bloodhound is not allowed off a lead for two reasons: he would soon leave his trainer behind, and since he has absolutely no road sense, he would be liable to be hit on the first road he had to cross. ¶The Bloodhound is a loving, gentle pet who should never be quarrelsome with people or other animals. He does not do especially well in the obedience department because his whole nature is to tell you where to go, not take directions *from* you. ¶The Bloodhound is not a casual dog owner's dog but rather a special breed for dedicated people. Good examples do not come cheaply, and $600 is not high. Bloodhounds are suited to country living. They like to be in the company of other animals and people. Their voices are glorious, and they are more apt to "sing" in greeting to someone they love than when on a trail. Bloodhound owners should consider training their dogs to trail and registering them with the police. Many children and confused old people have been saved by hounds owned by hobbyists. The Bloodhound does require a great deal of exercise, and his feeding must be scheduled and precise, since he is particularly subject to bloat. This gastric disorder of uncertain origin can kill an otherwise healthy dog within an hour.

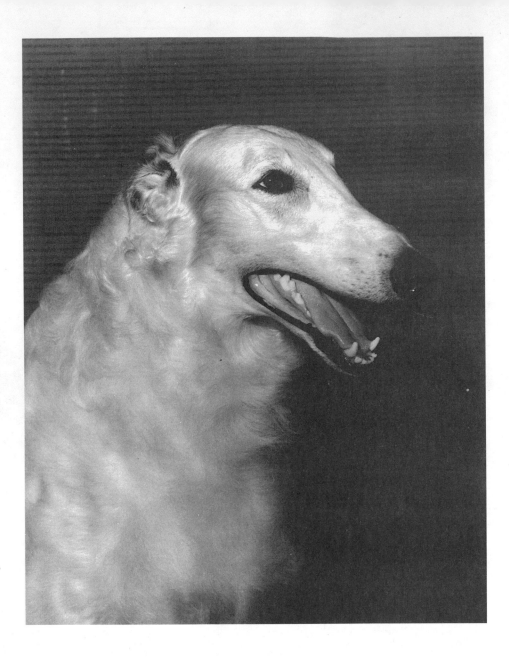

The Borzoi, originally known in the United States as the Russian Wolf-hound, is one of the most aristocratic of all dogs in style, bearing, and ancestry. Arabian Greyhounds, gazelle-coursing animals of great speed, were imported into Russia by members of the royal circle. When they failed to survive the Russian weather, others were imported and crossed with a native working dog. The result, after considerable effort, was what we know as the Borzoi. ¶Few dogs are as beautiful to behold as this magnificent hound, who is even more spectacular when seen in pairs. If a standing Borzoi is lyrical, the hound in motion is an epic poem. He floats when he gets into full stride. He is a powerful, aggressive, purposeful animal with deadly

Borzoi

Land of origin: RUSSIA

Original purpose: Coursing wolves and game animals

Recent popularity ranking by A.K.C. registration: 78th

Borzoi Club of America, Inc.
Karen Mays, Corres. Secretary
29 Crown Dr.
Warren, NJ 07059-5111

HEIGHT: Dogs to 31 inches   Bitches to 29 inches

WEIGHT: Dogs to 105 pounds   Bitches to 90 pounds

COAT
Long and silky but not at all woolly. May be flat or wavy or even somewhat curly. Neck well frilled, profuse, and curly. Feathering on hindquarters and tail, less on chest.

COLOR
Any color or combination of colors is acceptable.

Amount of care coat requires: 1 2 3 4 5 6 7 8 9 10
                                   •••••••

Amount of exercise required: 1 2 3 4 5 6 7 8 9 10
                                 ••••••••••••••••••••

Suitability for urban/apartment life: 1 2 3 4 5 6 7 8 9 10
                                          •••••

*If there is space and if exercise will be provided to suit the needs of this animal.

accuracy once he is set loose. He will run a wolf to the ground and kill it, whatever its size. This should be kept in mind when other dogs are around—a Borzoi in a fight is big trouble, not only because of size and power, but also because of the breed's extraordinary speed. ¶Any prospective owner should weigh carefully the exercise this animal must have. Since few city dwellers can provide an opportunity for the Borzoi to course, very long walks and, if there is a place where conditions are right, a chance to run are the minimal requirements. It must be remembered, though, that before a Borzoi is allowed to run, he must be thoroughly trained. He will be out of sight in seconds and well beyond a casual whistle of recall. The dogs certainly should not be allowed to molest native wildlife or other people's pets. ¶The Borzoi makes a good pet. He is generally a calm animal, considering his purpose and design, and is affectionate with youngsters and adults. Because of the animal's lightninglike reflexes, incredible speed, agility, and great size, any sign of aggressiveness toward people must be discouraged. A puppy should be trained early, and that training should be maintained throughout the dog's life. ¶The Borzoi is not always superb, however. There are an unfortunate number of poor examples around, animals who are too long for their height, with a disproportionate head, too short a tail, or who lack the liquid motion that so enhances the beauty of this breed; such specimens are to be avoided by knowing the parents of the animal and by not buying a puppy too young to be properly evaluated. Care in purchase is required, for relatively poor examples are found even in the show-ring. In the pet trade they can be horrendous. Beware of an inexpensive Borzoi.

Today's Dachshund is the descendant of a fiery German hunting dog of perhaps thirty-five pounds or more. He was used initially on badger, or so tradition goes (*Dachs* is the German word for "badger"), but also on a wide variety of other wildlife. He should exhibit the character and assertiveness this background suggests. ¶The Dachshund is a wonderfully responsive and loyal dog, seemingly a hound but with many terrierlike characteristics. He is intelligent, willing to learn, and a true participant. He loves play, and he travels well. Because of his short legs, he gets more exercise per block than almost any other breed you can name. He is, then, a perfect apartment dog. ¶The three coat styles require different degrees of care, of course, but it is never oppressive, for the naturally clean little Dachshund is never very large. The Miniature variety sports all three coats. He is a true lapdog and can be

Dachshund

Land of origin: GERMANY

Original purpose: Hunting, especially badger

Recent popularity ranking by A.K.C. registration: 8th

Dachshund Club of America, Inc.
Mr. Walter M. Jones, Secretary
390 Eminence Pike
Shelbyville, KY 40065

HEIGHT: Dogs to 9 inches   Bitches to 9 inches

WEIGHT:* Dogs to 20 pounds   Bitches to 20 pounds

COAT
Smooth variety—short, thick, smooth, shiny. Not coarse or too thick.

Wirehaired variety—uniform, tight, short, thick, rough, and hard. Good undercoat. Beard on chin. Eyebrows bushy.

Longhaired variety—soft, sleek, glistening, slightly wavy, feathered.

COLOR
Red or tan, red-yellow, yellow, brindle; deep black, chocolate, gray, or blue and white. Dappled. Foregoing for smooth variety. All colors permissible in wirehaired variety. Longhaired has same range as smooth except red and black is allowed and classed as red.

Amount of care coat requires:
Smooth: 1 2 3 4 5 6 7 8 9 10

Wirehaired: 1 2 3 4 5 6 7 8 9 10

Longhaired: 1 2 3 4 5 6 7 8 9 10

Amount of exercise required: 1 2 3 4 5 6 7 8 9 10

Suitability for urban/apartment life: 1 2 3 4 5 6 7 8 9 10

*Miniature Dachshunds are bred in all three coats (see above) and are shown as a division of the open class as "under 10 pounds" when twelve months or older.

carried anywhere. ¶Dachshunds get along well with children and with other animals, although when young they are very playful and can drive other animals up the wall. They soon learn their manners, though, and settle in as fine family pets. They are, in fact, often owned in pairs because they are such fun to watch. ¶Because they do have three very distinct coat styles, a wide range of colors, and a remarkable range in size, they are able to serve a variety of tastes. This coupled with their good nature and responsiveness has kept them consistently among the most popular of all breeds in the United States. People who own Dachshunds tend to keep right on owning them all their lives. ¶Dachshunds are so extremely popular that the mass-producers have had a field day, and there are some perfectly awful specimens offered for sale every day. Stick to the best specialty breeders and make sure you have the dog you set out to own—a fine example of a truly outstanding breed.

The American Foxhound may date as far back as De Soto's landing in Florida in 1539. Some records say that he brought a hound pack with him. We do know that English hounds were imported in 1650 and that these were foundation animals for what later appeared to be an American version of the English Fox-

hound. They were, in fact, better known as Virginia Hounds and were distinctly different from their English ancestors by George Washington's time. But English packs were imported in 1742 and 1770, and Washington was a subscriber to the latter importation. In 1785 Lafayette gave Washington some French hounds of similar size,

American Foxhound

Land of origin: ENGLAND, FRANCE, and AMERICA

Original purpose: Hunting and field trials

Recent popularity ranking by A.K.C. registration: 132nd

American Foxhound Club
Mrs. Jack H. Heck, Secretary
221 Oakwood Ave.
Dayton, OH 45419

HEIGHT: Dogs to 25 inches   Bitches to 24 inches

WEIGHT: Dogs to 70 pounds   Bitches to 65 pounds

COAT
Medium length, hard, close, typical of hounds.

COLOR
Any color—usually includes black, white, and/or tan.

Amount of care coat requires: 1 2 3 4 5 6 7 8 9 10

Amount of exercise required: 1 2 3 4 5 6 7 8 9 10

Suitability for urban/apartment life: 1 2 3 4 5 6 7 8 9 10
UNSUITED

and the Virginia Hounds were improved. In 1808 more came in from England and, in 1830, another pack from Ireland. ¶Over the intervening years more imports have helped improve the strength, durability, and versatility of what is now called the American Foxhound. He is still a little less sturdy than the English Foxhound, but he is a dog of great versatility with fine pet as well as field qualities. The American Foxhound is used today in field trials, as a trailing dog for armed fox hunters on foot, as a trailing dog in the mounted fox-hunting tradition, and as a general pack hound. Other popular hunting hounds in the South have been derived from the Foxhound, and his qualities appear among many American-developed scent hounds. ¶This is a dog of great speed and a jealous nature. He is unbeatable when it comes to determination, and no terrain will deter him once he is on a trail. His nose is very keen, and he ignores weather completely. Because he has been a pack dog all down through history, the American Foxhound, like his English cousin, gets along with other dogs. He is loyal to master and family and can be quite protective. He may be slow in taking up with strangers—he isn't silly or snappy, just cautious. The Foxhound is a field animal with hardened muscles, a creature of the hunt and the chase. Locked up and kept from running and using his incredible nose, he can go a little "stir crazy," and the dog who is kept that way should not be expected to show all of the fine qualities that a working dog will. ¶Many Americans split their time between the city and the country, and even people without a second residence spend long hours hiking and perhaps camping. For such owners the Foxhound is ideal. But only the very active city dweller should even consider this fine hound for a pet.

The English Foxhound's studbooks go back to the eighteenth century and have been well kept, for the breeding has been in the hands of masters of hounds. Any owner of an English Foxhound today should be able to trace that dog back to 1800 or before. ¶The well-boned, sturdy, and reliable English Foxhound on the aver- age tends to be somewhat stouter than his American counterpart to whose origins he contributed so much. The head is large but not gross. The neck is long and clean and should extend at least ten inches from the base of the skull to the shoulder. This is not a small dog. He is symmetrical in appear- ance and should have a bright and eager

English Foxhound

Land of origin: ENGLAND

Original purpose: Trailing, hunting

Recent popularity ranking by A.K.C. registration: 134th

HEIGHT: Dogs to 25 inches   Bitches to 24 inches

WEIGHT: Dogs to 70 pounds   Bitches to 62 pounds

COAT
Short, dense, glossy, and hard—typical of hounds.

COLOR
Black, white, tan, yellow; not important as long as basic hound colors are present.

Amount of care coat requires: 1 2 3 4 5 6 7 8 9 10

Amount of exercise required: 1 2 3 4 5 6 7 8 9 10

Suitability for urban/apartment life: 1 2 3 4 5 6 7 8 9 10
UNSUITED

look. Willingness is a prime characteristic of the breed. ¶Because Foxhounds have typical hound coats, they are clean and easily kept. They do shed, but that is seldom a problem unless the animals have been allowed to develop dry coats, a condition that is easily corrected. ¶Many of the things we have said about the American Foxhound are true of the English Foxhound as well. He is affectionate and loyal to his master and to his family. He is wary of strangers and wants to be sure of his ground before allowing too many liberties. He has a fine voice, of course, and can make a good watchdog. ¶All the Foxhounds—American, English, and their French counterparts—are trailing field dogs and have a limited tolerance for apartment living. It isn't the apartment that matters so much as it is the life-style of urban families. The Foxhound likes to curl up in front of a fire as much as the next dog does, but that comes after a lot of time acquiring aching muscles. All weather conditions suit the Foxhound, and miles and miles of sniffing the world is what he craves. You cannot take a find field dog, coop him up for weeks on end, and expect the classical Foxhound to show through. You will end up with a different kind of animal. ¶City dwellers who do not spend a great deal of time hiking or jogging in the country should think twice about this breed. One other thing: scent hounds like the Foxhounds get too interested in an exciting smell for their own good. They should be kept on leads anywhere near traffic, since they will put their nose down and go. They won't stop and look when they come to the curb, and many, indeed, have come to grief as a result.

Greyhound

Land of origin: Probably ancient EGYPT or ASSYRIA

Original purpose: Almost certainly hunting, coursing game

Recent popularity ranking by A.K.C. registration: 116th

Greyhound Club of America
Marsha Wartell, Corres. Secretary
3433 Cartagena
Corpus Christi, TX 78418

HEIGHT: Dogs to 27 inches   Bitches to 26 inches

WEIGHT: Dogs to 70 pounds   Bitches to 65 pounds

COAT
Short, smooth, and very firm.

COLOR
Not counted in judging. Often gray, white, or fawn. Can be solid or marked.

Amount of care coat requires: 1 2 3 4 5 6 7 8 9 10

Amount of exercise required: 1 2 3 4 5 6 7 8 9 10

Suitability for urban/apartment life: 1 2 3 4 5 6 7 8 9 10
UNSUITED

We will never know the origin of the Greyhound. This ancient breed may have started in Assyria or Egypt. Carvings on tombs show dogs almost identical in appearance to the Greyhound we know today. ¶Through most of history the Greyhound has been referred to as a coursing dog. The name *Greyhound* is of unknown origin. It could come from *Graius*, which means "Grecian," since the ancient Greeks thought highly of this splendid animal. The name also could come from the Old English words *grech* or *greg*, meaning "dog." ¶The Greyhound is not only the fastest dog in the world but one of the fastest four-footed animals. He has been bred for millennia to chase other animals. In modern times the Greyhound has displayed his incredible speed on race tracks and millions are bet on the outcome of these events. ¶There have been two "lines" of Greyhounds although they are the same breed of dog. The show lines display great elegance and high style. Presumably the dogs of these lines also show the same performance although they are seldom trained as track dogs are. The track dogs are bred for running, nothing else. Conformation is not a factor. ¶Since track dogs are generally "retired" between the ages of 2½ and 4 it is fortunate that the track greyhounds have not lost the breed's greatest true asset—temperament. Track dogs were formerly euthanized when their racing days were over but there has been enormous interest in them in recent years. They are placed through hundreds of volunteer adoption or "rescue" agencies and are proving to be among the most pleasant, reliable and accommodating of all dog breeds.

Although records exist of Harrier packs dating back to the middle of the thirteenth century in England, no one is certain of their origin. They may have come to the British Isles with the Normans, since hounds were in common use on the Continent well before they were in England, or they may have been developed in England. All kinds of theories are on record, some seemingly well supported. Dogs *similar* to the Harrier date back to ancient Greece, but the breed is not believed to be that old. ¶Harriers look like a bred-down version of the Foxhound, and many people believe that is exactly what they are. It would be hard to dispute that

Harrier

Land of origin: Unknown, most recently (since A.D. 1260) ENGLAND.

Original purpose: Hunting, especially hares

Recent popularity ranking by A.K.C. registration: 135th

HEIGHT: Dogs to 21 inches   Bitches to 20 inches

WEIGHT: Dogs to 50 pounds   Bitches to 45 pounds

COAT
Short, dense, hard, and glossy.

COLOR
Black, tan, and white—any natural hound color pleasingly distributed. Not highly considered in judging.

Amount of care coat requires: 1 2 3 4 5 6 7 8 9 10

Amount of exercise required: 1 2 3 4 5 6 7 8 9 10

Suitability for urban/apartment life: 1 2 3 4 5 6 7 8 9 10

point, for the Harrier does look and act exactly like a small Foxhound. It is certainly a riddle for which we will never have an answer. Hares have been run down with hounds since long before the activity was described by the historian Xenophon around 400 B.C., and since A.D. 1260 at least. Harriers have been considered highly desirable dogs for that style of hunting. ¶The Harrier is a neat, clean, well-put-together dog. He is naturally responsive and obedient, takes training well, and is friendly to man and animals alike. A well-bred and well-raised Harrier is a lovely family pet, although he is perhaps more naturally suited to country life than city dwelling. Still, if due regard is paid to the Harrier's natural desire to go, to run and sniff and feel the wind and the brush against his smooth, sleek hide, he still settle in anywhere with his master and give a flawless performance as a family dog. No one should, in all fairness, keep one of these dogs cooped up. Harriers do need long walks every day and frequent trips to the country. Families with dual residences are ideal. ¶Because the Harrier is naturally a pack animal, he gets along well with other dogs and cats and is fine for the multipet home. He is good around horses and other livestock as well, once he has been made to understand that they belong to the most important creature in a Harrier's life, his master. ¶The Harrier is nowhere near as well known as the Beagle in this country, and no doubt the Harrier and the two Foxhounds have suffered in popularity because they are so like the Beagle and possess few outstandingly different qualities that would enable them to upset one of the most popular of all breeds.

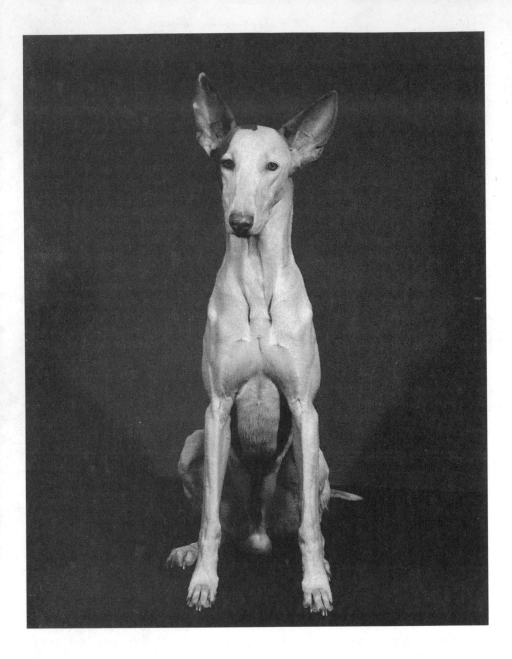

No one knows the real history of this very ancient breed. By the time of King Tutankhamen (1366 to 1357 B.C.) it already was immortalized in stone. Specimens may have been brought to Egypt from some other land long before the time of the boy king. For at least four thousand years they have survived around the periphery of the Mediterranean, but in recent years the greatest concentration has been found on the Balearic Islands off the coast of Spain. They are known by many names, but the concentration on the island of Ibiza seems to have labeled them at least as far as the English-speaking world is concerned. In Spain they are known variously as

Ibizan Hound

Land of origin: Probably EGYPT, then SPAIN

Original purpose: Coursing, hunting

Recent popularity ranking by A.K.C. registration: 127th

Ibizan Hound Club of the United States
Lisa Puskas, Secretary
4312 E. Nisbet Rd.
Phoenix, AZ 85032

HEIGHT: Dogs to 27½ inches   Bitches to 26 inches

WEIGHT: Dogs to 50 pounds   Bitches to 49 pounds

COAT
Short all over, shortest on head and ears—only slightly longer at back of thighs and under tail.

COLOR
White and red, white and lion, or solid white, red, or lion. Solids very desirable but rare.

Amount of care coat requires: 1 2 3 4 5 6 7 8 9 10

Amount of exercise required: 1 2 3 4 **5** 6 7 8 9 10

Suitability for urban/apartment life: 1 2 3 4 5 6 7 8 9 10

Podenco Ibicenco, Ca Eivissenc, Malorqui, Zarnelo, Mayorquais, Charnegue, and Chien de Baleares. On the island of Malta they are called Rabbit Dogs and on Sicily, Cirnecco dell'Etna. The name *Ibizan Hound* apparently has taken hold in the United States, though, and probably will not change. ¶This is one of the more recently recognized breeds listed by the American Kennel Club. Along with the Norfolk Terrier, recognition became official on January 1, 1979. ¶People who know this breed well speak of the Ibizan Hound as being exceptionally quiet and clean. He is responsive to his human companions but is reserved with strangers. He is particularly sensitive to change and will take his time to think things through, and this includes the arrival of new people on the scene. He is not "flaky" the way some sight hounds may be. He is, rather, sensible as well as sensitive, and steady in his habits. ¶The Ibizan Hound is, like the Greyhound, the Saluki, and the Afghan Hound, a dog of grace and dignity. He is fast and sleek and particularly adept at both high and broad jumps. He is, then, above all else an athlete—and a fairly large one, too. He must have exercise, like all the true coursing hounds. It would not be proper to keep this dog in an apartment unless he was assured of very long walks and an occasional trip to a safe area where he could be allowed to run. ¶The Ibizan Hound is not a sharp breed, but is a careful, determined friend to his master and family. It is too soon to tell how he will evolve in the United States now that his popularity is likely to rise. His mysterious and almost certainly unknowable beginnings are bound to add to his attractiveness. It is claimed that it was the Ibizan Hound (obviously known then by a different name) that was the model for the god Anubis, the guardian of Egyptian dead. He may be one of the few breeds, perhaps the only one, that was actually worshipped.

The mighty Irish Wolfhound is the tallest and one of the most powerful of all dogs. His origins are lost to us, although he was known and revered around the time of Christ. Records dating back to the third century A.D. suggest that the Celts may have brought him with them to Greece five hundred years earlier. ¶This great hound was developed for the hunt, to course wolves and even the elk of ancient Ireland. He is said to be able to run down a wolf and make the kill unaided. When coursing was the sport of kings, this regal dog was considered an appropriate gift from one king to another. There is a story of a war fought for the possession of a single specimen of

Irish Wolfhound

Land of origin: IRELAND

Original purpose: Hunting, coursing wolves and other large game

Recent popularity ranking by A.K.C. registration: 74th

Irish Wolfhound Club of America
Mrs. William S. Pfarrer, Secretary
8855 U.S. Route 40
New Carlisle, OH 45344

HEIGHT: Dogs to 32 inches and over   Bitches to 30 inches and over

WEIGHT: Dogs to 120 pounds and over   Bitches to 105 pounds and over

COAT
Rough, hard, and wiry. Longer on face.

COLOR
Gray, brindle, red, black, white, and fawn.

Amount of care coat requires: 1 2 3 4 5 6 7 8 9 10
                                   •••••

Amount of exercise required: 1 2 3 4 5 6 7 8 9 10
                                 ••••••••••••••••

Suitability for urban/apartment life   1 2 3 4 5 6 7 8 9 10
                                         UNSUITED

the breed. ¶The last of these dogs in their original form faced extinction about the time of the American Civil War. An officer in the British army—a Scot—set out to collect the few that remained in Ireland and rebuild the breed along ancient lines. He finally succeeded, and today's Irish Wolfhound closely resembles his ancestors. ¶Despite his being bred for violent purposes, the Irish Wolfhound is a gentle and reliable animal. He is well aware of his size and power and is extremely courageous. He is also intelligent and an excellent companion. He is not suited to city life, and even a small suburban home might be crowded with an animal of this size trying to find a place to relax. This is clearly a country dog, an estate dog, or a dog for the farm. He is good with children and will take a lot of punishment without displaying bed temper. He will be a deterrent to burglars, of course, and his presence can impart a feeling of security. Because of his enormous size and strength, it would be unthinkable to train him to attack. The look of him is enough. ¶The Irish Wolfhound is not an inexpensive dog to buy or keep. He requires a lot of food and a lot of room. A good example of the breed may cost $500 and up and should be purchased only from a reputable breeder. Like all hounds, the Irish Wolfhound does not like pulling up roots. Once he has settled into a home, he wants to stay there—for life—guarding it and sharing it with its human inhabitants. This is a splendid breed of dog for special situations only. He is for the home where there is the need and the means to own the largest dog in the world, and one of the most noble.

For the owner who envisions himself the master of a mighty wolflike beast of enormous power, the Norwegian Elkhound offers special possibilities. This great hunting dog of the North is not very large, less than half the weight of a real wolf, but he has many outstanding qualities and characteristics. ¶The Norwegian Elkhound accompanied the Vikings on their forays. He hunted with them, he herded flocks outside their villages, and he guarded man and animal alike against wolves and bears. Almost a legend now, the Norwegian Elkhound is one of the oldest and most romantic of breeds. ¶This is a northern breed, an animal well suited to rugged

Norwegian Elkhound

Land of origin: NORWAY

Original purpose: Guarding, herding, hunting big game

Recent popularity ranking by A.K.C. registration: 60th

Norwegian Elkhound Association of America, Inc.
Mrs. Diane Coleman, Corres. Secretary
4772 Mentzer Church Rd.
Convoy, OH 45832

HEIGHT: Dogs to 20½ inches   Bitches to 19½ inches

WEIGHT: Dogs to 55 pounds   Bitches to 48 pounds

COAT
Thick and hard, rather smooth lying. Longer outer coat and light, soft, woolly undercoat.

COLOR
Gray with black tips on long covering coat. Gray tones vary, but white or yellow are not desirable.

Amount of care coat requires: 1 2 3 4 5 6 7 8 9 10
                                   •••••••

Amount of exercise required: 1 2 3 4 5 6 7 8 9 10
                                 ••••••••••••••••

Suitability for urban/apartment life:*   1 2 3 4 5 6 7 8 9 10
                                            ••••••

*But only if regularly exercised to meet his demands.

weather and rugged terrain. He is a bold dog, impressively powerful and packed with seemingly endless energy. He has a superb sense of smell, and his hearing is reputed to be better than that of many other breeds. He is a hunting dog and one devoted to his master. He learns quickly and takes all kinds of training well, but he is also stubborn. A Norwegian Elkhound will have no difficulty in picking out an inappropriately soft hand. A wishy-washy owner will have a bad time of it and probably will not be able to master the dog. ¶The Norwegian Elkhound can be aggressive with other animals—but this happens rarely with human beings, unless they are strangers who threaten. Because he is such a powerful and assertive animal and will march chest out into any kind of a situation, the Norwegian Elkhound requires not only early and careful training but everlasting control as well. He is not a dog to be allowed to wander through a suburban neighborhood unattended. ¶Since he is a natural guardian of all that he loves, the Elkhound makes a perfect watchdog. He should never be taught to attack, and any tendency in that direction must be discouraged, but here is the answer for those who want an aggressive-sounding, alert, and purposeful dog who will sound the alarm in the night. ¶The Elkhound is a handsome animal; he has great dignity and purpose. An ideal companion for those he knows and trusts, he tends to take life seriously. He does not take friends, devotion, insults, or intruders lightly. He was put here with a job to do, and he spends the better part of each day attempting to fulfill his mission. He should only be purchased from the best available private kennel's stock. A mass-produced Norwegian Elkhound could be dangerous, or at least unpleasant.

The Otter Hound is a dog little known in this country. Probably in use in England by the reign of King John (1199–1216), he was bred in a straight line from a mixture of several different hounds (Harrier, Bloodhound, and others) to kill otters. A somewhat coarse or rough-looking dog, he has been so perfected as a single-purpose animal that he has never become a popular pet. Otter hounds were almost always trained to work in packs, and their precise response to commands was legendary in the last century, when otter hunting was in vogue. Those packs are now gone, as are most of the otters in England and Wales, and the breed is down almost to remnant

Otter Hound

Land of origin: ENGLAND and WALES; some arguments for FRANCE

Original purpose: Hunting otter

Recent popularity ranking by A.K.C. registration: 137th

Otter Hound Club of America
Dian QuistSulek, Corres. Secretary
Rt. #1, Box 247
Palmyra, NE 68418

HEIGHT: Dogs to 27 inches   Bitches to 26 inches

WEIGHT: Dogs to 115 pounds   Bitches to 100 pounds

COAT
Double; rough outer coat 3 to 6 inches long on back, shorter on legs. It must be coarse and crisp (hard). The undercoat is woolly and water-repellent. The coat is an important feature of this breed.

COLOR
Any color or combination of colors is allowed.

Amount of care coat requires: 1 2 3 4 5 6 7 8 9 10
••••••••

Amount of exercise required: 1 2 3 4 5 6 7 8 9 10
••••••••••••••••••

Suitability for urban/apartment life: 1 2 3 4 5 6 7 8 9 10
UNSUITED

level. The Otter Hound is one of those dogs who could vanish in the years ahead unless other qualities are accentuated. ¶It would be a shame to lose what has taken almost ten centuries to perfect. In fact, the Otter Hound shows qualities that should not be lost and could be adapted to other life-styles. He is loyal to his master, he has a very good nose, he is amazing in the water (he has webbed feet), and he can stand any weather and any water temperature. He would probably make a fine watchdog and should adjust well to an owner's family. But is is a tough fighter, and a brawl can quickly become a savage display. He therefore needs firm handling and constant supervision. ¶The Otter Hound is a large dog, often well over one hundred pounds, and his jaws are immensely powerful. His gait is easy and free, exhibiting great power and drive. He is a dog who never seems to tire, not letting up once he has a trail. He is out for blood and will not stop as long as he has a clue as to where the otter may be hiding. ¶Until breeders develop those qualities in the Otter Hound that would make him attractive for today's owner, he is better suited to country life. An Otter Hound and a city apartment are not the right combination. Owners should keep in mind that if their pet can't find otters (which he probably can't), he may practice on other wildlife and a few neighborhood cats. Otter Hounds, like all powerful and headstrong animals, must be under full-time control. History has taught us that they respond well to training, so there is no excuse for an ill-behaved Otter Hound.

Petit Basset Griffon Vendéen

Land of origin: FRANCE

Original purpose: Hunting

Recent popularity ranking by A.K.C. registration: 112th

Petit Basset Griffon Vendéen Club of America
Ms. Shirley Knipe, Secretary
426 Laguna Way
Simi Valley, CA 93065

HEIGHT: 13 to 15 inches (over 15^1/$_2$ inches a disqualifying fault.)

WEIGHT: 32 to 42 pounds

COAT
Rough and long without exaggeration. Harsh to the touch, with a thick, shorter undercoat. Beard, mustache, and long eyelashes. Casual, tousled look is required.

COLOR
White with lemon, orange and black in any combination. Tri-color or grizzle (black and white together) markings usual, but white for easy visibility required.

Amount of care coat requires: 1 2 3 4 5 6 7 8 9 10

Amount of exercise required: 1 2 3 4 5 6 7 8 9 10

*Suitability for urban/apartment life:**   1 2 3 4 5 6 7 8 9 10

*But only if exercised often and well.

The Petit Basset Griffon Vendéen or Petit (hereinafter PBGV) is a smart, tough little hound with a terrier's coat and not just a little of the terrier's fire. Often referred to as the "happy breed," he is all-for-the-game, whatever it happens to be. They are terrific with children as well as adults and get along perfectly well with cats and generally with other dogs. They are assertive, not likely to back off from a challenge but they are not petty or argumentative. They can be quite possessive of a food bowl, however. ¶The PBGV was developed between three and four hundred years ago to hunt, usually in packs, over rough terrain. It is a scent hound and although basset (which means low to the ground) is in his name he is really quite unlike the Basset Hound we know. The PBGV is smaller, well-haired, more agile, more terrier-like with much smaller ears. The breed as we know it today has been as popular in Denmark as in France and has only recently been appreciated outside of that relatively small portion of the Earth, first in England, then in Canada and now in the United States. ¶The happy, alert, busy-body PBGV can get along in almost any home situation as long as play and exercise are serious items on the family agenda. Two PBGVs can be even more fun than one, although almost any other hardy, robust dog can be a companion to a PBGV that has to be left for hours on end. This is a fine companion dog, not just a field breed. Its popularity in the United States and Canada is bound to grow.

The Pharoah Hound may be the oldest extant breed of dog in the world. If not it is certainly in the range of the other truly ancient breeds, the Saluki and Greyhound. The oldest known dog relic dates from the Stone Age and was found on the banks of the Nile. It is a disc and depicts two dogs that look very much like Pharoah Hounds. Tomb carvings in Egypt seem to show Pharoah Hounds as models for the dog-god Anubis. Classical antiquity is only one factor recommending this breed. ¶Few dogs are more sculptured and elegant than representatives of this sleek hound with their distinctive large ears and keen, intelligent amber eyes. The overall appearance and demeanor is noble. Because they hunt by both hearing and sight they are extremely alert and very fast on their feet. Their gait is free and flowing with the head held high. Their movement appears to be effortless. ¶Pharoah Hounds are

Pharaoh Hound

Land of origin: ANCIENT EGYPT, in all possibility, or in Middle East

Recent popularity ranking by A.K.C. registration: 133rd

Pharoah Hound Club of America
Rita L. Sacks, Corres. Secretary
P.O. Box 895454
Leesburg, FL 34789-5454

HEIGHT: Dogs 23 to 25 inches   Bitches 21 to 24 inches

WEIGHT: Not specified in standards

COAT
Short and glossy. Fine and close to slightly harsh. No feathering.

COLOR
Shades of tan to chestnut with white markings: white tip on tail highly prized. White "star" on chest, also on toes, slim white mark on center line of face allowed. White on neck, shoulders, back, or sides disqualifies.

Amount of care coat requires: 1 2 3 4 5 6 7 8 9 10

Amount of exercise required: 1 2 3 4 5 6 7 8 9 10

Suitability for urban/apartment life: 1 2 3 4 5 6 7 8 9 10

characteristically friendly and affectionate. They are also very playful and are too intelligent to ignore. They want to participate in everything going on around them. It is usually far better to allow an active and alert dog to share in activities under your management than to force them to invent their own games. ¶Very sedentary people who do not really want to share their lives with a dog may do better with a less *involved* breed. The Pharoah Hound does not take be being ignored. Decorative though they are, they need far more out of life than the opportunity to be that. What they really want is to run everybody else's life, too. ¶Like the other swift coursing dogs that are hunters by nature, Pharoah Hounds should be conditioned before being asked to accept small animals like kittens, that are likely to race around and dart out from under things. ¶Although Pharoah Hounds have apparently been around for thousands of years, they are quite new to the West. There was little interest in them in England before the 1960's. They were given breed status there in 1968 and in Canada in 1979. The A.K.C. standard for the breed was approved in 1983. ¶The Pharoah Hound is an interesting "new" breed that will grow in popularity, particularly among people with space for their dogs to move. The elegance of the breed is bound to not only attract attention but hold it. Dog fanciers who enjoy getting involved at the beginning of something exciting are sure to be drawn to this project. The fact that this is not only a handsome, gregarious pet but also one that was once the model for a god in the ancient world, is bound to bring new fans to the fold. Those with the experience say that the new Pharoah Hound adherents will never regret their decision.

This powerful guard and hunting dog of southern Africa is a cross between a number of European breeds brought there by settlers and a native dog known to us only as the Hottentot dog. That native African animal, probably little more than half wild, had a strange ridge of hair on his back that grew backward. Today's Rhodesian Ridgeback has inherited that unique characteristic, and hence the name. ¶The Rhodesian Ridgeback was bred to care for his master and his master's family. That meant standing off all comers, including armed human beings and predatory cats. The Ridgeback does not back down easily. He is reserved with strangers and

Rhodesian Ridgeback

Land of origin: SOUTHERN AFRICA

Original purpose: As combination hunting and guard watchdog

Recent popularity ranking by A.K.C. registration: 59th

Rhodesian Ridgeback Club of the United States, Inc.
Betty J. Epperson, Corres. Secretary
P.O. Box 121817
Ft. Worth, TX 76121-1817

HEIGHT: Dogs to 27 inches   Bitches to 26 inches

WEIGHT: Dogs to 75 pounds   Bitches to 65 pounds

COAT
Short and dense, sleek and glossy. Should never be woolly or silky.

COLOR
Light to red wheaten. Small white markings permitted.

Amount of care coat requires: 1 2 3 4 5 6 7 8 9 10

Amount of exercise required: 1 2 3 4 5 6 7 8 9 10

Suitability for urban/apartment life:* 1 2 3 4 5 6 7 8 9 10

*But not at all suitable unless given regular exercise sufficient for the individual dog's needs.

usually will not give another dog a second look. Should a dog challenge the Ridgeback, however, that is something else again. ¶The Ridgeback can be distinctly a one-person animal, although certainly a gentleman with the rest of the family. He is a natural watchdog and can be extremely intimidating when suspicious. He takes any weather and can go for twenty-four hours without water. A combination of working and hunting dog, he will pull down fleet-footed game or flush birds, whatever is asked of him. ¶The Ridgeback tends to be hardheaded. He will accept a balance with his master, but however much he may love him, he still will try for the upper hand. Good firm training starting early in puppyhood is required, and when it is accomplished, the reward is a good watchdog and family companion. This breed is too powerful, too bright, and too active to be anything but totally obedient. A Ridgeback with bad manners is unthinkable around other people. ¶Some people do attempt to keep Rhodesian Ridgebacks as apartment dogs, a bad idea except in the most unusual cases. A Ridgeback locked in an apartment all day is unlikely to mature into the animal he was bred to be. In fact, some city-kept Ridgebacks become downright "flaky" and can be all but impossible to manage. Wherever the animal is raised, he should go into the best obedience class available with his master. Don't leave the training of one of these splendid animals to chance or "instinct." ¶The Rhodesian Ridgeback has not yet hit its stride in popularity in the United States, but this is a breed on the rise. Every effort should be made to maintain quality of behavior as well as form in this unique dog from Africa.

The exotic Saluki may be the oldest breed of purebred dog in the world. Some people insist he is the dog the Sumerians knew and used almost seven thousand years before Christ—which would make him almost nine thousand years old. Whether or not he originated in ancient Sumer, the Saluki spread through-out the Middle East and parts of Asia. Before the birth of Western civilization the breed was already known as a coursing hound. ¶He is an incredibly fast dog, once used on gazelle and later on smaller game. He is also a dog of great stamina and endurance—no weather is too harsh and no terrain too rough. Like most coursing

Saluki

Land of origin: ASIA MINOR

Original purpose: Coursing

Recent popularity ranking by A.K.C. registration: 99th

Saluki Club of America
Donna J. Kappmeier, Secretary
12192 Gilbert St.
Garden Grove, CA 92641

HEIGHT: Dogs to 28 inches   Bitches to 24 inches

WEIGHT: Dogs to 60 pounds   Bitches to 55 pounds

COAT
Smooth, soft, silky, with slight feathers on the legs, at the back of the thighs, and on the ears.

COLOR
White, cream, fawn, golden, red, grizzle, and tan, tricolor (white, black, and tan), black and tan.

Amount of care coat requires: 1 2 3 4 5 6 7 8 9 10

Amount of exercise required: 1 2 3 4 5 6 7 8 9 10

*Suitability for urban/apartment life:**   1 2 3 4 5 6 7 8 9 10

*But only if a great deal of exercise is regularly scheduled.

hounds, he has a so-so nose (at least that is the reputation most often heard) but fine eyesight and almost unbelievable speed. Owners should keep in mind that, being a coursing dog, he will worry wildlife and small domestic animals if not supervised. A bolting rabbit cannot be resisted and neither, on occasion, can a cat. ¶The Saluki never fails to attract attention, in the show-ring or on the end of a street lead. He looks the part of the exotic hound, and his grace and free-flowing movement are distinctive and most attractive. ¶Although not demonstrative, the Saluki is a loyal friend who likes to work with and please his master. He is good with family, although small children and Salukis don't always make the happiest combination. Because there is a certain flare, there is also a flash point. Children must be taught how to behave around dogs like Salukis, and Salukis must be taught how to behave around children. ¶The Saluki is headstrong, like any hound who has had his own head for thousands of years, so any new owner should make his position of command clear. The Saluki needs a reasonable amount of obedience training. No one wants such a good-looking dog with that kind of venerable background rolling over and playing dead or begging, but neither does one want a Saluki who bursts through screen doors and breaks loose into heavy traffic. ¶It is questionable whether Salukis can ever get enough exercise living in an urban setting. Because of their high style and elegance, some people do keep them in the city, but they should be walked great distances and be taken regularly to a place where they can really go. ¶Exotic, expensive, and very handsome, the Saluki is a special dog for special owners.

The great Deerhound of Scotland is a true giant among dogs. He is in a class with the Irish Wolfhound (to which he may be related), the Borzoi, the Great Dane, and other massive breeds. Once restricted in ownership to earls and lords of higher rank, said to have been the ransom of kings and the cause of wars, the Deerhound is a part of the wild and romantic past of the Highlands. Stories about him are legion, and whether all or only partly true, they suggest a history that may be the single most noble in canine animals. ¶A dog sel-dom seen in America today, the Scottish Deerhound is an ideal companion. Although huge, he is even-tempered, calm, and some people say polite. He seems to understand his size and is careful not to inadvertently hurt anything smaller than himself. Not snappy, silly, or mean, he is a fine companion for children, although a toddler should be watched around an exuberant Deerhound pup. The Scottish Deerhound thrives on love and attention. As a watchdog, of course, his mere presence is enough to discourage anyone, and it

Scottish Deerhound

Land of origin: SCOTLAND

Original purpose: Hunting, particularly deer

Recent popularity ranking by A.K.C. registration: 119th

Scottish Deerhound Club of America, Inc.
Mrs. Joan Shagan, Secretary
545 Cummings Ln.
Cottontown, TN 37048

HEIGHT: Dogs to 32 inches or more   Bitches to 28 inches or more

WEIGHT: Dogs to 110 pounds   Bitches to 95 pounds

COAT
Harsh and wiry, to 4 inches long on the body and neck. Softer on head, breast, and belly. Not woolly. Thick, close lying, ragged, crisp to touch. Some strains have silky mixed with harsh.

COLOR
Dark bluegray is preferred. Also grays and brindles, yellow, sandy red, red fawn with black ears and muzzle. White is considered bad, so the less the better.

Amount of care coat requires: 1 2 3 4 5 6 7 8 9 10
                                                  ••••

Amount of exercise required: 1 2 3 4 5 6 7 8 9 10
                                               ••••••••••••••••••••

Suitability for urban/apartment life: 1 2 3 4 5 6 7 8 9 10
                                                               UNSUITED

need hardly be stressed that no one should ever encourage a Scottish Deerhound to be aggressive or more suspicious than he naturally is around strangers. He likes to be absolutely certain in his own mind that the incoming stranger is a welcome addition to the household. The Deerhound takes companionship and friendship seriously. ¶It should be kept in mind that although the Scottish Deerhound is a gentle and sensible animal, he is also a hunter, and for that task he has been bred for centuries. He was designed to tear to earth animals as large as 250-pound stags. It probably would not take much to get him to assume that role again. Gentle with other pets at home, a Deerhound can play havoc on other people's cats. Though a superb companion of man, a Scottish Deerhound who mis-behaves can be a gigantic pain in the neck. ¶The Scottish Deerhound obviously needs exercise. Cramped quarters without an opportunity to walk for miles and run until exhausted are not the style for this animal. One can suppose that there are huge, barn-like apartments left and imagine their owners or renters as physical people who walk miles every morning and night, so we cannot say that this breed is wholly unsuited to apartment life; Deerhounds are too loving of people and too adaptable for that. But certainly exercise should be a major consideration when thinking about this breed. The nonphysical owner cannot unmake the breeding, planning, and perfecting of centuries. The great, massive hound of Scotland will never really be a creature of pavement and traffic lights.

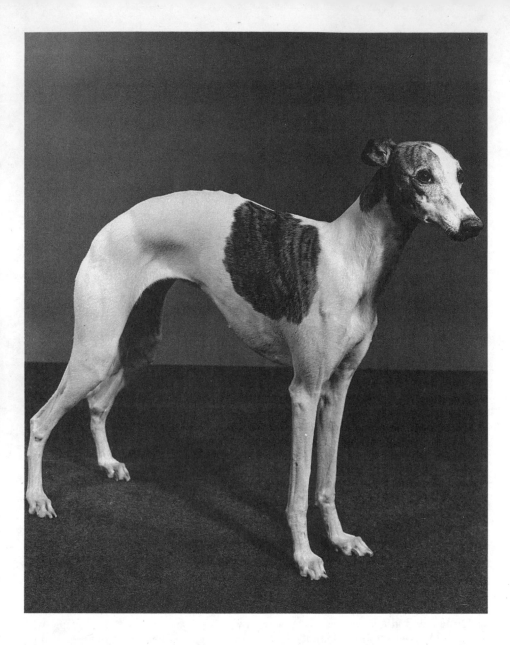

The Whippet is, in many people's opinion, one of the loveliest of all dogs. It
is impossible for one of these small sight
hounds, the fastest dog in the world in his
weight category, to assume an awkward
position. He always looks as if he just
stepped out of an Aubusson tapestry or off
the shelf as a piece of Sèvres porcelain.
He is an elegant as any dog can be. ¶The
Whippet was developed for gaming, and
for the "sport" of gambling as he raced
around small enclosures killing rabbits that
had no chance to escape. The more rabbits
the "miniature English Greyhound" could
kill or snap up (they were also called snap
hounds) the better. The Whippet today has
not lost that old taste for coursing, and he
should be carefully watched. He can take
off like an arrow and hit a stride of thirty-
five miles an hour almost instantly. A dog

Whippet

Land of origin: ENGLAND

Original purpose: Rabbit coursing and racing

Recent popularity ranking by A.K.C. registration: 62nd

American Whippet Club, Inc.
Mrs. Harriett Nash Lee, Secretary
14 Oak Cir.
Charlottesville, VA 22901

HEIGHT: Dogs to 22 inches   Bitches to 21 inches

WEIGHT: Dogs to 28 pounds   Bitches to 20 pounds

COAT
Smooth, close lying, and firm. Doesn't shed.

COLOR
Given in the A.K.C. standards as "immaterial." Very often seen in grays and tans, brindles and white.

Amount of care coat requires: 1 2 3 4 5 6 7 8 9 10

Amount of exercise required: 1 2 3 4 5 6 7 8 9 10

Suitability for urban/apartment life:* 1 2 3 4 5 6 7 8 9 10

*Provided the animal is given sufficient exercise.

moving at that speed may be assumed to be short on road sense. When anywhere near traffic, a Whippet is best kept on a leash. ¶There are few dogs that make better all-around family pets. Because a Whippet doesn't shed and is neat and clean, he is a pleasure to maintain; he is also easy to housebreak. For people who want to show a dog, the Whippet is grand in the ring, a born ham, and because of his small size he is easy to transport. He is, essentially, a family dog and won't really show his quality when kept in a kennel. This is a foot-of-the-bed dog for sure. He also likes to curl up in a blanket or its equivalent when he sleeps, so unless an owner wants all the beds in the house unmade, it is a good idea to leave the Whippet his own blanket. And don't step or lean on that blanket without checking—your Whippet won't make much of a lump inside it. ¶A Whippet is fine in an apartment—he is fine anywhere as long as the family is at hand—but he should be exercised. Long walks are needed every day, and periodically the dog should be taken to a wide open area—an abandoned beach is right—and allowed to run. You have never seen anything quite like a Whippet enjoying the power of his incredible body at full tilt. Despite what some people feel is a somewhat fragile appearance, the Whippet is hardy and durable. He is not at all keen on cold weather, however. ¶Whippets take to children naturally and are seldom mean. They are not yappy, although they can make good watchdogs. In a home where the Whippet is allowed to be *the* child, or at least one of the kids, this dog will flourish. Whippets don't like being left out. Given his attractive looks, that is about the last thing the Whippet has to fear.

{Group 3}

The Working Dogs

Akita

Alaskan Malamute

Bernese Mountain Dog

Boxer

Bullmastiff

Doberman Pinscher

Giant Schnauzer

Great Dane

Great Pyrenees

Greater Swiss Mountain Dog

Komondor

Kuvasz

Mastiff

Newfoundland

Portuguese Water Dog

Rottweiler

Saint Bernard

Samoyed

Siberian Husky

Standard Schnauzer

The Akita or Akita-inu is the heavy-duty work-dog of Japan. Named for the province of Akita on Honshu Island, this breed was used to hunt bear, boar, and deer and as a protector of life and limb. There are two other similar breeds in Japan—the Nippon-inu and the Shiba-inu—but they are somewhat smaller.

¶Four thousand years ago the inhabitants of Japan had a dog known to archaeologists as the *peat dog*. No doubt the Akita is a descendant of that animal. Also sometimes referred to as the Japanese Spitz, the Akita has a general Spitz-like appearance but is larger and stronger. The Akita has been likened to the Chinese Chow Chow, and it

Akita

Land of origin: JAPAN

Original purpose: Heavy hunting and guard duty

Recent popularity ranking by A.K.C. registration: 35th

Akita Club of America
Barbara Hampton, Secretary
7729 Rio Vista St.
Las Vegas, NV 89131

HEIGHT: Dogs to 28 inches   Bitches to 26 inches

WEIGHT: Dogs to 110 pounds   Bitches to 95 pounds

COAT
Double, with outer coat being somewhat on the harsh side.

COLOR
All colors permitted. White should not account for more than one third of total.

Amount of care coat requires: 1 2 3 4 5 6 7 8 9 10
                             •••••

Amount of exercise required: 1 2 3 4 5 6 7 8 9 10
                            ••••••••••••••••••

Suitability for urban/apartment life: 1 2 3 4 5 6 7 8 9 10
                                     ••••

is possible that the two have some ancestry in common, since commerce with the mainland followed the period when the peat dog was a part of every band, clan, and household. When highwaymen wandered the Japanese countryside, the Akita and his forebears no doubt played a very important role as watchdogs, a task this animal readily takes to still. ¶We have the Akita in America today because of military personnel stationed in Japan. A number of Akitas survived the war, and American servicemen were impressed with the breed's intelligence and his adaptability as both pet and guard dog. They began bringing examples back with them, and today the Akita enjoys full breed status from the American Kennel Club. ¶People who have come to know this new breed speak highly of his intelligence, his responsiveness to training, and his desire to please his master. Essentially a good-natured animal, this dog is still large, powerful, and assertive. There can be little doubt that an Akita who has been obedience-trained is much more desirable as a neighbor than one who has not. ¶Every indication suggests that the Akita will grow in popularity in the United States. It is to be hoped that breeders here will be as firm in their resolve to hold to the standards as their Japanese counterparts have been for centuries. Because of their hunting background and their fearless quality, Akitas are best maintained under tight control. They can be quite aggressive toward other dogs and should only be owned by people with some prior experience with large, tough-minded dogs. The Akita is not a casual pet.

No one knows the origin of the breed we call the Alaskan Malamute. The name is derived from the Russian name for the massive northwestern-most portion of North America—*Alashak* ("Vast Country")—and from one of the tribes that were found wandering there centuries ago—the Malemiuts, who had a sled dog of great stamina and loyalty. The breed is certainly one of the northern spitz dogs, but where it first originated and how it is related to the Siberian Husky, the Samoyed, and the sled dogs of Greenland and the eastern Canadian Arctic is unknowable. ¶Some sled dogs were bred for speed, and are indeed used in races today, but the Malamute is a freight hauler, a heavy-duty animal of great substance and endurance. Because these animals are naturally loyal to their owners, many of the examples kept as pets today are equally good watchdogs. Legend has it that every third or fourth dog generation the Innuit (the group to which the Malemiuts belong) tether their Mala-

Alaskan Malamute

Land of origin: Arctic region, usually given as ALASKA

Original purpose: As heavy-duty (freight) sled dog and camp guard

Recent popularity ranking by A.K.C. registration: 44th

Alaskan Malamute Club of America, Inc.
Stephen Piper, Corres. Secretary
3528 Pin Hook Rd.
Antioch, TN 37013-1510

HEIGHT: Dogs to 25 inches   Bitches to 23 inches

WEIGHT: Dogs to 85 pounds   Bitches to 75 pounds

COAT
Thick coarse guard coat, not very long and not soft. Dense undercoat 1 to 2 inches deep, oily and woolly. Guard hairs stick out, neck well maned.

COLOR
Light gray to black with white belly and white markings on feet, legs, and face. Only solid-colored dog allowed is all-white.

Amount of care coat requires:*   1 2 3 4 5 6 7 8 9 10

Amount of exercise required   1 2 3 4 5 6 7 8 9 10

Suitability for urban/apartment life:†   1 2 3 4 5 6 7 8 9 10

*Heavy brushing required in spring and early summer due to shedding.
†If enough exercise is given.

mute bitches out on the ice when they come into heat and allow wolves to service them. Whether or not that is true, the Malamute undeniably has wolflike qualities in his appearance. ¶The Alaskan Malamute is a magnificent animal, a fine pet who is good with children. He is solid and steady and has great endurance. Loyal unto death to his family, he is usually not one-personish. He is good with strangers, although he can be aggressive with strange dogs—not always, but that is a characteristic of some specimens. Of the northern spitz-like dogs, this breed is one of the best for the average household. ¶The harsh coat of the Malamute is best when not washed often, for washing tends to soften it and alter its desirable character. There is a coat-care consideration, though. That very dense undercoat is shed in spring and summer, and unless it is professionally stripped, it can drive the householder mad, for its shedding is endless. ¶The Alaskan Malamute is suited for a family with at least some active members, and in general for people who want a large, powerful, and wonderfully loyal pet. He is a heavy working dog and needs a great deal of exercise if he is to maintain condition and proper temperament. He will adapt to any living conditions as long as he is close to his human family, but confinement without proper exercise is cruel and foolish. ¶Great care should be taken in buying a Malamute, and only when two or three generations of a line are known should a final purchase be undertaken. There is a congenital malformation known as "dwarfism" in this breed, and it can crop up in alternate generations. A puppy should be evaluated carefully before purchase, and only the truly professional Alaskan Malamute breeder should be trusted.

The Bernese is a Swiss dog descended from dogs of ancient Rome. Two thousand years ago Roman legions crossed Switzerland into northern Europe accompanied by large and probably ferocious war and guard dogs. Inevitably some of these animals fell by the way, and some of them survived. From the latter it is believed that at least four large breeds evolved in the Alpine country alone. Three of them were used to herd sheep, but one was a draft animal, and that was the dog we today call the Bernese Mountain Dog. The name comes from the canton of Berne, where the weavers kept the dogs to draw their carts to market right up until quite modern times.

Bernese Mountain Dog

Land of origin: SWITZERLAND

Original purpose: As draft animal

Recent popularity ranking by A.K.C. registration: 68th

Bernese Mountain Dog Club of America, Inc.
Ms. Roxanne Bortnick, Secretary
P.O. Box 270692
Fort Collins, CO 80527

HEIGHT: Dogs to 27½ inches   Bitches to 26 inches

WEIGHT: Dogs to 70 pounds or more   Bitches to 65 pounds

COAT
Soft and silky with bright, natural sheen. Slightly wavy but never with actual curl.

COLOR
Jet black with russet brown to deep tan markings on all four legs, a spot just above forelegs, each side of white chest markings, and spots over eyes. Over-eye spots are expected and required. Brown on forelegs must separate black from white.

Amount of care coat requires: 1 2 3 4 5 6 7 8 9 10

Amount of exercise required: 1 2 3 4 5 6 7 8 9 10

Suitability for urban/apartment life: 1 2 3 4 5 6 7 8 9 10

¶The Bernese—seventy pounds and more, and almost twenty-eight inches tall—is a large animal. With his heavy coat and rugged constitution, he is an outside dog primarily and will do well in a kennel as long as he is shielded from sleet and freezing rain. He is hardy, healthy, and quite aristocratic. Adorable as a puppy, the Bernese matures into a steady, stable animal fearlessly loyal to his master. One-personish by nature, the Bernese will adjust to a family situation and accept family members and often-seen friends. Strangers, however, will be ignored, and are themselves better off if they ignore the dog until he is ready to attempt first overtures. The Bernese belongs to a few people and doesn't like to have his situation altered or expanded. He can be a good watchdog but should never be used for attack or other aggressive behavior. ¶The Bernese needs a lot of exercise and is happier in colder climates than in warm ones. He is not a satisfactory apartment pet. The big city with its restrictive environment is not Bernese Mountain Dog country. ¶The Bernese should be obedience-trained, and that training should start early and continue long. It is best if the owner takes the training sessions with the dog. In the Bernese Mountain Dog we have once again an animal too large to be tolerated as a brat. That kind of behavior may be cute and even acceptable (to a degree!) in a toy, but in a large, powerful animal like a Bernese it is quite intolerable. When it occurs, and certainly when it persists, the owner, not the dog, and certainly not the breed, is to blame.

The Boxer was derived in German from a number of strains common to Europe in the Middle Ages. Great Dane and English Bulldog may be included, and some of the mastiff line from Tibet is also likely. They all go back to what is called the Molossian stain, which undoubtedly came out of the Asian mountains to spread westward thousands of years ago. ¶This is a breed of enormous courage and stamina. Boxers were probably first bred for blood sports—baiting bulls and hunting boar and possibly dogfighting as well. They were bred for ferociousness, but that is gone now, and except for an occasional penchant for a good scrap, the Boxer is a gentleman.

Boxer

Land of origin: GERMANY

Original purpose: Probably for bullbaiting and other blood sports; later guard and companion

Recent popularity ranking by A.K.C. registration: 16th

American Boxer Club, Inc.
Mrs. Barbara E. Wagner, Corres. Secretary
6310 Edward Dr.
Clinton, MD 20735-4135

HEIGHT: Dogs to 25 inches   Bitches to 23½ inches

WEIGHT: Dogs to 75 pounds   Bitches to 70 pounds

COAT
Short, shiny, and smooth. It should lie tight to the body and never be curly, wavy, or woolly.

COLOR
Shades of fawn ranging from light tan to dark red and mahogany. Darker colors preferred generally. May also be brindled, with black standing out from fawn background. White markings often handsome, but generally not on back of torso. White face marking may replace dark mask.

Amount of care coat requires: 1 2 3 4 5 6 7 8 9 10

Amount of exercise required: 1 2 3 4 5 6 7 8 9 10

Suitability for urban/apartment life: 1 2 3 4 5 6 7 8 9 10

¶Alert, willing, and anxious both to participate and to please, the Boxer is an ideal family dog. He is affectionate, a fine watchdog, and good with children. He can be fine with other animals he knows and can be raised in a multianimal household. When he does fight, however, he is deadly serious. ¶A Boxer is by nature careful with strangers, although not snappy or silly. He checks things out thoroughly, and if he decides a stranger is all right, he is open and friendly. He is not complicated and sneaky. A Boxer lets you know what he has on his mind. The agility, fearlessness, and intelligence of this breed led to its being chosen as one of the first in Germany to work with the police. Boxers also have been used to lead the blind and for guard work. There is little this dog cannot learn to do. ¶Because they are so popular in this country, Boxers have been mass-produced, and that has been destructive to many lines. There are still so many fine examples of the breed being shown and sold as companion animals that no one need get stuck. Since a poorly bred Boxer may be ugly in disposition as well as in conformation, the prospective buyer should be willing to go far to buy from only the finest breeders. You must see the parents of a puppy and know something about them before you can properly judge the puppy itself. All Boxer puppies are adorable, but not all grow up to fulfill the breed's promise.

The Bullmastiff is not to be confused with the Mastiff. He is only 60 percent Mastiff; the rest is Bulldog. ¶This breed is one of the few animals actually bred to attack man. Once known as the "gamekeeper's nightdog," he was used to track and knock down poachers on private English estates. He was sometimes muzzled and was not meant to maul his victims, just keep them on the ground until the gamekeeper arrived to either thrash the man or arrest him. The Mastiff was tried for this task, but he was neither fast enough nor sufficiently aggressive. That is why the old Bulldog—a bigger, rough animal than the breed we know today—was blended in. ¶All of that is history. Today's Bullmastiff, while not exactly a dog to challenge in open combat, is usually a gentleman. He is not a fearsome beast, as he once may have

Bullmastiff

Land of origin: ENGLAND

Original purpose: Night patrol against game poachers on private estates

Recent popularity ranking by A.K.C. registration: 55th

American Bullmastiff Association, Inc.
Ms. MaryAnne Duchin, Secretary
Box 137D Burger Rd.
Melbourne, KY 41059

HEIGHT: Dogs to 27 inches   Bitches to 26 inches

WEIGHT: Dogs to 130 pounds   Bitches to 120 pounds

COAT
Short and dense, offering good protection against harsh weather.

COLOR
Red, brindle, or fawn, the latter usually with a dark face and ears. A small white spot on the chest is allowed but no other white markings. Originally darker dogs were favored because they were more difficult to see at night. Now lighter-colored animals are as highly regarded.

Amount of care coat requires: 1 2 3 4 5 6 7 8 9 10

Amount of exercise required: 1 2 3 4 5 6 7 8 9 10

Suitability for urban/apartment life: 1 2 3 4 5 6 7 8 9 10
UNSUITED

been from the poacher's point of view. (At that time poachers had the bad habit of shooting gamekeepers, which is why the Bullmastiff came into being.) He is fine with his owner's family and generally open and willing with strangers. It might be quite another thing, though, if a Bullmastiff's family seemed threatened, for this is an alert animal. He also happens to be without fear. It is doubtful that another dog could make a Bullmastiff back down once his hackles were up. For this reason he must be trained to live with other animals. Like the Bulldog, which constitutes nearly half his bloodline, he doesn't like other animals to challenge him. ¶There is no doubt that the sight of a Bullmastiff on the premises would be a deterrent to almost anyone, but in reality a dog is no harder than a man to disable with products like Mace and tear gas. No one should think that a Bullmastiff or any other breed will make their prop-

erty crimeproof, and for this reason the animal should never be attack-trained, nor should any aggressiveness toward people be tolerated. With giant breeds and super-dogs like Bullmastiffs, this is asking for trouble. Let the sight of him alone be the prime deterrent. A professional criminal will not deliberately put himself in a position to get hurt, so it is the innocent or minor-nuisance trespasser who is likely to be seriously hurt or killed by an attack-trained dog. ¶The Bullmastiff is a family dog, but he is hardly suited to apartment living. He is an estate dog, a dog person's dog, and a magnificent pet in the right setting. The fact that he will scare off lesser intruders is secondary. What is important is that the breed is a splendid one, represented by regal, powerful animals who are by nature devoted to their masters and without meanness or pettiness in their makeup.

The Doberman Pinscher is one breed whose history is well known. In the 1890s, Louis Dobermann of Apolda, Germany, developed the breed using old shorthaired shepherd stock mixed with Rottweiler and terrier—specifically, it is believed, the Black and Tan Terrier. The dog he was apparently trying for was the dog he got. The Doberman Pinscher has been from the beginning a superlative guard dog of noble appearance. ¶A medium-sized dog with an extremely alert bearing, the Doberman is as handsome as a dog can be. Intelligent, swift, a consummate athlete, he combines the trainability of the old shepherd stock, the inner fire of the terrier, and the positive attitude of the rottweiler. Louis Dobermann's mixture

Doberman Pinscher

Land of origin: GERMANY

Original purpose: Guard duty

Recent popularity ranking by A.K.C. registration: 19th

Doberman Pinscher Club of America
Mrs. Tommie F. Jones, Corres. Secretary
4840 Thomasville Rd.
Tallahassee, FL 32308

HEIGHT: Dogs to 28 inches   Bitches to 26 inches

WEIGHT: Dogs to 75 pounds   Bitches to 68 pounds

COAT
Smooth, short, hard, thick, and close. There may be an invisible gray undercoat on neck.

COLOR
Black, red, blue, and fawn. Sharply defined rust markings above each eye and on muzzle, throat, chest, legs, feet, and below tail. Small white marking on chest (under 1/2-inch square allowed). Fawn color is known as Isabella.

Amount of care coat requires: 1 2 3 4 **5** 6 7 8 9 10

Amount of exercise required: 1 2 3 4 5 6 7 8 9 10

Suitability for urban/apartment life:* 1 2 3 4 5 6 7 8 9 10

*But only if proper exercise is provided!

managed to preserve the best of each type he used. ¶The Doberman Pinscher is an active dog, and long, long walks are mandatory for his health and happiness. Many Doberman Pinschers are kept in apartments, and their rise in popularity according to American Kennel Club registrations has been meteoric. The reason for this great popularity lies in the fact that he is believed to be a deterrent dog. An amateur criminal probably will give wide berth to a home where a Doberman Pinscher is known to live, but a professional can incapacitate any dog on earth with a five-dollar tear-gas pen or poisoned bait. The use of Doberman Pinschers as crime deterrents by amateur owners is not to be encouraged. ¶The supremely handsome and incredibly loyal Doberman Pinscher is a controversial dog. One hears that he is a gentle, affectionate, and reliable pet, and also that he is a born killer and can never be trusted. The answer lies in the middle. ¶The Doberman Pinscher is an aggressive dog. The A.K.C. standards include the following statements: "The judge shall dismiss from the ring any shy or vicious Doberman" and "An aggressive or belligerent attitude towards other dogs shall not be deemed viciousness." ¶It is true that the Doberman Pinscher is more nervous than many other breeds—not always, certainly, but often. It is also true that the breed is intelligent and will take training readily from someone who knows what he is doing. The Doberman Pinscher is far too much dog for many people, especially casual or first-time owners. For owners who can accept the responsibility, the Doberman Pinscher is one of the great breeds of the working-dog group.

Most people do not seem to realize that the Giant, Standard, and Miniature Schnauzers are three distinct breeds, not just up-and-down versions of each other. Both the Standard and Giant Schnauzers are working dogs. ¶The *Riesenschnauzer* or Giant is not as old a breed as the Standard (which was painted by Dürer the year Columbus sailed for the New World) but is older by a good margin than the terrier we call the Miniature Schnauzer. ¶All the Schnauzers, apparently, were developed in either Württemberg or Bavaria, and the Giant probably was developed in and around Bavaria from smaller dogs obtained from Stuttgart. He was made into a power-

Giant Schnauzer

Land of origin: GERMANY

Original purpose: Cattle driving

Recent popularity ranking by A.K.C. registration: 79th

Giant Schnauzer Club of America, Inc.
Robin Greenslade, Secretary
12 Walnut Ter.
Salem, NH 03079

HEIGHT: Dogs to 27$\frac{1}{2}$ inches   Bitches to 25$\frac{1}{2}$ inches

WEIGHT: Dogs to 78 pounds   Bitches to 75 pounds

COAT
Hard, wiry, very dense; soft undercoat and harsh outer coat.

COLOR
Solid black or pepper and salt.

Amount of care coat requires: 1 2 3 4 5 6 7 8 9 10
•••••••••••••••••

Amount of exercise required: 1 2 3 4 5 6 7 8 9 10
••••••••••••••••••••••••••

*Suitability for urban/apartment life:**   1 2 3 4 5 6 7 8 9 10
•

*But only is suitable exercise is provided on a regular basis

ful drover to help get cattle to market. There is a strong belief today that the Flemish driving dog, the Bouvier des Flandres, and the black Great Dane were used with original Schnauzer stock to obtain the Giant we have today. The belief contains more than a little conjecture, however. ¶By World War I the Giant was in use by the police, and has been ever since. His progress in this country has been slow because the German Shepherd has been so extremely popular and the two dogs do overlap in use and appeal. The Giant Schnauzer is also much tougher than the average Shepherd, much more a real dog person's dog. ¶The Giant Schnauzer is a handsome dog of great strength and endurance. He is regal, standing very straight in a robust chest-first kind of way. He should never be shy or nervous, although he is characteristically very aggressive toward other animals. That should be kept in mind. ¶The Giant Schnauzer has been bred from the beginning to serve man, and that means he takes training very well and is extremely loyal. He is a guard dog, a watchdog, a working dog every inch of him. He is not a dog to be taken lightly or owned casually. ¶The Schnauzer's coat needs care. It needs pulling, trimming, and hard brushing. Only then will that splendid look be in evidence. The Giant Schnauzer is a dog that needs a great deal of exercise and should be owned by a family with at least one fairly athletic member. He can be a house dog, even an apartment dog, but long, long walks are in order every day and good runs whenever possible. Training is also mandatory, and anyone seriously considering this superior breed had better plan on some evenings at obedience school at the beginning. A well-trained Giant Schnauzer is a proud possession. One ill-trained or out of control is a lawsuit on the hoof.

The Great Dane is a true giant, one of the largest and most majestic dog breeds in the world. His history is not really known (a dozen mutually exclusive versions have appeared in print), but we do believe that his original purpose was to hunt boar. A dog of great power, courage, and endurance was needed for this dangerous sport, and that is what was bred into this German "mastiff." Actually, the dog we call the Great Dane may have been at the sport in something like his present form in the days of the pharaohs. ¶The ferociousness that must have gone into the original boar hunters is no longer apparent in the Great Dane. The dog we know is a gentleman, soft in manners, usually quiet, and very affectionate with his master and family. He is lovely with children if properly raised and not mean or petty with strangers, although he certainly is impressive as a watchdog. Needless to say, a dog

Great Dane

Land of origin: Ancient and unknown; GERMANY for last century or so

Original purpose: Boar hunting

Recent popularity ranking by A.K.C. registration: 34th

Great Dane Club of America, Inc.
Kathy Jurin, Corres. Secretary
1825 Oaklyn Dr.
Green Lane, PA 18054

HEIGHT: Dogs to 32 inches or more   Bitches to 30 inches or more

WEIGHT: Dogs to 150 pounds   Bitches to 135 pounds

COAT
Short, thick, smooth, and glossy. It should not stand off the body or be dull.

COLOR
Great variety—brindle (golden yellow with black), fawn or clean golden yellow with black
mask, steel blue, glossy black, harlequin (pure white with evenly distributed black markings).

Amount of care coat requires: 1 2 3 4 5 6 7 8 9 10

Amount of exercise required: 1 2 3 4 5 6 7 8 9 10

*Suitability for urban/apartment life:**   1 2 3 4 5 6 7 8 9 10

*Provided that long walks will be offered several times a day. It is particularly important that the
young Dane get enough exercise for condition and tone.

of this size should not be encouraged to be aggressive. ¶Some people, of course, keep Great Danes in city apartments—presumably, in many cases, to discourage burglars. That is a foolish plan, for anyone close enough to be hurt by a dog is close enough to totally incapacitate him. ¶The Great Dane really does need exercise. He can become stiff from improper exercise, resulting in poor muscle and bone development. Anyone keeping this giant in the city should plan on miles of walking every day, or hire someone to do it for him. No day should be skipped. ¶The Great Dane is sociable and fine within the family circle. When young he can be a bit "klutzy," and small children can be sent flying like tenpins. That should be kept in mind. As the Great Dane matures, he does so as a well-controlled, self-possessed animal who seems aware of his giant status. Aggressive or poorly managed Great Danes cannot be tolerated. The potential for really serious damage is far too great. ¶Unfortunately, Great Danes are not long-lived, and nine or ten good years with their families must be considered fortunate. Since older animals are subject to heart ailments and painful joint disorders, a quiet life is in order. Contrary to a widely held belief, Great Danes do not have to have their ears cut to be attractive or to be shown. In England the practice is illegal. ¶The Great Dane is one of the most handsome and regal of all dogs. He is a fine family pet, a good companion and protector of the home estate. He is, though, a giant; he needs room and an impressive quantity of food. He also needs obedience training, often at the professional level. A prospective owner should take all these factors into account.

The magnificent Great Pyrenees is a breed of enormous antiquity. Of the mastiff group, he probably came to the Middle East thousands of year ago from central Asia. There his ancestors existed during the Bronze Age, almost four thousand years ago, and also around the Baltic and Black Seas. Examples were carried across Europe and developed to the form we know today in the Pyrenees Mountains. Great Pyrenees have a long and noble history as guard dogs, sheep dogs, and bear and wolf fighters. They were favorites of the French court and other royal strongholds. There is a lot of history in this breed, and a lot of this breed in European

Great Pyrenees

Land of origin: Very ancient; MIDDLE EAST and EUROPE (Pyrenees Mountains)

Original purpose: Herding and guard work

Recent popularity ranking by A.K.C. registration: 46th

Great Pyrenees Club of America, Inc.
Charlotte Perry, Secretary
Rt. #1, Box 119
Midland, VA 22728

HEIGHT: Dogs to 32 inches   Bitches to 29 inches

WEIGHT: Dogs to 125 pounds   Bitches to 115 pounds

COAT
Fine, heavy white undercoat; long, flat, thick outer coat with coarse hair. Straight or slightly wavy.

COLOR
All white or mainly white with badger, gray, or tan markings.

Amount of care coat requires: 1 2 3 4 5 6 7 8 9 10
                           •••••

Amount of exercise required: 1 2 3 4 5 6 7 8 9 10
                          •••••••••••••••••••••••

Suitability for urban/apartment life: 1 2 3 4 5 6 7 8 9 10
                                      UNSUITED

---

history. ¶Great Pyrenees are giant dogs with more good qualities than we can catalog. They are loyal unto death to their family; they will tackle anything that threatens them. They are very affectionate and responsive to human moods. They take to children naturally and are generally safe and reliable. They are incomparable baby-sitters. Gentle and considerate with strangers (although cautious at first), they are not usually quarrelsome. They get along with other animals and have to be driven into a fight. Once they are in combat, though, few animals can best them. In the Middle Ages they were really invincible. ¶Undeniably, the Great Pyrenees are also among the handsomest of dogs. They are especially appealing as puppies, and once grown they move with enormous purpose and self-assurance. The Great Pyrenees does require exercise and this must be kept in mind. It is unfair to confine this dog for long periods and not give him a chance to move. It is not even healthy. Any family contemplating this breed should have very active members who are devoted to long, long walks and even romps in the country. ¶This is a breed with so many special qualities one is tempted to urge restriction of ownership and breeding to people understanding and deserving enough to be granted those privileges. Unfortunately, anyone can buy a Great Pyrenees, and anyone can breed them. Like all large dogs they are subject to hip dysplasia, and poor examples are seen everywhere the breed is found. Care should be taken in buying one of these splendid dogs, and only the best of the proven specialty breeders should be trusted. Crippled, snippy dogs will not be satisfying to the owner, and should never have been brought into the world in the first place.

The Greater Swiss Mountain Dog is down from the huge mastiffs the Romans introduced into the middle of Europe. This may be the oldest descendant of them all. It was a general farm utility/draft dog for centuries and was little known. Both the much better known St. Bernard and the German Rottweiler are down from this breed. ¶Around the turn of the century it was generally believed that the Greater Swiss Mountain Dog was extinct, replaced by machines and by smaller breeds. By 1910, however, enough specimens were located in remote Alpine villages and on farms to bring the breed back in Switzerland and Germany. In that year the breed was recognized

Greater Swiss Mountain Dog

Land of origin: SWITZERLAND

Original purpose: Herding, draft, guard, general farm utility

Recent popularity ranking by A.K.C. registration: Too recent—recognized in 1995.

Greater Swiss Mountain Dog Club of America, Inc.
DeAnne Gerner, Corres. Secretary
91 Schoffers Rd.
Reading, PA 19606

HEIGHT: Dogs 25$^1/_2$ to 28$^1/_2$ inches   Bitches 23$^1/_2$ to 27$^1/_2$ inches

WEIGHT: Not specified by standard but proportional to a full-bodied dog of these heights.

COAT
Top coat is dense, 1 to 1$^1/_2$ inches long. Undercoat typically thick and may show through on neck, belly, and underside of tail.

COLOR
Ground color is jet black—no other ground color allowed. Markings of rust and white on face, chest, neck, and legs. Symmetry highly desired. Rust over each eye.

Amount of care coat requires: 1 2 3 4 5 6 7 8 9 10

Amount of exercise required: 1 2 3 4 5 6 7 8 9 10

Suitability for urban/apartment life: 1 2 3 4 5 6 7 8 9 10
                                          UNSUITED

by the Swiss Kennel Club. ¶The Greater Swiss Mountain Dog is a true giant and is immensely powerful as befits a dog bred to pull carts and do other farm labor. Temperament is a critical factor, and although this dog should be bold, alert, and vigilant, it should never be nervous or aggressive. Dogs that display either characteristic are to be severely faulted, for they not only could be dangerous but are not living up to the rigid standards of the breed as regards temperament. The GSMD should never be shy, either, for timidity can lead to problems. This is a faithful, willing worker, appropriately protective and intelligent. A perfect dog for larger settings, the GSMD is a handsome nobleman of distinction. ¶There are relatively few of these magnificent dogs in the United States and it is to be hoped that only people skilled in managing and breeding special dogs of enormous character will become attracted to them.

The Komondor has been bred in Hungary in the form we know today for over a thousand years. He probably arrived there from central Asia a thousand years before that. The Komondor (plural form is *Komondorok*) is one of the oldest breeds in Europe and probably the best guard dog of all. He was not used as a sheep- herding dog, as is often stated. Smaller dogs did that work. The Komondor had the sole responsibility of driving away or killing wolves, bears, foxes, and any other animals that appeared to endanger the master's flocks. At this task the powerful and pur- poseful Komondor excelled. ¶As a puppy the Komondor is playful and typical, but as

Komondor

Land of origin: HUNGARY; before that, CENTRAL ASIA

Original purpose: Guarding flocks—*not* herding

Recent popularity ranking by A.K.C. registration: 122nd

Komondor Club of America, Inc.
Ms. Sandra Hanson, Corres. Secretary
W359 S10708 Nature Rd.
Eagle, WI 53119

HEIGHT: Dogs to 27 inches   Bitches to 25 inches

WEIGHT: Dogs to 95 pounds   Bitches to 85 pounds

COAT
Unique. Dense, weather resistant, double. Woolly, soft, and dense undercoat with long, coarse outer coat. Outer coat tends to cord and hang in characteristic ropes.

COLOR
White only. Any other color disqualifies.

Amount of care coat requires: 1 2 3 4 5 6 7 8 9 10

Amount of exercise required: 1 2 3 4 5 6 7 8 9 10

Suitability for urban/apartment life: 1 2 3 4 5 6 7 8 9 10
                                        UNSUITED

he matures, he hardens into a guard dog with undying loyalty and resolve. He is cautious with strangers and only slowly accepts even apparent friends of the household. The one-time or first-time visitor is watched quietly but without relaxation. Anyone who seems to threaten the tranquillity of the household might expect to get a chunk taken out of him—a large chunk. ¶The Komondor is serious but good with the family of his master. He is not especially nervous or snappy, and he is intelligent. Training is easy and should start early. It is practically impossible to call on a Komondor for more than he can deliver. His ability to learn and his determination to please and protect are apparently without limit. ¶The Komondor lives naturally in the open, in very harsh climates, and out-side quarters are a good idea for him even as a pet. There is no weather that will bother him, since he lives virtually encased in an impervious corded coat of white hair. It forms into hanging ropes, and the breed characteristically looks unkempt. That coat, though, is one of the more protective and efficient in the world of dogs. ¶Tough, hardy, alert, the Komondor needs a lot of exercise to stay in good condition. With the fear of crime as great as it is, some people have begun to think of the Komondor as a good guard in an apartment house. That is unwise for several reasons. An apartment is not a proper setting for so large an outdoor animal, and a guard-trained or even a naturally protective Komondor is much more than the average pet owner can handle.

The handsome white Kuvasz is another great guard dog out of central Europe. He undoubtedly came to Hungary from Tibet and was known throughout the Eastern countries (including the Middle East) for many centuries. In Hungary he flourished to become the darling of kings and nobles. While the nobility plotted against each other and planned their endless intrigues and assassinations, only the great Kuvaszok (that is the plural form) could be trusted. ¶The Kuvasz is said to have an uncanny ability to detect an enemy of his master even before the master himself realizes there is danger. The breed is fiercely loyal and protective. It is said of

Kuvasz

Land of origin: TIBET and HUNGARY

Original purpose: Guarding, and then some herding

Recent popularity ranking by A.K.C. registration: 102nd

Kuvasz Club of America
Connie Townsend, Corres. Secretary
3855 W. Pillar Rd.
Whitmore Lake, MI 48189-9687

HEIGHT: Dogs to 30 inches   Bitches to 28 inches

WEIGHT: Dogs to 115 pounds   Bitches to 90 pounds

COAT
Rather long on neck but shorter on sides. Slightly wavy.

COLOR
Pure white only is desirable. No markings. Occasionally seen yellow saddle is serious fault.

Amount of care coat requires: 1 2 3 4 5 6 7 8 9 10
•••••

Amount of exercise required: 1 2 3 4 5 6 7 8 9 10
••••••••••••••••••••••••

Suitability for urban/apartment life: 1 2 3 4 5 6 7 8 9 10
UNSUITED

this great dog that he is either a friend or an enemy for life. In the Middle Ages the Kuvasz was undoubtedly much larger than our present standard of thirty inches. Kuvaszok must have been very intimidating to commoners, who were forbidden to own them. ¶The dogs were used in packs for hunting from the fifteenth century on. Eventually they got into the hands of the common people and were used as guards and perhaps as herders of cattle and sheep. By that time the breed had evolved to about where we know it today. ¶The Kuvasz is probably related to the Komondor, for they do have traits in common. Both are great outdoor animals, and both are extremely loyal to a very small and select core of people. People thinking of the Kuvasz as a pet might consider carefully, if this is to be their first dog, whether or not they are up to the task. They are generally not. The Kuvasz is not a casual dog for the casual owner, nor is he a dog to be allowed to reign in the household. ¶This extremely handsome, very intelligent dog must be trained early and well and maintained that way, under constant supervision. A Kuvasz that gets the least out of hand is not only a nuisance but a potential menace. This is a dog for the firm, the strong, and the devoted among really experienced dog owners. It is a breed that is quite capable of being a little wiser than a man. There should never be any contest; the man must prevail and call all the signals. The very protective traits of the Kuvasz are things that must be kept in check, of course. No dog can be called upon to *always* know a friend from an enemy.

No one knows (and probably never will) where the Mastiff came from or how he was spread across the face of the world. There are lots of theories and some pretty fascinating bogus history, but it is conjecture at best. When Caesar invaded the British Isles in 55 B.C., the Mastiff was there alongside his British masters fighting against the Roman legions. As might be expected, examples of the breed were carried back to Rome. ¶The giant Mastiff (generically, the word *mastiff* implies a whole family of giant dogs) was bred for violence. He was a guard dog thousands of years ago, he was a war dog, a hunting dog for the largest game, and he was used in the

Mastiff

Land of origin: ENGLAND for 2,000 years, before that a mystery

Original purpose: Guarding, hunting, fighting, war

Recent popularity ranking by A.K.C. registration: 48th

Mastiff Club of America, Inc.
Betts HerlacheKieffer, Secretary
W3811 Culbertson Rd.
Seymour, WI 54165

HEIGHT: Dogs to 33 inches   Bitches to 31 inches

WEIGHT: Dogs to 185 pounds   Bitches to 175 pounds

COAT
Outer coat tends toward coarseness, with undercoat short, close lying, and dense.

COLOR
Apricot, silver fawn, or dark fawn brindle. Fawn brindle dogs to have fawn as background with brindle evenly distributed as dark stripes. Face the darker the better but always darker than body.

Amount of care coat requires: 1 2 3 4 5 6 7 8 9 10

Amount of exercise required: 1 2 3 4 5 6 7 8 9 10

Suitability for urban/apartment life: 1 2 3 4 5 6 7 8 9 10
                                                                    UNSUITED

pit in the most horrific of blood sports. It is more than a little strange that such a dog has developed into a generally docile animal. ¶In a setting large enough for this animal (an apartment is hardly right), he is a perfect pet. He is great with children, fine with almost anyone, and usually not quarrelsome with strangers, although he may be cautious until he has assured himself that all is well. He can be protective, which presents a problem because of his size. By nature obedient and responsive, the Mastiff will take training well and will be serious about the things he is asked to do. ¶Because he is so massive and so powerful, the Mastiff must be under control at all times. There are examples who are short with other animals, and they must be watched and, if possible, have trained out of them any sign of aggression. Other examples will be surrogate parents to the whole world and are provocation-proof. ¶It should be noted that the Mastiff and the Bullmastiff are two different breeds. The latter is a cross between the Mastiff and the English Bulldog. In error, many people use the names interchangeably. The Mastiff is much the larger of the two. ¶The Mastiff requires little coat care but does need exercise if he is to stay in good condition and not become stiff and lame. In situations where he must be tightly controlled, long walks are in order. He is best, of course, on a farm or a large estate, where he may exercise himself. These giants are rugged, hardy, and needless to say, very intimidating as watchdogs.

The Newfoundland is a giant of a dog, in appearance and nature every inch a "teddy bear." Named for the island off the east coast of Canada, the Newfoundland is undoubtedly descended from dogs brought there by European fishermen and later developed in England. ¶The Newfoundland is a working dog in fact as well as in classification (this is not the case with some breeds). This was a dog who was expected to help the islanders haul their nets, pull carts, and carry loads, and he became a legend in lifesaving. The number of men, women, and children the Newfoundland is said to have pulled from icy seas is endless. How much is fact and how much romance is hard to say. It is about the same situation we have with Saint Bernards and their mountain rescue stories. Some of the lore is known to be true, some is questionable, but the whole truth does not really have to be known. ¶The Newfoundland is a lover of a dog; he worships his master and his family. He is sensible with strangers and openly friendly once shown that his family is safe. Although not a nervous or even suspicious dog, the Newfoundland is very protective; with a dog of such size, that counts for

Newfoundland

Land of origin: NEWFOUNDLAND and ENGLAND

Original purpose: Hauling, carting, and sea rescue work

Recent popularity ranking by A.K.C. registration: 51st

Newfoundland Club of America, Inc.
Sandee Lovett, Corres. Secretary
5870 5 Mile Rd. NE
Ada, MI 49301

HEIGHT: Dogs to 28 inches   Bitches to 26 inches

WEIGHT: Dogs to 150 pounds   Bitches to 120 pounds

COAT
Outer coat moderately long but not at all shaggy. Flat and usually straight, although some wave is allowed. It should not curl. The undercoat is soft and dense, and much of it is lost in the summer.

COLOR
Black, with or without a little white on chest and toes and sometimes the tip of tail. Also bronze and shades of brown. White and black dogs are called Landseers.* Beauty in color and marking is highly rated in judging.

Amount of care coat requires: 1 2 3 4 5 6 7 8 9 10
                    ●●●●●●●●●●

Amount of exercise required: 1 2 3 4 5 6 7 8 9 10
                    ●●●●●●●●●●●●●●●●●●●●●●●●●

Suitability for urban/apartment life: 1 2 3 4 5 6 7 8 9 10
                                UNSUITED

*Dogs with the small white details on chest, toes, and tail tip are still considered black. The rare Landseers are truly pinto like.

something. ¶Fortunately, the Newfoundland is easygoing with other animals and, indeed, seems to want to have another dog or two around. He is in fact social and sensible in all matters and therefore ideal in a family situation. ¶Despite his heavy coat, the care of a Newfoundland is not a problem. A good work-over once a week will keep the coat from matting. If it is neglected, though, it can be a mess to straighten out. ¶The Newfoundland was built for water. He is a powerful swimmer and certainly more than strong enough to drag a man from the sea. No weather and no water temperature will bother this great dog, who seems to flourish in the worst possible weather. In fact, about all that fazes this dog is disapproval or lack of human response. ¶Because he is such a supreme gentleman, the Newfoundland will settle down anywhere his family wants him to. The city apartment isn't the best place, though, because most families simply can't supply enough walking time to satisfy the driving power of the Newfoundland's run and make up for the chance to break through heavy water in high wind. He is a breed that is much better in the open, much better out on the land or near the water than in an urban cave. If the family situation is right, and if there are frequent trips to the country, suburban life is fine. ¶The Newfoundland in spirit and size is one of the all-time great breeds. Owners remain owned and seldom will allow themselves to be without the companionship, sense of security, and feeling of style, taste, and pure unabashed love this dog provides.

Photo by Moments by Jane, Jane B. Donahue

It is probable that what we know as the Working Group's Portuguese Water Dog originated as a herding dog along the border between China and Russia almost a thousand years before Christ. There are a number of theories as to how this dog got to Portugal, but none of them will ever be proven. Whether they were carried westward by barbaric German tribes across Europe, or moved across North Africa by the equally savage Berbers, they did eventually reach the Iberian Peninsula and apparently flourished there in isolated communities of fisherfolk along the coast.

Portuguese Water Dog

Land of origin: PORTUGAL for centuries, but probably ASIA way back

Recent popularity ranking by A.K.C. registration: 84th

Portuguese Water Dog Club of America, Inc.
Ms. Joan C. Bendure, Corres. Secretary
6765 Platz Rd.
Fairview, PA 16415

HEIGHT: Dogs 20 to 23 inches   Bitches 17 to 21 inches

WEIGHT: Dogs 42 to 60 pounds   Bitches 35 to 50 pounds

COAT
Profuse but no undercoat or mane. Two varieties: wavy which is rather loose with some sheen and curly with compact cylindrical curls. The later is lusterless. Non-allergenic, non-shedding.

COLOR
Black, white, various tones of brown and black or brown combinations with white.

Amount of care coat requires: 1 2 3 4 5 6 7 8 9 10

Amount of exercise required: 1 2 3 4 5 6 7 8 9 10

Suitability for urban/apartment life:* 1 2 3 4 5 6 7 8 9 10

*But only if properly exercised.

¶In its time the Portuguese Water Dog has been a herding dog, a sporting dog, i.e., retriever, and a working dog. The last designation was the most recent, and thus the dog is legitimately classified today. The breed probably came from the same ancestral, genetic stock that gave us the Tibetan Terrier, the Poodle, and the Puli, and it is a likely ancestor of both the American and Irish Water Spaniels. It is a dog with a great deal of history built into it even if much of that is lost to us. ¶In Portugal this breed was evolved to go to sea. It pulled nets and swam ashore or between boats with messages. It is an extremely rugged dog with enormous stamina. It can tolerate just about any weather and work a terribly punishing schedule and still be cheerful about its lot in life. ¶The Portuguese Water Dog is marked for its great intelligence (remember it is probably related to the poodle) and its willingness to put itself to the service of man. It is an easy dog to train for anyone able to outwit it, and a happy companion best suited to live and work with people who are at least its match. To be blunt, this is not a *wimp's* dog. ¶Many people in a number of places over a span of at least three thousand years have had a stake in this historical breed, but it is out of the village now and off the boat and the farm and in the hands of a more gentle fate. It is devoutly to be wished that this new setting and different kind of enthusiasm will not degrade the superb working animal it has been, and turn it into a *wimpy* dog. ¶The Portuguese Water Dog is here to stay, of that there is no doubt. There will be styling changes over the years but hopefully the inside of the dog can stay the way it is. It has taken a long time to get there, time and human needs and also a lot of care and faith.

Rottweiler

Land of origin: ANCIENT ROME, then GERMANY

Original purpose: Driving livestock, pulling carts, guard and police work

Recent popularity ranking by A.K.C. registration: 2nd

American Rottweiler Club
Doreen LePage, Secretary
960 S. Main St.
Pascoag, RI 02859

HEIGHT: Dogs to 27 inches   Bitches to 25¾ inches

WEIGHT: Dogs to 90 pounds   Bitches to 85 pounds

COAT
Short, coarse, flat. Undercoat does not show through.

COLOR
Black with tan to mahogany markings on cheeks, muzzle, chest, legs, and over both eyes. Small white spot on chest or belly is allowed but not desired.

Amount of care coat requires: 1 2 3 4 5 6 7 8 9 10

Amount of exercise required: 1 2 3 4 5 6 7 8 9 10

Suitability for urban/apartment life: 1 2 3 4 5 6 7 8 9 10
UNSUITED

The Rottweiler has a noble and fascinating history. The ancestral form was carried through Alpine passes by Roman legions invading the center of Europe. The dogs were used to drive the cattle needed to feed the troops in countries where raiding was not profitable. Some of these dogs were left behind in Rottweil in Württemberg in southern Germany. The breed began about 1910. ¶The Rottweiler has been used with great success as a drover, guard, beast of burden, and police dog. He is highly intelligent and very willing, and he accepts virtually any training. Despite the hard usage to which the breed has been put throughout history, the Rottweiler today is affectionate, alert, and very good with his family. He is a natural watchdog and will be very cautious with strangers; with members of his family he tends to be a gentle, easygoing animal not given to temper or hysteria. He will tolerate other animals if they are raised with him and if he is made to understand that they are his master's property. ¶The Rottweiler is a rugged dog with stamina and a very purposeful approach to life. He is a serious animal and goes about things in an intelligent, deliberate manner. Training should start early and continue, for the breed's capacity to learn is apparently without limit. ¶Some people do keep Rottweilers in small suburban houses, and they will do well enough under those conditions if close to their family and if given plenty of exercise. They are better on a farm or large estate, though, for they are hard, outdoor animals. Exercise, wherever they live, is necessary for their good health. Too much confinement can make them tense and alter their disposition. ¶Some storefront "trainers" have been turning out so-called guard and attack-trained dogs, using the Rottweiler along with other large working breeds. These animals are to be avoided as potentially extremely dangerous.

The Saint Bernard, America's most popular giant breed, has a long and romantic history. Sometime after 1550, large working dogs were brought up to a monastery in the high Saint Bernard Pass in the Swiss Alps from the towns and villages below. They may have been obtained by the monks as companions or as watchdogs. The records have been lost that might reveal dates and reasons. We do not know the history of the breed before that, although it is often suggested that they were descended from the great Molossian dog from ancient Epirus (Greece), which in turn may have been descended from giant Asian breeds of the mastiff type. The dog imported by the monks, or rather brought up into the mountains, may have been the Talhund. All of this will probably forever remain theory and conjecture. ¶In time the dogs (not named Saint Bernard until the 1880s, a long time after Saint Bernard's death in 1153) came to do patrol work with the monks. They were used for testing trails and are said to have been able to predict storms and avalanches.

Saint Bernard

Land of origin: SWITZERLAND

Original purpose: Unknown—later, patrol and rescue work

Recent popularity ranking by A.K.C. registration: 39th

St. Bernard Club of America, Inc.
Cheryl Zappala, Corres. Secretary
1043 S. 140th
Seattle, WA 98168

HEIGHT: Dogs to 29 inches   Bitches to 27 inches

WEIGHT: Dogs to 170 pounds   Bitches to 160 pounds

COAT
Shorthaired version—very dense, close lying, smooth, tough, but not rough to touch.
Longhaired version—medium length, can be slightly wavy, not rolled, curled, or shaggy.

COLOR
White with red or red with white, various shades; brindle with white markings. Brown-yellow equal value to shades of red. Faces desirable dark. Never without white; solid and other colors faulty.

Amount of care coat requires:

Shorthaired: 1 2 3 4 5 6 7 8 9 10

Longhaired: 1 2 3 4 5 6 7 8 9 10

Amount of exercise required: 1 2 3 4 5 6 7 8 9 10

Suitability for urban/apartment life: 1 2 3 4 5 6 7 8 9 10
UNSUITED

They eventually were used to sniff out lost travelers. So much romantic literature was built on these stories that truth and fiction are difficult, if not impossible, to separate. ¶The Saint Bernard is a massive dog of enormous strength. He is traditionally calm and sensible and a fine pet in home situations where there is plenty of room. But he is too large for confined quarters; this is not a breed for the city apartment. He should get a great deal of exercise if his condition is to be maintained. Typical of large dogs, he is not very long-lived, and he appears far too often with hip deformities due to the careless breeding and mass-production engendered by his great popularity. ¶In recent years the press has reported Saint Bernards turning sour and attacking people. This is so contrary to the character of this breed that it must again be laid at the feet of bad breeding and greed. Some of the worst puppy factories ever raided by humane groups have turned out to be farms on which Saint Bernard puppies were being turned out by the crateful. The breed has been subjected to great cruelty, and there are very bad and even dangerous examples around. ¶Only the very finest specialty breeders should be trusted to supply a dog who can truly reflect the intelligent, quiet, sensible, and affectionate nature of this superior breed. And potential owners should not allow themselves to be mesmerized by the "cuteness" of a Saint Bernard puppy. That puppy very quickly becomes an absolute giant of a dog.

The magnificent Samoyed is an extremely ancient dog whose true origins are lost in the mists of the Arctic. Apparently for thousands of years he has been the companion of the Samoyed peoples, who have roamed the northern reaches of Asian Russia. A dog of the tundra, he is hardy and durable and extremely useful in many ways. ¶No one is sure how the Samoyed was first used. He was utilized variously to herd reindeer and to guard the flocks and herds against wolves, bears, perhaps even tigers. He was used to guard the wandering nomads, too, and later the villages and other permanent settlements. He has been used right up to the present time

Samoyed

Land of origin: ARCTIC RUSSIA

Original purpose: Protection, herding reindeer, pulling sleds

Recent popularity ranking by A.K.C. registration: 43rd

Samoyed Club of America, Inc.
Julie Robertson, Corres. Secretary
P.O. Box 520853
Salt Lake City, UT 84152

HEIGHT: Dogs to 23½ inches   Bitches to 21 inches

WEIGHT: Dogs to 65 pounds   Bitches to 50 pounds

COATDouble. Undercoat soft, short, thick, and very dense. Outer coat long, harsh, straight from body without curl. Should glisten.

COLOR
Pure white, white and biscuit, cream, and all biscuit. No other colors allowed at all.

Amount of care coat requires: 1 2 3 4 5 6 7 8 9 10
●●●●●●●●●●●●●●●●

Amount of exercise required: 1 2 3 4 5 6 7 8 9 10
●●●●●●●●●●●●●●●●●●●●●●

Suitability for urban/apartment life:* 1 2 3 4 5 6 7 8 9 10
●●●●

*Provided adequate exercise is given on a regular basis.

for pulling sleds, and indeed there has not been a major Arctic or Antarctic expedition utilizing sled dogs that hasn't had the Samoyed out front with the best of them. The Samoyed, naturally a jolly animal, puts himself into the sled game as readily as he does any other. More than anything else he wants to be part of the action whatever the cost in exertion or even danger to himself. ¶Several characteristics distinguish this truly splendid breed. He is an extremely intelligent dog, perhaps the most intelligent of all sled dogs. He is beautiful—some people say the single most beautiful of all dogs, although we would have to view that as subjective. No one, though, can deny the pure splendor of a Samoyed in fine coat. ¶The great Samoyed by his very nature gets along well with people and other animals. He is a natural with children and is rarely mean or nasty. The standard called for in the American Kennel Club breed guide seems to say it all. Under disposition it says: "Intelligent, gentle, loyal, adaptable, alert, full of action, eager to serve, friendly but conservative, not distrustful or shy, not overly aggressive. Unprovoked aggressiveness to be severely penalized." ¶Despite the fact that the Samoyed is a northern dog and is happiest in cold climates, and even though he is a very active dog, he can survive in an apartment with a properly loving family. He should be exercised a great deal and especially when the weather is harsh. It is never too cold for a Samoyed, and there is never enough running and plowing through snow. The coat, of course, is the breed's crowning glory and must be seen to. Brushing, dry cleaning, and only occasional bathing are the techniques whereby a Samoyed maintains his position at the top level of canine splendor.

The Husky is a striking dog—handsome and solid—and a devoted pet. He is naturally friendly and usually does not make the best watchdog despite his fine size and "wolflike" appearance. ¶The Husky is seldom quarrelsome with people and is usually very good with other animals in the family. He can return to being a hunter, and some will take to molesting stock. This can be a difficult habit to break. It is obviously most undesirable. ¶The Husky is not the easiest dog in the world to train, and anyone contemplating this active, outdoor breed should plan on intensive obedience training. It is particularly important that a Husky be taught to come when called. They are often tramps at heart and will look at their owner beguilingly and then take off tail held high while the owner fumes and rages helplessly. It is not wise to allow Huskies to roam, anymore than it is any other dog, for it is then that they get

Siberian Husky

Land of origin: SIBERIA

Original purpose: Pulling sleds

Recent popularity ranking by A.K.C. registration: 18th

Siberian Husky Club of America, Inc.
Mrs. Fain B. Zimmerman, Corres. Secretary
65 Madera Dr.
Victoria, TX 77905-4847

HEIGHT: Dogs to 23½ inches   Bitches to 22 inches

WEIGHT: Dogs to 60 pounds   Bitches to 50 pounds

COAT
Double, and medium in length. Generally smooth lying and not harsh to the touch. Not to be trimmed or clipped. Undercoat sheds out in summer.

COLOR
All colors are allowed, from black to white. Interesting and very handsome face markings are usual. Eyes may be brown or blue or even one of each.

Amount of care coat requires: 1 2 3 4 5 6 7 8 9 10
•••••••••••••••

Amount of exercise required: 1 2 3 4 5 6 7 8 9 10
••••••••••••••••••

Suitability for urban/apartment life: *   1 2 3 4 5 6 7 8 9 10
••••

*Not really suitable to urban life unless given a great deal of exercise every day with special long weekend and holiday romps.

into trouble. ¶Huskies are so intent on human companionship and so openly affectionate that many people have taken to keeping them in apartments and small, restrictive suburban homes. Locked up alone during the day, a Husky can become destructive. He isn't by nature that kind of dog, and although human relationships are more important to a Husky than anything else, he is better off in cooler climates and in open country—after he has had intensive obedience training. From the very beginning the Husky will try to test the pecking order, and if an owner is indecisive or unassertive, the Husky will be very pleased to be on top. From there on, it is straight downhill until the dog is a first-rate nuisance to everyone. ¶Huskies are excellent family dogs and generally fine with children. Most Huskies love snow and harsh weather, but believe it or not, there are individual animals who hate to get their feet wet or spend much time in the snow (it is not hard to tell how many generations *that* strain has been out of Siberia). But for the typical Husky there is no temperature that is too low. He can tolerate anything from the Arctic to the Antarctic. ¶In the spring it is wise to have as much of the Husky's undercoat pulled as possible. It will come away by the handful. The shedding is constant until that coat is gone. ¶The Husky is only to be recommended to the owner or family that will work with their dog, teach and maintain his manners, and keep the animal from wandering too far afield. A Husky is more than a casual pet. He may be enchanting, but he can also be a destructive pest. The difference lies more with the owner than with the dog.

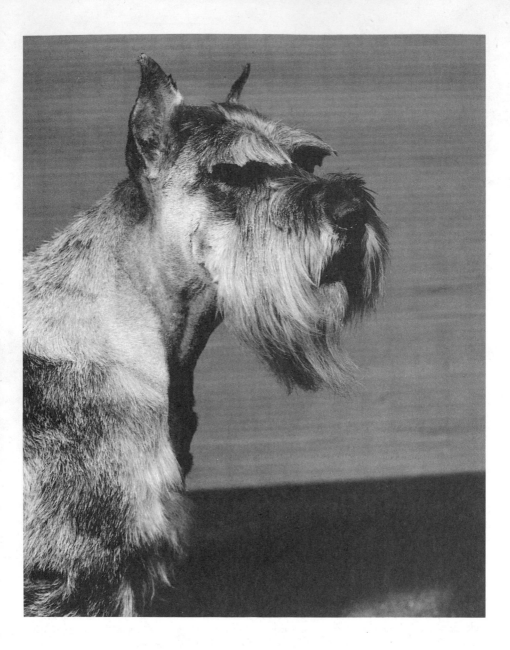

The Schnauzer is known in this country in three sizes—the Giant, the Standard, and the Miniature—and each is considered a separate breed. They are not all shown in the same group. Of the three breeds, the Miniature is by far the most popular, ranking fourteenth in the country, compared with the Standard's position as ninety-third and the Giant's as seventy-ninth. ¶The Schnauzer has long been known in Germany and was painted by Dürer, Cranach, Reynolds, and many other artists, usually as part of a noble portrait. They were companion animals as well as ratters, hunters, guards, retrievers—almost anything a dog could be called upon to do. They are

Standard Schnauzer

Land of origin: GERMANY

Original purpose: As companion, ratter, hunter, guard, and retriever

Recent popularity ranking by A.K.C. registration: 97th

Standard Schnauzer Club of America
Liz Hansen, Secretary
P.O. Box 153
Kampsville, IL 62053

HEIGHT: Dogs to 19½ inches   Bitches to 18½ inches

WEIGHT: Dogs to 37 pounds   Bitches to 35 pounds

COAT
Tight, hard, wiry, and thick. Soft, close undercoat and harsh outer coat.

COLOR
Pepper and salt or pure black. Many shades of pepper and salt from dark iron to silvery highlights. Black as strong as possible. Black rarer in this country.

Amount of care coat requires: 1 2 3 4 5 6 7 8 9 10

Amount of exercise required: 1 2 3 4 5 6 7 8 9 10

*Suitability for urban/apartment life:**   1 2 3 4 5 6 7 8 9 10

*But only if properly exercised on a regular basis.

---

among the most intelligent of all dogs, and this has apparently always been the case. In America the Miniature is classed as a terrier, while the Standard and Giant are shown as working dogs, of which the Germans undoubtedly approve. ¶It is believed that the Schnauzer originated from crosses of a black German Poodle and a gray spitz-type dog. The original stock may have been *pinscher* with these other types crossed in. The breed is old enough that these facts cannot be determined. ¶The Standard Schnauzers are solid, square, highly active animals with great affinity for human beings and human activities. As house pets they are participators and niche fitters. They make the best of all possible worlds out of every situation and have the ability to endear themselves and attract attention. They love to play and

they love to work, and they enter into every situation with boundless enthusiasm. They are rugged and tough and will take on all comers. They are excellent watchdogs although not overly suspicious. ¶Their fine form must be seen to at least twice a year by someone with professional grooming skills, but their day-to-day care is not oppressive. They are, as they say in the horse world, easy keepers. ¶Standard Schnauzers are fine house dogs and can be kept in an apartment if given plenty of exercise. They are so fast and so quickly caught up by an idea that care must be taken to keep them on a lead anywhere near traffic. They are, nonetheless, eminently trainable in all things appropriate to the companion dog. Early and intensive obedience training is necessary.

{Group 4}

The Herding Dogs

Australian Cattle Dog

Australian Shepherd

Bearded Collie

Belgian Malinois

Belgian Sheepdog

Belgian Tervuren

Border Collie

Bouvier des Flandres

Briard

Collie

German Shepherd

Old English Sheepdog

Puli

Shetland Sheepdog

Cardigan Welsh Corgi

Pembroke Welsh Corgi

The Australian Cattle Dog was developed very deliberately by stockmen in that country beginning about 1830. The records show an original cross between a dog called the Smithfield with the feral dog of Australia, the dingo. The Smithfield was too much of a barker to be of much use with cattle and the idea was to get the bark out of the dog. That worked well enough but it also put a bite in, an unfortunate characteristic. The cross was then bred with smooth blue-merle collies brought over from Scotland. That pretty much got the bite out, but put the bark back in. Dalmatian and Kelpie were added and then a native herding dog. The Queensland heeler emerged as a quiet, controllable, non-biting herding dog that was companionable and about as smart as you could want a dog to be. The name was eventually changed and that is the dog we call the Australian Cattle Dog today. ¶This masterpiece of genetic engineering was not perfected along lines of beauty but pure function. The Australian Cattle Dog is compact, robust, and has seemingly unlim-

Australian Cattle Dog

Land of origin: AUSTRALIA

Recent popularity ranking by A.K.C. registration: 63rd

Australian Cattle Dog Club of America
Joyce Rowland, Secretary
874 N. Holliston Ave.
Pasadena, CA 91104

HEIGHT: Dogs 18 to 20 inches   Bitches 17 to 19 inches

WEIGHT: Range of 33 to 50 pounds

COAT
Moderately short, straight outer coat of medium texture with a short, dense undercoat. A good brushy tail.

COLOR
Blue: Blue or blue-mottled with or without markings of blue or tan.
Red: Red speckle all over with or without dark red markings on head. Even head markings a plus.

Amount of care coat requires: 1 2 3 4 5 6 7 8 9 10
                                   ••••

Amount of exercise required: 1 2 3 4 5 6 7 8 9 10
                                 ••••••••••••••••

Suitability for urban/apartment life: 1 2 3 4 5 6 7 8 9 10
                                          ••••

ited stamina. It is always able, always willing, and terribly serious about is assignments. It is generally very slow about accepting strangers but it is incredibly loyal to its master, its family, its stock, and its turf. It is a dog that takes well to obedience training and should be offered a lot of training from its early months on. It is too smart and inventive to be left to its own resources. Its work program is better as an assignment than as a solution to its own boredom. ¶The Australian Cattle Dog is not remarkable for its elegance and indeed that has never been the intent of its breeders and fanciers. It will be interesting and perhaps a little sad to see what happens to this breed over the next quarter of a century. The Australian Cattle Dog can be kept in an apartment but out of fairness to the genes that have been built into it the dog should

be exercised regularly and often. It is simply not the dog to lock away like a toy. In its present form it is a young breed still close to its origins and those origins meant work. The play the non-stock-owning owner may substitute for work had best seem like work, things the dog can feel it is expected to do. An Australian Cattle Dog that is not allowed to feel as if it is fulfilling a role will be a sad dog. ¶There is an undeniable sense of adventure in getting involved with a newly recognized breed just beginning to grow in popularity. It is, though, really a challenge for an experienced dog person. The Australian Cattle Dog, tough, loyal, resilient, and possessive is not an ideal first dog. It is a doggy dog and requires more than feeding and petting. It needs managing. That is a plus when the owner is up to the task.

Australian Shepherd

Land of origin: SPAIN and the UNITED STATES

Original purpose: Sheepherding

Recent popularity ranking by A.K.C. registration: 40th

United States Australian Shepherd Association
Sherry Ball, Secretary
P.O. Box 4317
Irving, TX 75015

HEIGHT: Dogs 20 to 23 inches   Bitches 18 to 21 inches

WEIGHT: Not specified, but proportionate

COAT
Double. Undercoat varies in length according to climate. Outer coat, medium in texture, straight or wavy—moderate feathering. Mane more pronounced in dogs. Must be appropriate to a working shepherd.

COLOR
None preferred from list of blue merle, black, red merle, red—any with or without white markings sometimes with tan to copper points. White markings on face, chest legs, and neck but not on torso.

Amount of care coat requires: 1 2 3 4 5 6 7 8 9 10
                                   •••••••••

Amount of exercise required: 1 2 3 4 5 6 7 8 9 10
                                 •••••••••••••••••••••••

Suitability for urban/apartment life: 1 2 3 4 5 6 7 8 9 10
                                          UNSUITED

The Australian Shepherd, hereafter the Aussie, is not a dog of Australia despite his name. He originated in Spain long ago and was brought here by the Spanish in the early 16th century and later by the Basques to do what the breed had always done, protect and guide flocks of sheep. ¶The Aussie is typically a very intelligent dog because herding a large number of animals requires a dog that can improvise and solve problems. As befits his profession the Aussie is extremely active and highly motivated to work. These desirable traits in a shepherd make him a questionable city or even suburban dog. He not only wants to work, he needs to work. He typically has an even disposition and is good natured and not silly or quarrelsome. The Aussie has more important things on his mind. Shyness, any degree of timidity or aggression are considered great faults in this breed and are not to be tolerated. ¶This well balanced, agile, easy-moving guard and shepherd is a splendid companion. He is handsome and loyal and eager to please, and above all he is willing to work. If you don't frustrate him in that, he is a fine pet. Aussies do well with strangers after they have been given a chance to think things over and draw their own conclusions. They don't like to be pushed. They are good with children but, again, they shouldn't be expected to be immediately demonstrative. Although hardly dull they are initially reserved but soon enough come around and show off their essentially good natures. The Aussie is a capable, sensible dog in all things and takes training and social responsibility well.

This relatively recent addition to the roster of breeds recognized by the American Kennel Club is a British sheepdog. American registration became effective October 1, 1976, but the breed itself may be the oldest of English droving dogs. Certainly it is much older than the Old English Sheepdog. ¶ The "Beardie," as his fanciers refer to him, is a herding dog first, a pet second. He is a natural herder and drover. Children, especially small tots, must expect to be directed, guided, and nudged to where the family Beardie thinks they should be. He is generally excellent with children and ultimately friendly with strangers the family accepts. ¶ The Bearded Collie makes a perfectly awful guard dog. This is not part of his makeup, although he

Bearded Collie

Land of origin: SCOTLAND and ENGLAND

Original purpose: Drover

Recent popularity ranking by A.K.C. registration: 89th

Bearded Collie Club of America, Inc.
Ms. Diana Siebert, Corres. Secretary
1116 Carpenter's Trace
Villa Hills, KY 41017

HEIGHT: Dogs to 22 inches   Bitches to 21 inches

WEIGHT: Dogs to 55 pounds   Bitches to 45 pounds

COAT
Double—undercoat soft, furry, and close; outer coat harsh, strong, flat, *not* woolly, *not* curly.

COLOR
Slate gray, reddish fawn, black, all shades of gray, brown, and sandy. May or may not have typical white Collie markings on head, chest, neck, legs, feet, and tail tip.

Amount of care coat requires:*   1 2 3 4 5 6 7 8 9 10

Amount of exercise required: 1 2 3 4 5 6 7 8 9 10

Suitability for urban/apartment life:†   1 2 3 4 5 6 7 8 9 10

*Slightly more during first two years.
†If properly exercised *every* day.

is a satisfactory watchdog. He will bark at a strange sound in the night, but don't expect a Beardie to go for a stranger's throat, even an unwelcome stranger. Tail wagging is more likely. ¶The breed is slow to mature, and a Beardie's coat for the first two years requires about forty-five minutes of vigorous brushing a week. After two years, about twenty minutes a week will do. In the breed's favor is the fact that Beardies shed very little. ¶This dog is active; he has a long, lean body and he does not normally run to fat. He has an easy, free movement and does require exercise. Any Beardie maintained in the suburbs or city should get an absolute minimum of half an hour to an hour of real exercise every day. That double coat means the Beardie can take any weather, certainly more than his master is

likely to appreciate. A run in an open field is really what a Bearded Collie needs and wants, and for that reason I prefer to see this breed in the country. Still, the dog is not so large that he is a handicap in an apartment, and he is flexible enough to manage the situation as long as he is loved and is walked—a lot. Running is better than walking, when possible. ¶It was predictable that the Bearded Collie would be recognized by the A.K.C., and he is surely a dog destined for stardom. The breed club has been so meticulous that the A.K.C. was able to adopt its studbook outright when the decision was made to give the breed full recognition. One hopes those standards will be maintained and that popularity will not harm this fine, old herding dog from the British Isles.

The Belgian Malinois is one of three virtually identical Belgian sheepherding dogs that differ only in color and to some degree in coat (see also the Belgian sheepdog and the Belgian Tervuren). All three breeds evolved from the basic shepherd stock of Holland, Belgium, and France that was known as *Chien de Berger*, an animal bred for loyalty, endurance, and intelligence. The livelihood and therefore the lives of the sheepherding people depended in no small part upon the quality of their dogs. Dog owning was not a luxury. You fed an animal who earned its keep, and the herding dogs of Europe, in the Middle Ages, earned their keep and more. Bandits,

Belgian Malinois

Land of origin: BELGIUM

Original purpose: Sheepherding

Recent popularity ranking by A.K.C. registration: 85th

American Belgian Malinois Club
Susan Morse, Corres. Secretary
278 Lower Creek Rd.
Ithaca, NY 14850

HEIGHT: Dogs to 26 inches   Bitches to 24 inches

WEIGHT: Dogs to 60 pounds   Bitches to 55 pounds

COAT
Short and straight with a dense, protective undercoat. Somewhat longer around neck and on tail and back of thighs.

COLOR
Fawn to mahogany with black overlay; black muzzle and ears. Lighter underneath but not washed out. White on toe tips and *small* white spot on chest permitted.

Amount of care coat requires: 1 2 3 4 5 6 7 8 9 10
                                      ••••

Amount of exercise required: 1 2 3 4 5 6 7 8 9 10
                                  ••••••••••••••••••••••

Suitability for urban/apartment life:*   1 2 3 4 5 6 7 8 9 10
                                             ••••

*But must be exercised regularly and seriously.

stock thieves, and wolves prowled the countryside, and it took no small amount of canine courage to protect flocks and families against intrusion and ruin. ¶The Belgian Malinois, like the other two breeds, is obviously related at some point to the German Shepherd. The earlier shepherd dogs of western Europe were not bred for color and style but for performance, and it is only in relatively modern times that an effort has been made to standardize them. The Malinois is a short-haired mahogany dog, the Belgian Sheepdog a black breed, and the Belgian Tervuren a longer-haired, mahogany-russet breed. ¶The overall impression the Belgian Malinois gives is of a square and well-balanced dog. The male is masculine looking, and the bitch unmistakably feminine. The expression is alert, sure, and inquiring. The Belgian Malinois wants to know what you want, whether you are a friend or a stranger. If you are a stranger, the dog certainly wants to know that you are not a threat to the household he was born to protect. ¶Because they are natural watchdogs and at times openly suspicious of people they do not know, these dogs should be trained early and well. They were used to drive wolves and feral dogs away from the flocks, so they had fear bred out of them. They can be quick to fight, and when they do, there is no stopping them. They will fight to the death. ¶The Belgian Malinois is a fine, intelligent, and affectionate dog. The least known of the three Belgian breeds in this country, it is still close to its original form. Anyone looking for a breed that has not been watered down by mass-production might well turn to this fine herding dog. As a herding dog, however, it is a breed more suited for open country than for city life, and it should be given a great deal of exercise every day.

Until 1959 all three breeds of Belgian sheepherding dogs were known in this country as Belgian Sheepdogs. The breed we know today as the Belgian Sheepdog (properly also called the Groenedael) had been here since 1907, when the first five specimens were imported. The dog we today know as the Belgian Malinois arrived here in the late 1940s, the Belgian Tervuren in 1954. By 1959 the American Kennel Club has separated the three into distinct breeds, and only the black (with occasionally a very little bit of white), medium-to-long-haired dog is today called and shown as the Belgian Sheepdog. ¶These intelligent dogs have been used extensively for police work in Europe and other parts of the world, including the United States, and

Belgian Sheepdog

Land of origin: BELGIUM

Original purpose: Sheepherding

Recent popularity ranking by A.K.C. registration: 92nd

Belgian Sheepdog Club of America, Inc.
Marilyn Russell, Corres. Secretary
154 Main Rd. S.
Hampden, ME 04444

HEIGHT: Dogs to 26 inches   Bitches to 24 inches

WEIGHT: Dogs to 60 pounds   Bitches to 55 pounds

COAT
Guard hairs long, straight, and very abundant, particularly around neck, back of front legs;
long trimming on hindquarters and on tail. Dense undercoat very protective.

COLOR
All black, or black with restricted amounts of white: moderate strip or patch on chest, between
pads of feet, on tips of rear toes only, and gray or white on chin and muzzle. White on tips of
front toes a fault.

Amount of care coat requires: 1 2 3 4 5 6 7 8 9 10

Amount of exercise required: 1 2 3 4 5 6 7 8 9 10

*Suitability for urban/apartment life:** 1 2 3 4 5 6 7 8 9 10

*But must be exercised regularly and seriously.

indeed may have been the first breed in Europe to be trained for such work. They are loyal and willing animals who want to please their masters; they are affectionate with people they know but are suspicious of strangers. They were used as patrol and courier dogs in World War I, and hundreds gave their lives in battle. They are without fear and will attack anything they feel threatens their family and their holdings. They are possessive and territorial, as goes with being an outstanding guardian of home and flock. The Belgian Sheepdog is not at all casual about his responsibilities. ¶When one considers that the German Shepherd ranks third in this country in popularity (by 1994 A.K.C. registrations) and the Belgian Sheepdog ninety-second, one realizes how unspoiled and still true to purpose and form this dog probably is. Anyone who finds that distinction appealing and who wants to work toward maintaining such early and original perfection might well consider this intelligent breed. ¶The Belgian Sheepdog requires a lot of exercise. He is a rough, tough outdoor animal designed to handle any weather and any assignment. To coop him up and deny him an opportunity to move, to protect, and to participate in an active, outdoor life is to start the breed on the road to disintegration. Training of the Belgian Sheepdog should start early and continue long, and his distrust of strangers should be carefully supervised. He is far too intelligent an animal to be allowed to get the upper hand. Once you surrender it, you might never be able to get it back.

This is the breed known in France and Belgium as the *Chien de Berger Belge*. It is a stunningly handsome version of the black Belgian Sheepdog, different only in color. Before the 1880s, when dog shows became popular and tended to direct attention to a dog's appearance, European shepherds were not concerned with conformation. They were looking for dependability and durability, and they had that in their *Chiens de Berger* no matter what they looked like. But by the 1880s fencing and corralling were commonplace, and the wolves were gone. It was time to start dressing up the working breeds in dependable finery. ¶The Belgian Tervuren, like

Belgian Tervuren

Land of origin: BELGIUM

Original purpose: Sheepherding

Recent popularity ranking by A.K.C. registration: 96th

American Belgian Tervuren Club, Inc.
Ms. Nancy Carman, Corres. Secretary
4970 Chinook Trl.
Casper, WY 82604

HEIGHT: Dogs to 26 inches   Bitches to 24 inches

WEIGHT: Dogs to 60 pounds   Bitches to 55 pounds

COAT
Guard hairs long, straight, and very abundant, particularly around neck, back of front legs; long trimming on hindquarters and on tail. Dense undercoat very protective.

COLOR
Attained at 18 months: rich fawn to russet mahogany with black overlay. Hairs two-colored (black tipped). In males, pronounced on shoulders, back, and rib section. Chest mixture of black and gray. Mask and ears largely black. Tail with darker tip. Lighter underbody but not washed out.

Amount of care coat requires: 1 2 3 4 **5** 6 7 8 9 10

Amount of exercise required: 1 2 3 4 5 6 7 8 9 10

Suitability for urban/apartment life:*   1 2 3 4 5 6 7 8 9 10

*But must be exercised regularly and seriously.

his very close cousins, the Belgian Malinois and the Belgian Sheepdog, is an elegant-looking animal with a lively and graceful gait. His whole attitude is one of willingness, even eagerness to work, to please, to belong. He is obedient when trained well and early and has a long memory for friends and foes. He can be a fighter, because he was made to drive off or kill the feral dogs that ranged across Europe spreading rabies and terror, but his possessiveness and fearlessness must be held in check. Although they are fine base-line qualities, they are not needed the way they once were. ¶Once again, we find in the Belgian Tervuren an animal still close to some original ideal pragmatically arrived at a long time ago in a very rough world, but a breed little known in this country. Only the fine points of appearance have been modified or clarified in modern times—in the last century—and the rest is still probably pretty close to original design. This has great appeal for many people, and so does the fact that the spoilers have not yet chosen this breed for their quick-dollar machinations. ¶The Belgian Tervuren, like his first cousins, needs a great deal of exercise and is of limited appeal in the city. By nature a watchdog, he is best in the suburbs or country, where he still should be controlled and not allowed to fight with other dogs, as some specimens are likely to do. Early and careful obedience training are in order for this herding dog of western Europe.

The Border Collie is the premiere sheepherding dog, in most fanciers' estimation. It is tireless, agile and determined. But most of all it is highly motivated, intelligent and trainable. ¶The breed, as we know it, evolved in Scotland, where they are still very much in use. The stock came from all over England, Wales and Scotland. The canine craft of herding sheep is an ancient one and the Border Collie is probably as advanced as it ever got. The Romans brought the first sheepherding dogs to the British Isles and the Celtic clans picked up on the idea and began developing their own shepherds. And today we have the Border Collie.

172 THE ROGER CARAS DOG BOOK

Border Collie

Land of origin: ENGLAND/SCOTLAND

Original purpose: Sheepherding

Recent popularity ranking by A.K.C. registration: Too newly recognized—1995.

HEIGHT: Dogs 19 to 22 inches   Bitches 18 to 21 inches

WEIGHT: Not given in standards—well proportioned

COAT
Two varieties—Rough and Smooth—both double, soft, dense, weather resistant.
Forelegs feathered in Rough.

COLOR
All white not allowed. Traditionally black with white blaze, collar, stockings, and tail tip.
Sometimes with tan pointings. A variety of primary body colors and markings allowed—bi-color,
tri-color, merle, and sable. Secondary in judging to other considerations.

Amount of care coat requires: 1 2 3 4 5 6 7 8 9 10

Amount of exercise required: 1 2 3 4 5 6 7 8 9 10

Suitability for urban/apartment life: 1 2 3 4 5 6 7 8 9 10
                                  UNSUITED

¶There is a serious problem with the breed and it can really only be resolved in one way for full satisfaction, with a secondary solution very much second best. On the one hand the loyal, faithful Border Collie is a superb combination. Obedience training comes easily to it and there is just no better dog to walk or hike with. They can be hyper-sensitive to gunfire and thunder but they are generally stable, gentle, and not quarrelsome. As befits a sheepherding dog they get along with other animals, cats and other dogs included. But, and here is the rub, they simply have to work. They are so motivated that cramped quarters and no responsibilities will make them hyper and perhaps silly. They belong on a farm where they can take charge as their genes tell them to. We have a flock of geese and our Border Collie spends his day marching them around when he isn't herding grandchildren, other dogs, and incoming automobiles. At night he collapses with exhaustion. The alternative—nearly constant exercise. It can include jogging, hiking, or working at something, but never force a Border Collie to be idle or given the feeling of not being needed. The outcome will be unfair to owner and dog alike.

The cattle-herding people of the northern French hill country and southwestern Flanders needed a really tough dog to guard, herd, and drive their animals. The Bouvier des Flandres emerged as that animal. He is a rough and intelligent dog who was of help to the small farmer and the butcher alike. The itinerant strangers and packs of feral dogs who wandered those hills all needed to be watched, and occasionally attacked, and the Bouvier was the right dog for the job. Afraid of nothing, undeterred by any kind of weather or terrain, and boundless in his devotion to his master, the Bouvier set about his task with particular skill and energy. ¶The seventy-

Bouvier des Flandres

Land of origin: FLANDERS and NORTHERN FRANCE

Original purpose: Cattle herding, driving, and guarding

Recent popularity ranking by A.K.C. registration: 64th

American Bouvier des Flandres Club, Inc.
Sandy Lyon, Corres. Secretary
1880 Jahns Dr.
Wheaton, IL 60187

HEIGHT: Dogs to 27¹/₂ inches   Bitches to 26¹/₂ inches

WEIGHT: Dogs to 70 pounds   Bitches to 65 pounds

COAT
Rough and tousled. Able to tolerate any weather. Outer coat harsh, rough, and wiry; very, very thick. Undercoat fine and soft.

COLOR
Fawn to black, salt and pepper, gray, and brindle. White star on chest permitted. Chocolate brown with white spotting not desired.

Amount of care coat requires: 1 2 3 4 5 6 7 8 9 10
                                   •••••••••

Amount of exercise required: 1 2 3 4 5 6 7 8 9 10
                                 ••••••••••••••••••••••••••

Suitability for urban/apartment life:*   1 2 3 4 5 6 7 8 9 10
                                            •

*But exercise is a serious matter and must be regular.

pound Bouvier des Flandres served faithfully in World War I as well. He was an ambulance dog and a messenger. That war, however, nearly did the breed in. The areas where he was best loved and where most of the significant breeding was going on were devastated by the battles that raged back and forth. Most of the stock was lost, and many examples were carried off to Germany. A few good specimens survived, though, and one who belonged to a U.S. army veterinarian was special. Ch. Nic de Sottegem appears as a forebear in perhaps most of the pedigrees seen here today. ¶The Bouvier can be a family dog and is usually good with children. He is loyal and obedient when trained and is a watchdog. But he is also rough-and-tumble and hard to maintain in close quarters. He really is a dog for the countryside, although a suburban neighborhood will do as long as the dog is well trained and well controlled. It must be remembered that the Bouvier des Flandres was used to drive away whole packs of stray dogs, and he is not likely to back down from a fight. Like many herding and driving breeds, the Bouvier des Flandres is protective and territorial, and that can lead to fights, even though the strange dog's intentions are inoffensive. This must be watched, for the Bouvier is far too powerful to be allowed to perform his ancient responsibilities unchecked. ¶A good household pet if there is an opportunity for plenty of exercise, the Bouvier is an interesting large dog with a long and noble tradition of service to man.

The Briard is probably the oldest of the true French sheepherding dogs. These animals originally were used to protect flocks against thieves and feral dog packs. They have exceptional hearing, are extremely agile, and are loyal. They are still the top-rated sheep dog in France and are in use all over the country. Although often known as *Chiens Berger de Brie*, they are popular well beyond Brie. They have had their place of eminence for over seven hundred years, which speaks well for their qualities. ¶The Briard does not learn as quickly as some of the other herding dogs, but once he has been trained, he is trained for life. Further, nothing will deter him.

Briard

Land of origin: FRANCE

Original purpose: Sheepherding

Recent popularity ranking by A.K.C. registration: 107th

Briard Club of America, Inc.
Janet G. Wall, Secretary
547 Sussex Ct.
Elk Grove Village, IL 60007-4211

HEIGHT: Dogs to 27 inches   Bitches to 25$^{1}/_{2}$ inches

WEIGHT: Dogs to 80 pounds   Bitches to 74 pounds

COAT
Long, stiff, and slightly wavy.

COLOR
All solid colors allowed with the exception of white. Dark preferred—black, black with some white hairs, dark and light gray shades, tawny. Or two of these in combination but with no spots—transition between colors to be gradual and symmetrical.

Amount of care coat requires: 1 2 3 4 5 6 7 8 9 10
                                           ● ● ● ● ● ● ● ● ●

Amount of exercise required: 1 2 3 4 5 6 7 8 9 10
                                     ●

Suitability for urban/apartment life: 1 2 3 4 5 6 7 8 9 10
                                                      UNSUITED

He can stand any terrain and any weather, and he has enormous endurance. He is so willing a worker that his short career as a cart dog proved undistinguished, as he tended to overdo and hurt himself. The Briard served well in World War I, carrying supplies and munitions to the front. ¶The Briard is a quick mover—he turns fast, as suits a sheepherder. These dogs are definitely not keen on strangers and tend to remain suspicious even after some time has passed. They are not yappy and silly about newcomers, but they will watch quietly for some sign that they are needed. As natural watchdogs, they can be quite protective. ¶Because they have been bred through so many centuries as active field dogs, they do need exercise to remain happy and in good shape. They cannot be kept easily in an apartment. In any circumstances there must be active members of the family to take them on long walks and runs, and more than once a day. In general, the Briard is a well-mannered dog, stoic and reserved. He is a good breed with children that he knows. He does not tend to stray, preferring to stay near the property of his master so that he can protect it. ¶The Briard is not the most elegant of breeds, but he does have a nice square, solid appearance. He looks as purposeful as he is, and in the right setting he makes a good family pet and household guardian. Training has to start early and last long. Once you have brought your Briard to the right point of training, though, you have an exceptionally well-mannered canine friend.

Rough-Coated Collie

Smooth-Coated Collie

The Collie dates back several hundred years to the Scottish Highlands, and given the antiquity of sheepherding, the breed undoubtedly had much earlier origins on the Continent. No one will ever sort out the early history of the Collie, for no records were kept by breeders of herding dogs. These animals were essential to their masters' livelihood rather than to their sense of aesthetics. ¶There are two varieties of Collie, the rough and the smooth, with the former being the more popular. Records indicate that as late as the end of the last century the two varieties might appear in the same litter, but some authorities believe that the two had different origins. Today, though, they are considered varieties of the same breed, and all the rest must remain conjecture. ¶The standards for the two forms are the same except for the coat, and therein lies a world of difference. The Rough-Coated Collie requires a great deal of care if he is to look as he should. His coat is long and dense and

Collie

Land of origin: SCOTLAND

Original purpose: Herding, farm work

Recent popularity ranking by A.K.C. registration: 30th

Collie Club of America, Inc.
Carmen Leonard, Secretary
1119 South Fleming Rd.
Woodstock, IL 60098

HEIGHT: Dogs to 26 inches   Bitches to 24 inches

WEIGHT: Dogs to 75 pounds   Bitches to 65 pounds

COAT
Well-fitting, straight, and harsh outer coat with very dense soft, furry undercoat. Very abundant and the dog's "crowning glory" in the rough-coated variety. The smooth variety has a hard, dense, and smooth coat.

COLOR
Four varieties: sable and white (sable running from light gold to dark mahogany), tricolor (predominantly black with white and tan markings), blue merle, and white. The latter is really predominantly white with sable or tricolor markings. Colors are the same for both coat styles.

Amount of care coat requires:

Rough: 1 2 3 4 5 6 7 8 9 10
•••••••••••••••••••••••

Smooth: 1 2 3 4 5 6 7 8 9 10
•

Amount of exercise required: 1 2 3 4 5 6 7 8 9 10
••••••••••••••••••••••••••

Suitability for urban/apartment life: * 1 2 3 4 5 6 7 8 9 10
•••••

*Provided that enough exercise is given every day.

soon will become a hopeless tangle unless brushed out regularly. The Smooth-Coated variety requires virtually no care, but he is not at all popular with American fanciers of the breed. ¶The Collie is a herding dog designed for living in the open. He requires a lot of exercise on a regular basis, for working dogs are creatures of habit. No one should think of owning a Collie unless he plans to exercise him and care for him properly. ¶By nature the Collie is careful with strangers—not hostile, just cautious. He is very affectionate with family and with people he knows well. He is loyal, a good watchdog, and sensible in all things. Like many other breeds, the Collie has suffered from extreme popularity. As a result of books, films, and television series starring Collies, the breed consistently has been one of the most popular in America. Many breeders far more interested in dollars than in the welfare of their breed have capitalized on the demand, and there are many substandard specimens around. They can be unreliable and nervous, the last things one should expect of a fine Collie. ¶Perhaps as much as with any breed in America today, great care should be taken when buying a Collie. Only the most responsible breeders should be considered. Collies are shown in two varieties, rough and smooth, but aside from their coats, the same standards prevail.

The highly popular German Shepherd was derived over a period of several hundred years of native herding and from general farm dogs in Germany and surrounding areas. From the beginning of this century his worldwide popularity has grown steadily. He is the third most popular purebred dog in America. ¶The German Shepherd is first, last, and always a working dog designed to serve man in any way needed. A herding dog, a guard dog for livestock, a police dog, a military dog, a dog to lead the blind and pull carts—this sturdy, intelligent animal has never been outclassed by any task or any other breed. He is the preeminent herding dog, and his popularity clearly reflects that fact. ¶A shy or nervous German Shepherd is not to be

German Shepherd

Land of origin: GERMANY

Original purpose: Farm work, herding, guard work

Recent popularity ranking by A.K.C. registration: 3rd

German Shepherd Dog Club of America, Inc.
Blanche Beisswenger, Corres. Secretary
17 West Ivy Lane
Englewood, NJ 07631

HEIGHT: Dogs to 26 inches   Bitches to 24 inches

WEIGHT: Dogs to 85 pounds   Bitches to 70 pounds

COAT
Double and of medium length. Outer coat should be dense, straight, harsh, and close lying.
Never silky, soft, woolly, or open.

COLOR
Most are permissible, but not white. Black and tan, gray, or black are common.

Amount of care coat requires: 1 2 3 4 5 6 7 8 9 10

Amount of exercise required: 1 2 3 4 5 6 7 8 9 10

Suitability for urban/apartment life:*   1 2 3 4 5 6 7 8 9 10

---

*But only if properly exercised.

---

forgiven, for the standards clearly state that such personality faults are to be severely penalized. A really nervous German Shepherd is a dangerous animal and should not have access to innocent bystanders. ¶It is true that 80 percent or more of reported purebred dog bites are caused by German Shepherds. That is because bites by large dogs are more apt to be reported than nips by small dogs, and because the German Shepherd is so very popular. It is also unfortunately true that many inexpert people keep these animals as deterrent dogs. Too many accidents obviously happen as a result. ¶The German Shepherd can be taught just about anything, and one thing often taught this animal, most unfortunately, is to attack. Private citizens have no more right to an attack-trained German Shepherd than they have to a Luger in a shoulder holster. Laws are going to have to be enacted to regulate the rental and sale of attack dogs. ¶A German Shepherd raised as a pet and well trained is as fine a canine companion as anyone could possibly want. Intelligent, alert, a perfect watchdog, careful with strangers but not petty or mean—he is loyal unto death to his family and will do anything to protect family children. That does not have to be built in, it is already there. ¶The German Shepherd requires a lot of exercise to maintain condition, and his coat should be brushed regularly to keep its sheen. The breed is very susceptible to hip dysplasia, with about a 65 percent heritability factor. ¶It is not easy nor is it inexpensive to locate a fine example of this breed. When you succeed, you have a superb dog. When you fail (and the exploiters win), you have a mess! Only the very best breeders should be consulted, and no German Shepherd should ever be purchased from a puppy mill.

The Old English Sheepdog is English, without doubt, but not quite as old as his name might imply. The breed probably emerged in the latter half of the eighteenth century, although the groundwork was laid somewhat earlier. The ancestry of the breed is not known. Many people insist on Collie as the foundation stock, while others opt for a Russian dog known as the *Owtchar*. If it was Collie, it was probably what we now know as the Bearded Collie. ¶The dog was a sheepdog, again as the name implies, but not so much a herding animal as a drover. The dog's task was to help drive sheep and probably other livestock to market. The peculiar ursine gait, a wonderful

Old English Sheepdog

Land of origin: ENGLAND

Original purpose: Driving livestock

Recent popularity ranking by A.K.C. registration: 52nd

Old English Sheepdog Club of America, Inc.
Kathryn Bunnell, Corres. Secretary
14219 E. 79th St. S.
Derby, KS 67037

HEIGHT: Dogs to 25 inches   Bitches to 24 inches

WEIGHT: Dogs to 65 pounds   Bitches to 60 pounds

COAT
Profuse but not excessive; hard textured, not straight, but shaggy and never curly. Not soft or flat. Undercoat forms waterproof pile.

COLOR
Shades of gray, grizzle, blue, or blue merle with or without white markings. No brown or fawn allowed.

Amount of care coat requires: 1 2 3 4 5 6 7 8 9 10

Amount of exercise required: 1 2 3 4 5 6 7 8 9 10

Suitability for urban/apartment life: 1 2 3 4 5 6 7 8 9 10
UNSUITED

---

ambling shuffle, speaks of great stamina. The Old English Sheepdog lives inside a protective shield of a coat and should not be stripped of that coat unless it becomes hopelessly matted. Unfortunately, this is a common occurrence. So the Old English Sheepdog's coat does require maximum care. It should be brushed every day to help keep it clean and free from mats. ¶The Old English Sheepdog is not at his best in confinement, though he is a house dog. Ideal on a farm, he will do well in a suburban home but not in an apartment. He must get plenty of exercise in all kinds of weather. A dog that is closely confined and not exercised can become lame and may be very "flaky" to deal with. Such a bumptious pest is cute for only a very short time. Naturally obedient and decidedly pleasant, the Old English Sheepdog will reflect the care and consideration with which he has been raised. Not meant to be chained or left alone in close quarters, he will be destructive and uncontrollable only if driven to it by conditions he could be expected to tolerate poorly. ¶The Old English Sheepdog has skyrocketed in popularity in recent years, and there are an inevitable number of poor examples of the breed on the market. Get to know the parents of the dog you are considering. Only puppies from solid, pleasant, and even-tempered stock should be considered. It is a shame to become disenchanted once your puppy has started to grow. And no one should consider the breed unless they have studied it well. This is a large, demanding, working dog who requires extensive obedience training. Only then will he keep his promise as a pet. He is not an ideal first dog.

The Puli is another of the superior shepherd's dogs from Hungary, where they have been in use for at least a thousand years. No one knows where they came from or what their ancestral stock might be. There is a strong argument for the Tibetan Terrier, since the two breeds bear a resemblance, and the Hungarian dogs generally are believed to have come from the East. Arguments that the breed arose from stock from Lapland and Iceland are less convincing. It is a problem that will not be solved, for no records were kept, and the movement of dog breeds and groups of breeds apparently was constant over thousands of years. ¶The Puli is an agile, active

Puli

Land of origin: HUNGARY

Original purpose: Sheepherding

Recent popularity ranking by A.K.C. registration: 117th

Puli Club of America, Inc.
Ms. Barbara Stelz, Secretary
5109 Kathy Way
Livermore, CA 94550

HEIGHT: Dogs to 19 inches   Bitches to 18 inches

WEIGHT: Dogs to 35 pounds   Bitches to 32 pounds

COAT
Unique. Dense, weather resisting, double. Outer coat long, never silky. May be straight, wavy, or somewhat curly. Undercoat soft, woolly, dense; mats into cords. Seen either combed or uncombed with hair hanging in neat even cords.

COLOR
Solid colors only, dark preferred. Black, shades of gray, and white. Blacks are rust or weathered. Some mixing in grays but overall effect must be of solid-colored dog.

Amount of care coat requires: 1 2 3 4 5 6 7 8 9 10

Amount of exercise required: 1 2 3 4 5 6 7 8 9 10

Suitability for urban/apartment life:* 1 2 3 4 5 6 7 8 9 10

*Must be exercised a great deal.

outdoor dog who is as much a herder today as he ever was in history. A Puli shows his best qualities when being worked. Tough, extremely intelligent, and readily trained by anyone who knows what he is doing, this breed is not for the casual or indifferent owner. A Puli is more than just careful with strangers, he tends to be openly suspicious. He makes, therefore, a first-rate watchdog. He must be regulated, though, lest watchfulness becomes aggressiveness. Although not large, the Puli is like spring steel, probably because the breed is said to have run across the backs of sheep, even to have ridden them. There is no doubt that this is a special breed for special purposes. ¶The coat of the Puli (the plural form is *Pulik*) is another special characteristic.

It tends to cord like that of the Komondor and is protection against all weather. The puli never has to come inside. They haven't invented weather he cannot thrive in. ¶If one is to match himself in dog-handling skills to the dog he buys, the first-time owner (or one with very limited patience) should go slow with this breed. Unless managed well and really appreciated for his superior abilities to learn and respond, the Puli will not only be wasted on such an owner but become a nuisance. This breed is headstrong, assertive, and very expert at what it does—handling other animals and guarding the master's territory. It is thought to be one of the most intelligent of all breeds.

The Shetland Sheepdog or "Sheltie" is more than a very small Collie, although the two breeds have some ancestry in common and do resemble each other in conformation. The Sheltie has qualities of his own and very great charm. The ancestral stock carried to the islands from mainland Scotland was the Hill Collie, a smaller animal than the one we know as the Collie today. Various small breeds were crossed in over the years, including some spaniels and a small herding dog from Iceland. Eventually Collies were used again to give the dog a final shape and proper coat. There has been more than a little controversy as to what this breed should look like and how big it should be. ¶The Shetland Sheepdog, despite his diminutive

Shetland Sheepdog

Land of origin: SCOTLAND and SHETLAND ISLANDS

Original purpose: Sheepherding and as watchdog

Recent popularity ranking by A.K.C. registration: 13th

American Shetland Sheepdog Association
Mr. George Page, Corres. Secretary
1100 Cataway Pl.
Bryans Road, MD 20616

HEIGHT: Dogs to 16 inches   Bitches to 15 inches

WEIGHT: Dogs to 16 pounds   Bitches to 15 pounds

COAT
Double—outer coat is long, straight, and harsh; undercoat is short, furry, and very dense.
Hair on face, feet, and ear tips smooth. Mane and frill abundant and impressive.

COLOR
Black, blue merle, and sable ranging from golden through mahogany. White or tan markings.
More than 50 percent white disqualifies. Brindle also not allowed.

Amount of care coat requires: 1 2 3 4 5 6 7 8 9 10

Amount of exercise required: 1 2 3 4 5 6 7 8 9 10

Suitability for urban/apartment life:*   1 2 3 4 5 6 7 8 9 10

*But must be properly exercised

size, is a smart herding animal and was and would be again fine with sheep. He also works well with hogs and goats. He is fast and alert and responds well to training. He is responsive to human moods and demands and always strives to fit himself in. He was used at the outset as a watchdog, and that is a quality he has not lost. A Shetland today, reserved with strangers but not snappy, is a dog who can be depended upon to give the alarm. He has a loud and insistent bark. Some Shetlands, in fact, tend to overdo it! ¶The Shetland Sheepdog requires grooming; that resplendent dog we see in the show-ring will not be apparent in the casual owner's living room unless he is brushed regularly and kept in fine trim. It is not a hard job or a long one, since this is a small and obedient dog, but it is a job that should be seen to every day. The Shetland also requires exercise. He is a delightful apartment dog, fine with chil-

dren, small, neat, and easily trained, but he has descended from working dogs of harsh country and harsh weather, and that part of him must be seen to as well. Long daily walks are in order and, whenever possible, good country romps. ¶The superior little Shetland Sheepdog can live anywhere as long as he has love and a reasonable amount of attention. He should be trained early and well—something he naturally loves anyway—and taught not to be unnecessarily yappy. A good watchdog is one thing, a noisy nuisance is another. Beware of the mass-production breeders, for the Shetland Sheepdog is one of the most popular breeds in the country, and terrible examples abound. Seek sound advice and do your homework if you intend to add a Shetland Sheepdog to your family. Avoid obviously shy specimens. That can mean poor breeding or bad early handling.

The Cardigan Welsh Corgi is a very ancient breed said to have come to southern Wales as early as 1200 B.C. He is believed to have arrived there in the company of central European Celts and to have had common ancestry with the Dachshund. The breed was used for everything a pastoral people might need—rushing small game, herding, guard work, chasing away neighbors' cattle, ratting, and general vermin work. This dog has enough fire and stamina to handle all these assignments, and he is intelligent enough to take any training required to excel at each task in turn. ¶The Cardigan Welsh Corgi, "the Corgi with the tail," is a tough little animal

Cardigan Welsh Corgi

Land of origin: WALES

Original purpose: Herding cattle, guarding, flushing small game

Recent popularity ranking by A.K.C. registration: 91st

Cardigan Welsh Corgi Club of America, Inc.
Ginny Conway, Corres. Secretary
14511 Trophey Club Dr.
Houston, TX 77095-3420

HEIGHT: Dogs to 12 inches   Bitches to 11¹/₂ inches

WEIGHT: Dogs to 25 pounds   Bitches to 20 pounds

COAT
Medium length, dense, slightly harsh, but never wiry or silky. Weather resistant.

COLOR
Red, sable, red brindle, black brindle, black, tricolor blue merle. White markings on neck, chest, face, feet, and tail tip usual. Pure white disqualifies, and predominant white heavily faulted.

Amount of care coat requires: 1 2 3 4 5 6 7 8 9 10
                                      ••

Amount of exercise required: 1 2 3 4 5 6 7 8 9 10
                                  •••••••••••••

*Suitability for urban/apartment life:**   1 2 3 4 5 6 7 8 9 10
                                            ••••••••••••••••••••••••

*Proper amount of exercise necessary.

who can raise havoc with other animals. He is utterly fearless and quick and smart in his movements, despite his short legs. He is territorial and protective of his master's property, and that can lead to confrontations. The Cardigan Welsh Corgi should be trained early and well. He is an exceptionally long-lived dog and should be reminded of his training regularly. He has a natural desire to please his master and wants to fit in with everything that is going on around him. He tends to be careful with strangers and even a little too suspicious at times. It is to the owner's advantage to keep that characteristic in check. Being a watchdog, which the Cardigan surely is, is enough. Barking is all that is needed. ¶The Cardigan Welsh Corgi is above all things intelligent. He watches his master, constantly seeking clues as to what is expected and what will win praise. He responds instantly in his own flashy way, without being hyper and silly. Not quite as soft in nature as the Pembroke Welsh Corgi—there are inevitably many exceptions to that, however—he is a bit one-personish, but the man who has that friendship has a loyalty that cannot be beaten. The love of a Cardigan Welsh Corgi is a special privilege. ¶The Cardigan Welsh Corgi is not as well known in this country as the Pembroke Welsh Corgi, a very different dog. In 1978 the American Kennel Club reported the registration of 2,349 new Pembrokes and only 339 new Cardigans. Fewer registrations generally mean less interest on the part of the mass-production breeders, but care is still advised so that a satisfying example of the breed may grow up in your home.

The Pembroke Welsh Corgi has a wholly different ancestry from the Cardigan Corgi. He came to the British Isles with the Flemish weavers imported by Henry I in 1107. The weavers settled in Wales, and the little Schipperke-like dog they brought with them evolved into a cattle dog. The Pembroke Welsh Corgi, then, is descended from spitz-type dogs and is not as old as the other Corgi. There was a great deal of interbreeding, but that is not done today. Fanciers of each breed want to keep their favorite distinct, as it should be. Any similarity noted today is a result of interbreeding in Wales up to the last century. ¶There are easy distinctions

Pembroke Welsh Corgi

Land of origin: FRANCE, then WALES from twelfth century on

Original purpose: As general farm dog—cattle herding

Recent popularity ranking by A.K.C. registration: 37th

Pembroke Welsh Corgi Club of America, Inc.
Joan Gibson Reid, Corres. Secretary
9589 Sheldon Rd.
Elk Grove, CA 95624

HEIGHT: Dogs to 12 inches   Bitches to 11 inches

WEIGHT: Dogs to 30 pounds   Bitches to 28 pounds

COAT
Short, thick, weather-resistant undercoat with a longer, more coarse outer coat. Wiry, marcelled, or thin coat is very serious fault.

COLOR
Red, sable, fawn, black, or tan, with or without white markings. White allowed on legs, chest, neck, muzzle, underparts, and as blaze on head only. Blue or smoky cast very serious fault.

Amount of care coat requires: 1 2 3 4 5 6 7 8 9 10
                                                ••••

Amount of exercise required: 1 2 3 4 5 6 7 8 9 10
                                              •••••••••••••

*Suitability for urban/apartment life:**   1 2 3 4 5 6 7 8 9 10
                                                        ••••••••••••••••••••••••

*Proper amount of exercise necessary.

to be made between the two Corgis: the Cardigan has rounded ear tips and a good tail, while the Pembroke has pointed ear tips and a very short tail, no more than two inches. The two are quite similar in size and outline, however. ¶The Pembroke Welsh Corgi is a gentle, sensible, and even-tempered dog. He is a dog for the farm, the suburbs, and the city apartment. He is affectionate, and although he can be a good little watchdog, he is not quarrelsome or foolish and is never mean. It is stated in the standards of the breed that shyness or viciousness are grounds for immediate disqualification, and judges are admonished to dismiss any dog showing these undesirable characteristics. ¶Corgis travel well and are fine with children. They are, in fact, as close to being ideal pets as can be found. They have spunk and fire and enormous charm. Naturally obedient, they take training well and are very hardy. They are exceptionally long-lived, and specimens approaching twenty years are not unknown; certainly the middle to late teens could be considered normal. They are naturally healthy but should be exercised well to maintain both health and condition. They are so pleasant you can take them anywhere, and it would be the unusual Pembroke Welsh Corgi who could not fit in with other animals. They are very often owned in pairs and are especially pleasant that way. ¶Be careful in buying a Corgi and rely only on the best breeders to provide you with a satisfactory example of this marvelous companion animal.

{Group 6}

The Terriers

Airedale

American Staffordshire Terrier

Australian Terrier

Bedlington Terrier

Border Terrier

Bull Terrier

Cairn Terrier

Dandie Dinmont Terrier

Fox Terriers

Irish Terrier

Kerry Blue Terrier

Lakeland Terrier

Manchester Terrier

Miniature Bull Terrier

Miniature Schnauzer

Norfolk and Norwich Terriers

Scottish Terrier

Sealyham Terrier

Skye Terrier

Soft-Coated Wheaten Terrier

Staffordshire Bull Terrier

Welsh Terrier

West Highland White Terrier

Once known as the Waterside Terrier, this distinctive animal is today the king of all existing terrier breeds. He is the largest and, in many people's opinion, the most admirable. ¶The Airedale is descended from a cross between a hunting terrier and the Otter Hound; the latter animal helped improve the nose and performance in the water. The resulting terrier was used on fox, badger, weasel, otter, water rat, and other lesser game. It was a breed much beloved and one fostered down to our own time with devotion. ¶As a terrier, the Airedale is by nature courageous and bold. He is also aggressive, cut much calmer than most other terriers and never silly or overexcitable. He will attack anything he is sent against and is one of the best all-time

Airedale

Land of origin: ENGLAND

Original purpose: Hunting small- and medium-sized game

Recent popularity ranking by A.K.C. registration: 49th

Airedale Terrier Club of America
Dr. Suzanne H. Hampton, Corres. Secretary
47 Tulip Ave.
Ringwood, NJ 07456

HEIGHT: Dogs to 23 inches   Bitches to 22 inches

WEIGHT: Dogs to 50 pounds   Bitches to 45 pounds

COAT
Double. Hard, dense, and wiry, lying close to the body. A light, soft undercoat. The outer coat may be slightly wavy.

COLOR
Tan and black or tan and dark grizzle. Some red mixture in black acceptable, as is a small white blaze on the chest.

Amount of care coat requires: 1 2 3 4 5 6 7 8 9 10
                                  ••••••

Amount of exercise required: 1 2 3 4 5 6 7 8 9 10
                                ••••••••••••••••••••••••

Suitability for urban/apartment life:*   1 2 3 4 5 6 7 8 9 10
                                          ••••••••••••••

*With proper exercise.

ratters. ¶With his master and family the Airedale is an affectionate, gentle, and loyal animal. He is a first-rate watchdog and thrives on rough and tumble play with children. It is unusual for an Airedale to be mean or nasty. He wants to be a part of everything that goes on in the household, and he expects the right to check out strangers. He just likes to be sure, and in security matters he seems to prefer his own judgment to that of a mere human. He easily softens with nonthreatening strangers, though, and is usually too aloof to take exception to a minor insult from a lesser dog. But be careful of an Airedale who has been egged on, for he is a terror when the fight erupts. Fortunately, he generally elects to pass. ¶Airedale owners resemble religious converts in the intensity of their affection for this breed; they become missionaries. This apparently has been going on for a long time, since the Airedale remains a popular breed, although less so than in the past. ¶There is the temptation to suggest that because the Airedale is both a dog of considerable substance and active like all terriers, he is not suited to city life. That is not quite true. While probably very happy with a lakeside home in the country, the Airedale will settle down to an urban routine as long as he has his family around him. It remains important, however, that he get a great deal of exercise, and ideally that means several miles every day. Obedience training is highly desirable, for an ill-mannered Airedale would be more than just a nuisance. Given half a chance, this is one dog who will prove himself under any circumstances to be a gentle, loyal, and noble friend. It is more than his size that makes him king of the terrier kind.

The American Staffordshire Terrier (formally known simply as the Staffordshire Terrier) is not to be confused with the Staffordshire Bull Terrier or the Bull Terrier, both recognized as separate breeds. ¶The American Staffordshire Terrier was derived from the English Bulldog (which in the early nineteenth century looked more like today's American Staffordshire Terrier than today's Bulldog) and a terrier. The exact identity of that terrier is not known although many claims are heard. The cross was originally called the Bull-and-Terrier Dog and then by at least half a dozen other names. It wasn't until 1972 that the name American Staffordshire Terrier was adopted.

American Staffordshire Terrier

Land of origin: ENGLAND

Original purpose: Fighting bulls and other dogs

Recent popularity ranking by A.K.C. registration: 73rd

Staffordshire Terrier Club of America
Mr. H. Richard Pascoe, Secretary
785 Valley View Rd.
Forney, TX 75126

HEIGHT: Dogs to 19 inches   Bitches to 18 inches

WEIGHT: Dogs to 50 pounds   Bitches to 45 pounds

COAT
Short, stiff, and glossy. Lies close to the body.

COLOR
Any color, solid or parti. All white, more than 80 percent white, black and tan, and liver are not desired.

Amount of care coat requires: 1 2 3 4 5 6 7 8 9 10

Amount of exercise required: 1 2 3 4 5 6 7 8 9 10

*Suitability for urban/apartment life:**   1 2 3 4 5 6 7 8 9 10

*Only if properly exercised.

¶The early history of this dog and related breeds is a nightmare. They were used for the cruelest of blood sports, and much of that image has come down with these breeds. American Staffordshire Terriers can be good pets, loyal, affectionate, and responsive. They accept training but must always be considered suspect around other animals, for they are terriers, and like all dogs in this group they don't just get into a scrap, they go for the finish. Owners should keep this in mind and not allow their dogs to make a decision as to whether to fight or not. Take it for granted that your dog is probably going to be fine with people but at least questionable with other dogs and with cats. ¶The American Staffordshire Terrier does not require any grooming (an occasional wipe with a harsh cloth will bring out the coat's natural luster) and will be a quiet, sensible apartment dweller if taken on a good walk a couple of times a day. He does make a good watchdog and is an interesting pet for a person able and willing to train and supervise him. He should not be allowed to wander in the suburbs and should not be teased if chained or fenced in. He is a highly questionable choice for an inexperienced dog owner.

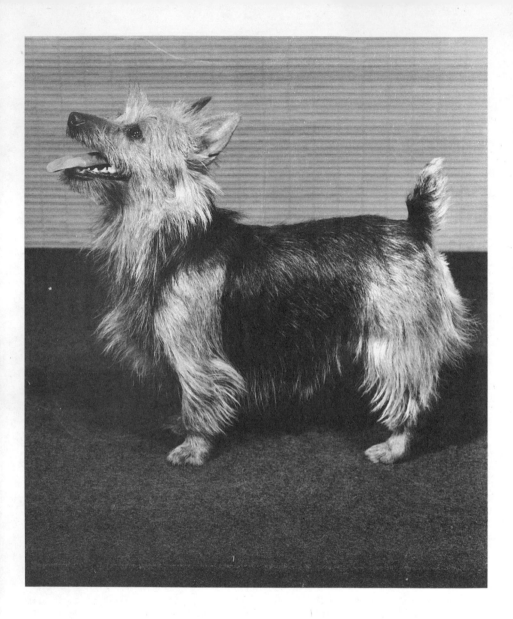

The Australian Terrier (not to be confused, as so often happens, with the Silky Terrier, a toy dog, also from Australia) is a blend of many other terrier lines. It is quite possible that more different breeds were used to create the perky Australian Terrier than went into any other modern purebred dog. At the very least the Scottish, the Cairn, the Dandie Dinmont, the Irish, the Skye, and the Yorkshire Terriers all went into its makeup. The original parent stock was what was known as the Broken-Haired Terrier, sometimes also known as the Rough-Coated. What emerged was a distinctive Australian creation, one of the smallest of the working terriers. ¶The

Australian Terrier

Land of origin: AUSTRALIA

Original purpose: Companionship and hunting small game

Recent popularity ranking by A.K.C. registration: 97th

Australian Terrier Club of America, Inc.
Ms. Marilyn Harban, Corres. Secretary
1515 Davon Ln.
Nassau Bay, TX 77058

HEIGHT: Dogs to 10 inches   Bitches to 10 inches

WEIGHT: Dogs to 15 pounds   Bitches to 14 pounds

COAT
Outer coat harsh and straight, about 2¹/₂ inches long. Undercoat short and soft. Topknot distinctive feature.

COLOR
Blue black or silver black with rich tan (the deeper the better). Sandy or red markings on head and legs.

Amount of care coat requires: 1 2 3 4 5 6 7 8 9 10

Amount of exercise required: 1 2 3 4 5 6 7 8 9 10

Suitability for urban/apartment life: 1 2 3 4 5 6 7 8 9 10

Australian Terrier is a dog of fire and stamina despite his small size. Barely more than a toy, he can hold his own under any weather and terrain conditions. He has been used on small game in the Australian outback, although the impetus behind his development was undoubtedly the search for a superior companion dog. He was first shown in Melbourne in the middle 1880s and has since attracted attention and devoted followers in a number of countries. ¶The Australian may be close to the perfect small house and apartment dog. Small enough not to intrude, he is a loyal pet with charm and personality. He isn't a heavy shedder and knows instinctively how to fit in and ingratiate himself. He will hold his own with other animals without being silly and quarrelsome. He makes a good watch-dog and will return affection in kind and in depth. Although he is an active little dog by nature, he isn't hyper and doesn't need long walks. He is quite satisfied being a homebody but will participate in any outdoor activities offered him. He is fine on a farm, great in the suburbs, and almost flawless in an apartment. ¶Although not yet a fad in this country, the Australian Terrier undoubtedly will grow in popularity over the years, and care should be taken to obtain specimens only from the most reliable sources. This is not a breed to be mass-produced, for it would not hold its present fine style. This terrier was evolved so recently and from such a variety of lines that only careful breeding will enable it to solidify all it has gained from the care taken so far.

This spunky little terrier has had a number of names down through the years. He evolved in the north of England from stock that has never really been identified. Known as the Rothbury Terrier and the Northumberland Fox Terrier, he was admired both in England and Wales for his great pluck. He would fight any other dog or any vermin, and was used in pits and demonstrations against his own kind as well as against badgers, rats, foxes, and anything else that would put up a fight. ¶The fire behind that behavior still burns in the Bedlington Terrier, and he generally does better in a one-animal household. He will fight anything that intrudes on his pro-

Bedlington Terrier

Land of origin: ENGLAND

Original purpose: For use on vermin

Recent popularity ranking by A.K.C. registration: 111th

Bedlington Terrier Club of America
Mr. Robert Bull, Corres. Secretary
P.O. Box 11
Morrison, IL 61270-7419

HEIGHT: Dogs to 16½ inches   Bitches to 15½ inches

WEIGHT: Dogs to 23 pounds   Bitches to 22 pounds

COAT
Crisp but not wiry—stands out from skin. Not to exceed 1 inch when shown. Has tendency to curl.

COLOR
Blue, sandy, liver, blue and tan, sandy and tan, liver and tan.

Amount of care coat requires: 1 2 3 4 5 6 7 8 9 10

Amount of exercise required: 1 2 3 4 5 6 7 8 9 10

*Suitability for urban/apartment life:** 1 2 3 4 5 6 7 8 9 10

*If properly exercised.

prietorship. A good pet when properly raised, he will be fine with children and is not bad with strangers, if a little cautious. But he doesn't want any other animals around to steal his thunder. In owning a Bedlington, that should be kept in mind. He should not wander where he is likely to encounter other dogs and cats. Away from other animals, he can be quite placid. ¶The Bedlington can make an ideal pet for a couple whose children are grown and who want to share their home with a devoted friend. Because he is a highly spirited terrier, he should be exercised regularly. He needs those long, steady walks on a lead, and he needs a good romp in the country whenever there is an opportunity. He should not be let free near traffic, however, because if he sees another animal, he might take off in pursuit, letting his spirit rather than his good sense guide him. ¶The Bedlington's coat must be seen to if he is to have that appealing if deceptive "little-lamb" look. That does require some instruction to be done well. Many owners prefer to let a professional groomer see to the job. Unique in appearance and full of fire, will, and devotion, the Bedlington Terrier is an interesting pet for the right household.

The Border Terrier is the least-known terrier in the United States. In 1978 the American Kennel Club reported only 136 new specimens registered in this country. And that is a shame. ¶This is a hardy, tough little action terrier from the border country between England and Scotland. For several hundred years this wiry dynamo has been used to drive away and kill foxes and other animals that might tamper with the lambs. Extremely alert and active, this dog can tolerate any weather, any terrain, and will run behind a horse for hours. When a fox is spotted, he will chase it to ground and kill it from above or below, wherever he can catch the quarry. He can

Border Terrier

Land of origin: ENGLAND and SCOTLAND

Original purpose: Killing foxes and vermin

Recent popularity ranking by A.K.C. registration: 86th

Border Terrier Club of America, Inc.
Mrs. Laurale Stern, Secretary
832 Lincoln Blvd.
Manitowoc, WI 54220

HEIGHT: Dogs to 13 inches   Bitches to 12 inches

WEIGHT: Dogs to 15½ pounds   Bitches to 14 pounds

COAT
Short, dense undercoat with very wiry outer coat that is close lying. No curl or wave. Thick, loose hide.

COLOR
Red, grizzle and tan, blue and tan, or wheaten. A small amount of white allowed on chest but not on feet.

Amount of care coat requires: 1 2 3 4 5 6 7 8 9 10
                                 ••••

Amount of exercise required: 1 2 3 4 5 6 7 8 9 10
                               ••••••••••••••••••

Suitability for urban/apartment life:*   1 2 3 4 5 6 7 8 9 10
                                         ••••••••••••••••••••••••

*But must be properly exercised regularly.

burst through any tangle of wire or brush because his loose skin keeps him from getting trapped. He will climb any wall or overcome any obstacle to get at his enemy. ¶The tough little Border Terrier is a hard-working field animal and cannot always be expected to double in brass as a pet. He is, though, loyal to his master and anxious to please. If raised in a home, he will respond because he is intelligent and eminently trainable. ¶It must always be remembered that the Border Terrier has been bred to kill other animals. That is his original calling, and that can lead to trouble unless the dog is held in some kind of check. Border Terriers need early training and a strong-willed master to see to it that deportment is given high priority. The dog is so active and so assertive that if ill-mannered, he could become the neighborhood pest or even menace. That need not be, however, since the breed is so bright and anxious to please. A good trainer can do wonders with this dog, the largest single problem being his penchant to go after other animals, cats included. ¶This rare dog is attractive and spunky and could enjoy popularity in this country at some future time. Anyone now contemplating the purchase of one should see to it that plenty of exercise is provided. The breed is active enough, and having one go "hyper" for lack of proper exercise is surely unnecessary.

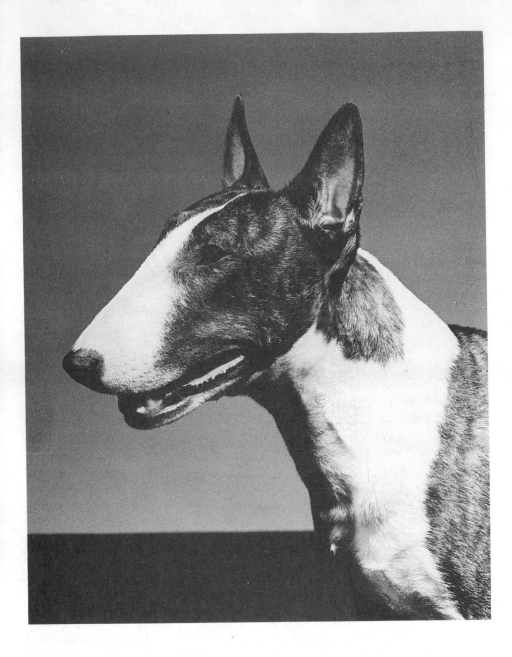

The Bull Terrier is a much maligned dog. It is true that he was originally bred for blood sports, but those were rougher times. There is a kind of nobility to the breed, and he is not a nasty creature at all. But neither is he a wise choice for an inexperienced owner. He should not be one's first dog. ¶The Bull Terrier, a cross between the Bulldog and an extinct variety of white terrier with some Pointer blood thrown in, is a powerful and assertive animal who will answer the ancient call of his kind only if challenged. When that happens, he can kill almost any dog alive. Bull Terriers, because there is always the danger that they will be provoked into a fight,

Bull Terrier

Land of origin: ENGLAND

Original purpose: Fighting

Recent popularity ranking by A.K.C. registration: 76th

Bull Terrier Club of America
Mrs. Becky Poole, Corres. Secretary
2630 Gold Point Cir.
Hixson, TN 37343

HEIGHT: Dogs to 22 inches   Bitches to 21 inches

WEIGHT: Dogs to 60 pounds   Bitches to 50 pounds

COAT
Short, hard, flat, and glossy.

COLOR
Two varieties. White—all white or white with some markings on head. No other markings allowed. Colored—any color other than white or any color with white markings as long as white does not predominate. Brindle is preferred color.

Amount of care coat requires: 1 2 3 4 5 6 7 8 9 10

Amount of exercise required: 1 2 3 4 5 6 7 8 9 10

Suitability for urban/apartment life:* 1 2 3 4 5 6 7 8 9 10

*If taken on really long walks several times a day.

must at all times be kept under control and never allowed to wander. They don't necessarily look for trouble, but trouble has a way of presenting itself. Unfortunately, Bull Terriers don't just get into fights, they finish them. ¶With people Bull Terriers can be affectionate, playful, and loyal. They make excellent watchdogs. There is something about them that frightens unwelcome people away. ¶The Bull Terrier eats a great deal and must be walked often and long. They are not a good breed for inactive people. They require an active, lively family who wants to romp, run, and tussle. Activity is the keynote of this dog's existence. ¶As for appearance, there are people who detest it and people who love it. That seems to be true of the breed in general—no one just *likes* a Bull Terrier, they either hate or adore him. ¶Some people insist that there is a greater difference between the disposition of dog and bitch in this breed than in any other. However that may be, the bitch is certainly a softer dog, milder and perhaps easier to train and manage. ¶The Bull Terrier is a fine old breed of special merit and problems. It is one that should be owned only by people prepared to appreciate the quality, history, and character of the animal and to meet the responsibility of ownership. The Bull Terrier is potentially a first-class companion within the home but a menace as well as a nuisance if not trained and controlled as well as loved and admired. This breed is not to be confused with the American Pit Bull, currently being bred in this country for use in illegal dogfights. Dogfighting has been outlawed in both the United States and England, and the Bull Terrier has not been bred for that purpose, except clandestinely, for a long time.

The Cairn is one of Scotland's super little working terriers, and for hundreds of years he has been used to pursue vermin. He has a game, hunting spirit and is bold and fearless, but he is also a little hardheaded. Some writers insist that the Cairn is the ancestral breed for the Scottie, the West Highland White, and the Skye. He certainly has contributed to all those and to others that we don't even know in this country. ¶The Cairn Terrier has managed to survive fads and quirks and remains, thanks to the determination of his fanciers, much the dog he was hundreds of years ago on the Isle of Skye. He has a broader head than most terriers and a relatively short,

Cairn Terrier

Land of origin: ISLE OF SKYE, SCOTLAND

Original purpose: Killing vermin

Recent popularity ranking by A.K.C. registration: 45th

Cairn Terrier Club of America
Christine M. Bowlus, Corres. Secretary
8096 Chilson Rd.
Pinckney, MI 48169

HEIGHT: Dogs to 10 inches   Bitches to 9¹/₂ inches

WEIGHT: Dogs to 14 pounds   Bitches to 13 pounds

COAT
Hard and weather resistant. Double—outer coat profuse and harsh, undercoat short, soft, and close.

COLOR
Any color except white. Dark ears, muzzle, and tail tip are desirable. Often seen wheaten, grizzle, and tan.

Amount of care coat requires: 1 2 3 4 5 6 7 8 9 10

Amount of exercise required: 1 2 3 4 5 6 7 8 9 10

Suitability for urban/apartment life: 1 2 3 4 5 6 7 8 9 10

pointed muzzle. He is built close to the ground, but he is not heavy. At least he should not give that impression. The whole feeling should be of an alert, intelligent, active, and assertive dog. And all those things are true. ¶Cairns are perfect house pets and are fine in an apartment. They require only a reasonable amount of exercise, although any time a good romp is available, it should be encouraged. They shed, but not very much, and they are devoted to their master. They can be a little one-personish, but certainly not to the point of being a nuisance or menace. They are generally cheerful, they are always busybodies, and they want to be in on everything going on in their household. Let there be no mistaking the point: The house where a Cairn lives is *his* property. Cairns make good little watchdogs. ¶The Cairn coat is very important to the animal's appearance, but no real clipping is involved. The coat is tidied and brushed; for top show form a little trimming is required. The hair on that broad head is all-important. Although the coat can have a slight wave, any tendency to silkiness or to curl would be a severe fault. ¶The Cairn is hardy and ready to go at all times. Weather doesn't bother him, and he is a very responsive animal, sensing almost magically the moods of his owner. He watches and waits and takes his cues automatically. He is an ideal dog for a single person or a couple without children who want to add a spot of eternal cheerfulness to their life.

The Dandie Dinmont has the distinction of being the only dog named for a fictional character. Dandie Dinmont was a farmer in Sir Walter Scott's novel *Guy Mannering*. The farmer Dinmont kept six rough-coated terriers who had been developed in the border country of England and Scotland, and they became known, because of the great popularity of the novel, as Dandie Dinmont's dogs. ¶The Dandie Dinmont is a wonderful little character with great purpose and assertiveness. Once a hunting terrier, he is now a companion animal who is characteristically devoted to his master and who is fine with family members. Not mean or petty, the Dandie Dinmont can be reserved and cautious with strangers. ¶This is not the typical terrier;

Dandie Dinmont Terrier

Land of origin: SCOTLAND and ENGLAND

Original purpose: Otter and badger hunting

Recent popularity ranking by A.K.C. registration: 124th

Dandie Dinmont Terrier Club of America, Inc.
Caroline Darracott, Secretary
25 Ridgeview Rd.
Staunton, VA 24401

HEIGHT: Dogs to 11 inches   Bitches to 10 inches

WEIGHT: Dogs to 24 pounds   Bitches to 22 pounds

COAT
Double—twice as much crisp outer hair as soft undercoat. Hair on head, including topknot, silky. Important judging and appearance point.

COLOR
Pepper or mustard—many intermediate shades in both color groups. Pepper from dark bluish black to light silver gray. Mustards from reddish brown to pale fawn. Head may be creamy white.

Amount of care coat requires: 1 2 3 4 5 6 7 8 9 10

Amount of exercise required: 1 2 3 4 5 6 7 8 9 10

*Suitability for urban/apartment life:** 1 2 3 4 5 6 7 8 9 10

*If properly exercised.

he has none of the terrier's square shape. He is a low-to-the-ground little roughneck with a large head and great, dark appealing eyes. They should be hazel and have deep luster. The Dandie Dinmont's coat requires care on a regular basis, or it will be a mess and have to be stripped. It takes months for a coat to grow back once it has been pulled. The coat is crisp but not really wiry, and the head fur is soft and silky. That topknot is a must. ¶Although a hunting dog, the Dandie Dinmont is very adaptable and will do well in an apartment. The size, of course, is perfect, and he makes a good watchdog, although he is not yappy or foolish. Anyone contemplating this breed should plan on two basic requirements—coat care and exercise. He is fine on a farm, in a suburban household, or in a city apartment, but the Dandie Dinmont does require both of these attentions from his human family if he is to be healthy and happy and keep his appealing good looks. ¶The training of the Dandie Dinmont should start early and continue on a regular basis. The dog can be headstrong and even overly assertive if allowed to go unchecked as a puppy, but this is an intelligent breed that will respond to training by a strong but sensitive owner. A well-behaved Dandie Dinmont is much more pleasant to have around than one who is wild and uncontrolled, but that is true of all breeds. The Dandie Dinmont is not a popular breed yet in this country (that is apt to change at any time), and the breed standards have been well maintained by specialty breeders. It is a good idea to deal directly with them when seeking your puppy.

Smooth-Coated Fox Terrier

Wirehaired Fox Terrier

There are, of course, two Fox Terriers, the Smooth and the Wirehaired. Since June, 1985 they have been considered two separate breeds by the AKC. They probably arose from totally different stocks, and the Wirehaired is undoubtedly the older form, although the Smooth became known first in the show-ring. It was once common practice to cross these two breeds, and although that is no longer done, the dogs are identical except for coat. They do have virtually the same personality; they are the same size and are judged by all the same point standards, again except for coat. ¶The Fox Terriers, Wirehaired and Smooth, are clowns. Play is the thing, night and day without letup. Anyone contemplating these breeds should be pre-pared to participate, to toss balls, and to have a marvelous little busybody butting into his life at every turn. The Fox Terriers are devoted, loyal, fine watchdogs, and very good with family members. They are apt to be stand-offish with strangers. They seldom walk but go at everything at full gallop. They can be protective, and that has to be controlled. ¶Although once hunting dogs (when the hounds had run the rabbit to the ground, the Fox Terriers were sent in for the kill), they are now chiefly companion animals. The instinct to kill is still there, however, and that should be taken into consideration. The Fox Terriers can learn to live in a multianimal household, but the puppy should be introduced carefully and with constant supervision. ¶The

Fox Terriers

Land of origin: WALES and ENGLAND

Original purpose: Fox hunting and companionship

Recent popularity ranking by A.K.C. registration: 56th (wire) and 82nd (smooth)

American Fox Terrier Club
Mr. Martin Goldstein, Secretary
P.O. Box 604
South Plainfield, NJ 07080-0604

HEIGHT: Dogs to 15½ inches   Bitches to 14½ inches

WEIGHT: Dogs to 18 pounds   Bitches to 16 pounds

COAT
Smooth variety—smooth, flat, hard, dense, and abundant.

Wirehaired variety—broken, hard, and wiry but not silky or woolly. The more wiry the better.

COLOR
Basically white with black or black and tan markings. Not very important except red, liver, and brindle are not desirable.

Amount of care coat requires:

Smooth: 1 2 3 4 5 6 7 8 9 10

Wirehaired: 1 2 3 4 5 6 7 8 9 10

Amount of exercise required: 1 2 3 4 5 6 7 8 9 10

Suitability for urban/apartment life: 1 2 3 4 5 6 7 8 9 10

*If the appropriate amount of exercise is given.

Fox Terriers can live anywhere people can—farm to urban metropolis—and as long as their human families are near, they will be happy. Since these breeds are "hyper" to begin with, it stands to reason that if they are denied proper exercise they will really act up. Improperly worked Fox Terriers become absolutely silly with their spring-steel legs and boundless good humor. That energy *has* to be worked off, and a bouncing rubber ball is one good way of doing it, *if* there is a place to do it. Although eminently trainable, the stylish Fox Terriers may not always respond as quickly as you want them to when you say, "Come." It is therefore essential to keep them on leads in the city lest a tragedy occur. Many a Fox Terrier has spotted a cat or another dog he was unable to resist, and a Fox Terrier in the middle of a mad dash may not check for cars and buses. ¶The Fox Terriers are long-lived animals and fine with children. There are plenty of bad examples of both breeds around, and care should be taken about source and blood-lines. A good example of either breed is as fine a pet as a dog can be.

The Irish is one of the oldest of the terrier breeds, and his origins are a matter of conjecture. He so strongly resembles the Irish Wolfhound in shape and character that there is a temptation to think of him as the great hound bred down in size—far down to be sure. The Irish Terrier, however, is an authentic terrier type in both appearance and nature. ¶The energetic, racy red terrier from Ireland is a perfect companion animal. Once he gives his love, it is assigned until death. There is no hardier dog than this and none more adaptable—as long as his master is at hand. A large country estate is fine with an Irish Terrier, but so is an apartment or a small

Irish Terrier

Land of origin: IRELAND

Original purpose: Probably sporting

Recent popularity ranking by A.K.C. registration: 106th

Irish Terrier Club of America
Cory Rivera, Corres. Secretary
22720 Perry St.
Perris, CA 92570

HEIGHT: Dogs to 18 inches   Bitches to 18 inches

WEIGHT: Dogs to 27 pounds   Bitches to 25 pounds

COAT
Dense and wiry, rich but not soft or silky. Skin barely shows when hair is parted with fingers.
Curly or kinky coats very objectionable.

COLOR
Solid colored; bright red, golden red, red wheaten, or wheaten. *Small* patch of white on chest is
allowed but not desirable. Black hair found in puppies should not last into adulthood.

Amount of care coat requires: 1 2 3 4 5 6 7 8 9 10

Amount of exercise required: 1 2 3 4 5 6 7 8 9 10

Suitability for urban/apartment life:* 1 2 3 4 5 6 7 8 9 10

*But only if properly exercised every day.

---

suburban house. What matters is that the right people live there as well. ¶With the children of the household the Irish Terrier is a perfect playmate, but he is also apt to be protective, and that is something that has to be held in check. Not every kid who comes running into the yard to tackle or wrestle the owner's child is an enemy—but an Irish Terrier may not always be able to make that distinction. This is one breed for whom "no" must mean "NO!" ¶This Irishman has been used as a land and water retriever, and at both jobs he not only excels but thoroughly enjoys himself. He is a born hunter and is death on vermin, but here again the red terrier may not always agree with the neighborhood's definition of vermin. That, too, must be held under some kind of control. What it amounts to is that if you avail yourself of one of these superior terriers, you are going to have to make some of the decisions and pass the news along to your friend. An Irish Terrier should be trained early and well and constantly given refresher courses. ¶During World War I the Irish Terrier was famous as a patrol and courier dog and proved utterly fearless in all situations. No one can reckon how many men survived that holocaust as a direct result of this noble element in the Irish Terrier's character. ¶Show dog, ratter, big-game hunter, war dog, companion, household guard, and playmate—all these things describe the Irish Terrier. The breed is still as good as it is because of the efforts of the fanciers who love it above all others. Turn to them for help if you decide to buy one of these splendid dogs for your own family and home. Be sure to give your Irish Terrier a great deal of exercise; he both needs and deserves it.

The Kerry Blue Terrier is an animal of enormous style and character. He is a substantial dog with temper and temperament. Whether shown "in the rough" as he is in his native Ireland or in a refined shape as he is in the United States, he is handsome and regal. ¶It is sometimes claimed that the Kerry Blue (he came from County Kerry) is descended from the Soft-Coated Wheaten Terrier. Whatever his origin, there is little he has not done in the way of dog's work. He has been used as a water retriever, a trailing dog, a herder, and a general farm utility dog. He has even been trained to a limited extent for police work in the British Isles. ¶The Kerry Blue

Kerry Blue Terrier

Land of origin: IRELAND

Original purpose: General utility herding, retrieving, and trailing

Recent popularity ranking by A.K.C. registration: 101st

United States Kerry Blue Terrier Club, Inc.
Jo Ann Custer, Corres. Secretary
602 W. Fernwood Dr.
Toronto, OH 43964

HEIGHT: Dogs to 20 inches   Bitches to 19½ inches

WEIGHT: Dogs to 40 pounds   Bitches to 34 pounds

COAT
Soft, dense, and wavy. Never harsh, wiry, or bristly.

COLOR
Important: from deep slate to light blue gray. Quite uniform. Darker areas on muzzle, head, ears, tail, and feet.

Amount of care coat requires: 1 2 3 4 5 6 7 8 9 10

Amount of exercise required: 1 2 3 4 5 6 7 8 9 10

Suitability for urban/apartment life:*   1 2 3 4 5 6 7 8 9 10

*If properly exercised.

Terrier is hardy, can tolerate any weather, and is long-lived. At eight years, when some other breeds are nearing the end of their lives, this terrier is still a young animal. ¶The Kerry Blue is not keen on strangers and can be a little tricky to read at times. He has been known to bite, but this tendency can be offset by early and intense obedience training. Certainly, it is essential that an owner establish at the beginning that there is a chain of command within the household and that the dog is not at the top. The Kerry Blue Terrier would like that position and will try to take it. This is a breed that can explode with other animals, and owners are obligated to keep their pets under firm control—on a leash. If a Kerry Blue Terrier decides he doesn't like another dog he passes in the street, it may take a lot more than a voice command to get the two apart. ¶The Kerry Blue Terrier is a very devoted friend and can be fine with his owner's family. He will be stubborn if allowed to be, and there again early training is essential. ¶None of this is to say that the Kerry Blue Terrier isn't a fine pet as well as a watchdog or show dog in the right household, but he is the kind of dog who can prove to be more than the new owner reckoned on. He is so assertive, strong-willed, and loaded with character that inexperienced dog owners should be warned about what they are getting into. The Kerry Blue Terrier is a pushover for a real dog person, but it takes some years of experience to earn that title. ¶His long life, his high style, his great character and personal power have made the Kerry Blue Terrier something of a cult dog with people well acquainted with the breed. He remains something of an enigma to almost everybody else.

The Lakeland Terrier, a product of the English Lake District, was once known as the Patterdale Terrier. He is one of the oldest of the English working terriers and is typical of that type of dog. He is utterly fearless, impossible to tire, and full of game and fire. He was used to chase foxes and otters to ground and is a deadly adversary.

The desire to hunt is as strong in today's dog as it was a century or two ago. ¶The Lakeland is not common in this country, but that is probably due to the fact that he is a working terrier and is not as often reduced to being a plain companion animal as other small terrier breeds. He is more stable than many other terriers, calmer and

Lakeland Terrier

Land of origin: ENGLAND

Original purpose: Fox hunting

Recent popularity ranking by A.K.C. registration: 115th

United States Lakeland Terrier Club
Susan B. Werner, Secretary
4259 Bear Hollow Trl.
Haymarket, VA 22069

HEIGHT: Dogs to 14½ inches   Bitches to 13½ inches

WEIGHT: Dogs to 17 pounds   Bitches to 16 pounds

COAT
Double—soft undercoat with a hard, wiry outer coat.

COLOR
Blue, black, liver, black and tan, blue and tan, red, red grizzle, grizzle and tan, or wheaten. Light tans very much preferred over mahogany-like tones.

Amount of care coat requires: 1 2 3 4 5 6 7 8 9 10

Amount of exercise required: 1 2 3 4 5 6 7 8 9 10

*Suitability for urban/apartment life:**   1 2 3 4 5 6 7 8 9 10

*If properly exercised.

a good deal more sensible. He is also good-natured and especially good with children whom he knows. He is devoted to his master but slow to take up with strangers. Before entering into an in-depth relationship, the Lakeland wants to *know* that it is a good move. The Lakeland seems to shy away from shallow relationships with people, preferring all or nothing. ¶The Lakeland is strong on land and in the water, probably the strongest of all terriers in his weight class. He works with and therefore generally can live with other dogs; he has been used in England with Otter Hounds and Foxhounds as well as Harriers. ¶Young Lakeland Terriers were highly prized in the Lake District a century or more ago and were kept for breeding purposes. It was some time before examples were really known outside of this small, somewhat secluded region. The tendency to keep the dog at home was strengthened by the fact that the northern districts—counties like Northumberland, Cumberland, and Westmoreland—had their own working terriers and seldom needed to draw upon the outside. Perfecting was done from within, and attention was paid to performance, not to color or conformation. Many of those old working terrier breeds are lost to us today, and, indeed, we don't even know their names. The Patterdale survived, however, to become the powerful and congenial animal we have today. Rare though it may be on this side of the Atlantic, it is a breed to be held in esteem.

Manchester Terrier

Land of origin: ENGLAND

Original purpose: Ratting

Recent popularity ranking by A.K.C. registration: 95th

American Manchester Terrier Club
Ms. Diana Haywood, Secretary
52 Hampton Rd.
Pittstown, NJ 08867

HEIGHT:* Dogs to 16 inches   Bitches to 15 inches

WEIGHT: Dogs to 22 pounds   Bitches to 16 pounds

COAT
Short and smooth. Should be thick, dense, close, and glossy. Never soft to the touch.

COLOR
Well-defined jet black and rich mahogany tan. White considered very bad and will disqualify if over 1/2 inch in any dimension.

Amount of care coat requires: 1 2 3 4 5 6 7 8 9 10

Amount of exercise required: 1 2 3 4 5 6 7 8 9 10

Suitability for urban/apartment life: 1 2 3 4 5 6 7 8 9 10

*See also Toy Manchester Terrier.

The Manchester Terrier is identical (except in size) to the Toy Manchester Terrier. The dimensions given for the two forms are as follows:

	HEIGHT	WEIGHT
Standard	To 16 in.	To 22 lbs.
Toy	To approximately 7 in.	To 12 lbs.

The two are simply size variations of the same breed, although they were once considered two separate breeds. (The ears are cropped in the Standard but not in the Toy.) ¶The breed probably first emerged in Manchester when a coarse Bland and Tan Terrier was crossed with a Whippet to produce a superior gaming dog for the rat pits and for practical use along the waterfront. (Today's Manchester Terrier was also once called the Black and Tan but is, under any name, far more refined than that older parent breed.) ¶The Manchester in either size is a superior companion animal. He is like a fine racehorse—trim, neat, and with the look of perfection about him. Not only is he affectionate, responsive, and intelligent, but he is also clean, virtually odorless, and fits well into any family situation. He is fine in an apartment and will be satisfied with a limited amount of outdoor exercise. He would still make a good ratter on the farm, but he is almost exclusively a companion animal today. ¶In an effort to derive the Toy version from the Standard, there was some crossbreeding with the Italian Greyhound, but that practice was abandoned. The smaller version is now well established. ¶The Manchester Terrier in either size is a good watchdog and a very understanding friend. Only the finest breeders should be trusted, for this is a breed that must not be mass-produced, nor should its standards be abused.

Miniature Bull Terrier

Land of origin: ENGLAND

Original purpose: Companionship

Recent popularity ranking by A.K.C. registration: 121st

Miniature Bull Terrier Club of America
Marilyn Drewes, Corres. Secretary
17 Fremont Rd.
Sandown, NH 03873

HEIGHT: 10 to 14 inches

WEIGHT: Not specified except to be in proportion.

COAT
Short, flat, harsh with a fine glossy look.

COLOR
Two varieties, although unlike the Bull Terrier of standard size, they are shown together: *White*—to be pure white. Skin pigmentation and markings on the head are not penalized. *Colored*—any color allowed but must predominate over white markings.

Amount of care coat requires: 1 2 3 4 5 6 7 8 9 10

Amount of exercise required: 1 2 3 4 5 6 7 8 9 10

Suitability for urban/apartment life: 1 2 3 4 5 6 7 8 9 10

The Miniature Bull Terrier or MBT is a fiery smaller version of the incredibly brave Bull Terrier of standard size. The standard Bull Terrier runs 21 to 22 inches at the shoulder while the Miniature is 10 to 14 inches. With the proportionate loss of bulk (a third or more) we end up with a neat, conveniently-sized dog of style, dash and great courage. For all of that the MBT should be even-tempered and reasonable even with dealing with other animals. Fire in the case of the MBT does not equate with cranky or mean-spirited. ¶The MBT is an athlete down from a long line of athletes and should be agile and quick and should move with force and drive. This is, after all, a terrier breed and should be both snappy (in appearance only!) and proud. MBT, like all terriers, love games, crave interaction and hate being excluded from the human activity around them. They adore tennis balls or their equivalent, and they not only need but love long walks, the brisker the pace the better. ¶This breed is an expression of a simple idea—we live in smaller dens now, and dogs that we love should come in convenient sizes for those of us for whom space can be a problem. The MBT is not a toy, by any means, it is a mid-size reduction, a true miniature. The bloodline is, of course, Bull Terrier and the standard sized dog has been bred back in in the past to add gene pool diversity. Although the MBT is distinctly a breed apart new owners can expect to find in the MBT all the qualities they admired in the larger dog. Nothing has been lost.

The Miniature Schnauzer was derived in part from the larger forms of Schnauzer by carefully crossing the smallest available specimens with Affenpinschers. It was recognized as a distinct breed by the end of the nineteenth century. ¶The Miniature Schnauzer strongly resembles the larger dogs, but he is the ideal small house or apartment dog. He is long-lived, intelligent, and affectionate. He seems to naturally adore children, and children generally adore him! Whatever is available in the way of space, love, and attention he will take. He loves to play, he seems to be made of springs, and he never tires. Indoors or out he insists on being a part of everything

Miniature Schnauzer

Land of origin: GERMANY

Original purpose: Companionship

Recent popularity ranking by A.K.C. registration: 14th

American Miniature Schnauzer Club, Inc.
Mrs. Susan R. Atherton, Secretary
RR2, Box 3570
Bartlesville, OK 74003

HEIGHT: Dogs to 14 inches   Bitches to 14 inches

WEIGHT: Dogs to 15 pounds   Bitches to 14 pounds

COAT
Double—hard, wiry outer coat and a close undercoat. Usually plucked—length usually not less than 3/4 inch.

COLOR
Salt and pepper, black and silver, or solid black. Tan shading is allowed.

Amount of care coat requires: 1 2 3 4 5 6 7 8 9 10

Amount of exercise required: 1 2 3 4 5 6 7 8 9 10

Suitability for urban/apartment life: 1 2 3 4 5 6 7 8 9 10

that is going on around him. He sulks when omitted. ¶The Miniature Schnauzer is one of the most popular dogs in America, having ranked in the top ten for years. His popularity is based on his easy keeping qualities and his good disposition. He does like long walks but can survive without them when the weather is bad (he can take the weather, but his master can't always keep up); he is easily trained for any regimen. He is naturally happy and healthy, and if you see more Miniature Schnauzers waiting in the veterinarian's outer office it is just because there are so many of them around. ¶The Miniature Schnauzer is perfectly willing to become a first-class food brat if that is what you want him to be. He responds to what is offered and takes advantage of all opportunities. If you want to feed him chopped chicken livers on imported English biscuits, that is fine with him, but so will kibble be if that is what you have to offer. This is a smart little animal, and a lot of owners feel the need to spoil them. ¶Because the Miniature Schnauzer is so popular, there have been an awful lot of marginal breeders (and that is being kind). Hence, anyone wanting an example of this breed as it was meant to be is going to have to avoid the obvious pitfalls. This is a superlative companion animal, and there are fine breeders all across the country willing to place their puppies in good homes. What the buyer gets is what the buyer is willing to seek out; take the trouble to evaluate and to know what you are getting.

Norfolk Terrier

Norwich Terrier

These Norwich and Norfolk Terriers are among the smallest of terriers in size and among the largest in spirit. The gait, stance, and personality of each reflects the true English terrier blood and supports the supposition that both Border Terrier and Irish Terrier blood went into the making of these breeds. The Norwich and Norfolk Terriers are not old breeds, but they do have some special qualities. Developed in England in the 1880s, the original version quickly became a fad dog with undergraduates at Cambridge University. There are still some people who believe the breed (now breeds) should be known as Cantab Terriers in honor of this early support. But actually, at that time their forerunner was known as the Jones Terrier; it wasn't until after World War I that the name *Norwich Terrier* came into use. By 1964 breeders in England had achieved two breeds, Norwich and Norfolk. ¶Until 1978 the American Kennel Club recognized the Norwich Terrier as the only breed and allowed two ear styles—the prick or upstanding and the drop. In 1979, though, the A.K.C. followed the British example and recognized only the prick-ear variety as the Norwich, calling the drop-ear the Norfolk. They are now two separate breeds for

Norfolk and Norwich Terriers

Land of origin: ENGLAND

Original purpose: As pets, companions, and for some hunting

Recent popularity ranking by A.K.C. registration: 103rd (Norwich) and 109th (Norfolk)

Norwich and Norfolk Terrier Club
Linda D. Haring, Corres. Secretary
695 Glendale Blvd.
Mansfield, OH 44907

HEIGHT: Dogs to 11 inches   Bitches to 10 inches

WEIGHT: Dogs to 14 pounds   Bitches to 12 pounds

COAT
Close lying, hard, and wiry. Distinct undercoat, outer coat straight. No curl, and not silky.

COLOR
Shades of read, wheaten, black, tan, and grizzle. Small white markings on chest only allowed.

Amount of care coat requires.   1 2 3 4 5 6 7 8 9 10
        ••

Amount of exercise required: 1 2 3 4 5 6 7 8 9 10
        •••••••••••••

Suitability for urban/apartment life: 1 2 3 4 5 6 7 8 9 10
        ••••••••••••••••••••••

purposes of registration and showing. The dogs are virtually identical in the United States, except for the ears, but the British standard does call for the Norfolk to have a slightly longer neck. It will be interesting to see if that difference stands here and what other differences, if any, emerge. ¶The Norwich and Norfolk are incredibly responsive to their environment and their family. They can be exclusively attached to one person if that is what is expected of them, but they can also be family dogs. They are all personality and quickly capture the hearts of anyone who comes to know them. They want to be in on absolutely everything that is going on around them. For the family with or without children, the Norwich or Norfolk can be the almost ideal breed. Each is small and neat and travels well, and is assertive enough to handle himself in almost any situation. Their hard, always straight and wiry coat requires little care. It doesn't retain dirt,

and these dogs are cleaner than most. ¶Although perfectly fine in an apartment if well exercised, these breeds are best suited for the country or suburbs. They naturally love horses and farm life. Both live with other animals, cats included, but it should be remembered that some of the earliest examples in America were used for hunting. The Norwich and Norfolk love a good chase and will bedevil small wildlife if given an opportunity to do so. Too small to become a real stock killer, they should be trained to guard small farm animals rather than pursue them. This is the kind of training a Norwich or a Norfolk can take, since they are loyal, great little watchdogs, and take to obedience training as if it were the grandest pastime on earth. Some enthusiasts believe that the Norwich has the softer disposition of the two. Now that the breeds are free to go their separate ways, it will be interesting to see how the two develop.

The arguments are endless over the origins of this rather old Scottish breed. Some say the Scottish Terrier is the original Skye Terrier, who is not to be confused with the dog we know by that name today. Other historians have different ideas. In fact, the details of the Scottie's evolution in the Highlands are uncertain, for records were seldom kept. We do know the breed comes from the Highlands; it is respectably old and has long been highly regarded. ¶The Scottish Terrier, or, as it is commonly addressed, the "Scottie," is a game, close-to-the-ground, working terrier who must have been a holy terror on vermin. He is, like all dogs of this line, without a

Scottish Terrier

Land of origin: SCOTLAND

Original purpose: Sporting after small game

Recent popularity ranking by A.K.C. registration: 38th

Scottish Terrier Club of America
Evelyn D. Kirk, Corres. Secretary
2603 Derwent Dr. SW
Roanoke, VA 24015

HEIGHT: Dogs to 10 inches   Bitches to 10 inches

WEIGHT: Dogs to 22 pounds   Bitches to 21 pounds

COAT
Rather short (about 2 inches)—dense undercoat with very hard outer coat. Should be *very* wiry to the touch.

COLOR
Steel or iron gray, brindled or grizzled, black, wheaten, or sandy. White marking not desired, but *small* amount on chest allowed.

Amount of care coat requires: 1 2 3 4 5 6 7 8 9 10
                                    ••••••••••••••

Amount of exercise required: 1 2 3 4 5 6 7 8 9 10
                                  •••••••••••

*Suitability for urban/apartment life:**   1 2 3 4 5 6 7 8 9 10
                                            •••••••••••••••••••••••••

*If properly exercised.

semblance of fear. He is also hardy and will take any terrain, any weather, and any number of hours afield. He will back away from nothing as long as he can still draw a breath. ¶The Scottie is a dour character, as befits his origin, and takes loyalty to his master and mistress seriously. If they have children, he will behave well as long as he is raised with them. He is very slow to accept strangers at all, much less take up with them, and he is never happier than when he is alone with his own family. The rest of the world, man and animal alike, could vanish, and the Scottie wouldn't care a bit. Some people find this aloofness (for that is the best description) one of the Scottish Terrier's most attractive characteristics, and indeed it does make one respect the breed. ¶The Scottie should be trained early and well. Because he can threaten strangers and can be a scrapper, the Scottie should learn how to obey instantly. Strangers should be advised to give the dog time and let him make the overtures. ¶Young Scotties are extremely appealing and very demonstrative. Few breeds have cuter youngsters. That jumping and licking display tends to disappear in the adults, and one should not be misled. The adult Scottie is a square, solid, determined, and intelligent dog; he remains reserved except with those he really knows and loves. Because the puppies are so very appealing, prospective buyers should be careful to know the line well. Cute puppies do not always turn out to be splendid dogs.

The Sealyham was developed between 1850 and 1890 in Haverfordwest, Wales. The breed's benefactor—really its designer—was Capt. John Edwardes. The ancestral stock used by Captain Edwardes is not known. After the Sealyham's first show appearance in 1903, it caught on. By 1908 a club had been formed in Wales to further interest in the breed. The breed was recognized in this country in 1911; although it has never been a terribly popular dog, it has been admired. ¶The A.K.C. standards sum up the breed well: "The Sealyham should be the embodiment of power and determination, ever keen and alert, of extraordinary substance, yet free

Sealyham Terrier

Land of origin: WALES

Original purpose: Gaming and hunting vermin

Recent popularity ranking by A.K.C. registration: 129th

American Sealyham Terrier Club
Judy E. Thill, Secretary
13948 N. Cascade Rd.
Dubuque, IA 52003

HEIGHT: Dogs to 10^1/$_2$ inches   Bitches to 10^1/$_2$ inches

WEIGHT: Dogs to 24 pounds   Bitches to 23 pounds

COAT
Soft, dense undercoat and wiry outer coat. Never silky or curly.

COLOR
All white. Lemon, tan, or pale badger marking allowed on hear and ears.

Amount of care coat requires: 1 2 3 4 5 6 7 8 9 10
••••••••••••••

Amount of exercise required: 1 2 3 4 5 6 7 8 9 10
•••••••••••

*Suitability for urban/apartment life:** 1 2 3 4 5 6 7 8 9 10
••••••••••••••••••••••

*Provided that enough exercise is given regularly.

from clumsiness." ¶Like most terriers, perhaps all, the Sealyham is a natural watchdog, and a stranger is unlikely to approach unannounced. Extremely loyal to his family, the Sealyham is likely to be cautious with strangers, animals included. He is fast, tough, determined, and hardy. He needs exercise and loves a good romp. He has a proud carriage and looks just splendid plowing on ahead at the bottom end of a leash. The Sealyham does not shed much and makes an almost ideal house and apartment dog. However, his coat needs care, and the dog looks fine only when properly groomed. The Sealyham is easily trained, although if he detects weakness he will play it and be stubborn. He recognizes a master once his worth is demonstrated. ¶Other terriers appeared in the United States earlier—dogs like the Scottish Terrier—and that perhaps has held the Sealyham back somewhat. But with our enormous urban population and the desire of people in apartments for watchdogs who are also trouble-free pets, it is predictable that the Sealyham will continue to grow in popularity. His character and qualities are so ideally suited to the urban life-style that he will surely take off and move up on the charts. People thinking seriously of this dog, however, should remember his need for plenty of exercise. The occasional visit to the country will be appreciated.

The terriers generally are not particularly old, but the Skye goes back at least four hundred years, making him one of the oldest. He was the product of the rough, harsh islands off Scotland, particularly the Isle of Skye in the northwest, where he reached the form we know long, long ago. ¶By the middle 1500s the Skye was known in London, where he quickly became a favorite at court and, quite naturally, down through the ranks of nobility until even commoners recognized him as fashionable. For two hundred years at least he ranked as a kind of king among terriers, but then newer breeds began to take over. Perhaps the shorthaired terrier coat of the

Skye Terrier

Land of origin: ISLE OF SKYE, SCOTLAND

Original purpose: Sporting, hunting

Recent popularity ranking by A.K.C. registration: 126th

Skye Terrier Club of America
Karen Sanders, Secretary
11567 Sutters Mill Cir.
Gold River, CA 95670

HEIGHT: Dogs to 10 inches   Bitches to 9¹/₂ inches

WEIGHT: Dogs to 25 pounds   Bitches to 23 pounds

COAT
Double—undercoat soft, woolly, and short; outer coat hard, straight, flat, and very long.

COLOR
Black, blue, gray (dark or light), silver platinum, cream, or fawn.

Amount of care coat requires: 1 2 3 4 5 6 7 8 9 10

Amount of exercise required: 1 2 3 4 5 6 7 8 9 10

Suitability for urban/apartment life: 1 2 3 4 5 6 7 8 9 10

*Only if enough exercise is provided on a regular basis.

younger breeds was more attractive because it meant less work. Still, the Skye, less popular now than in the past, has his fanciers, and they are tenacious in their devotion. ¶The Skye Terrier was almost certainly developed to fight tough vermin and run them to ground. How much of that original purpose was based on necessity and how much on sport is hard to say, for man has always claimed much of his sport as necessary. However that may have been, the Skye was a tough roughneck of a go-to-ground dog, and that original terrier fire and determination is still in him. ¶The Skye's coat requires care, and anyone considering this handsome, stylish dog should keep that in mind. They are not self-keep-

ers; they need help to look their best. ¶The Skye Terrier is a devoted pet and needs a great deal of attention. Reassurance and the opportunity to interact with human family members must come frequently. An ignored Skye Terrier is an unhappy dog. Because of his devotion to family and his stylish appearance, the Skye is a fine city dog—but only if long walks are provided. That is a commitment the new Skye owner must make and keep. ¶Because he ranks rather far down in popularity, the Skye is generally available from only a few specialty breeders. That is a good thing, too, for this is a dog with a long history and a heritage worth preserving.

Although the Soft-Coated Wheaten Terrier has been known in Ireland for centuries, he is new to our shores. Here is a breed that is just about to catch on. ¶No one knows the ancestry of this Irish farm terrier. He has just "always been there." He *may* be an ancestral form of the Kerry Blue Terrier, but that is not known for sure.

Whether it is true that the dogs who swam ashore from the ill-fated Spanish Armada are part of this dog's past is not known either. ¶The Soft-Coated Wheaten Terrier is an all-purpose farm dog, a fine companion for children, and a first-rate watchdog. He is also adept at herding, hunting, and chasing any vermin to ground and dis-

Soft-Coated Wheaten Terrier

Land of origin: IRELAND

Original purpose: All-purpose farm work

Recent popularity ranking by A.K.C. registration: 66th

Soft Coated Wheaten Terrier Club of America
Richard Tomlinson, Corres. Secretary
4428 Provine Line Rd.
Princeton, NJ 08540

HEIGHT: Dogs to 19 inches   Bitches to 18 inches

WEIGHT: Dogs to 45 pounds   Bitches to 40 pounds

COAT
Abundant, soft, and wavy. Should appear natural and not overtrimmed or styled.

COLOR
Clear wheaten; may be shaded on ears and muzzle.

Amount of care coat requires: 1 2 3 4 5 6 7 8 9 10
••••••••••

Amount of exercise required: 1 2 3 4 5 6 7 8 9 10
•••••••••••••••••••

Suitability for urban/apartment life:* 1 2 3 4 5 6 7 8 9 10
••••••••••••••••••••••••

*If properly exercised.

patching them. He is spry, resilient, and intelligent. He will take any training and remember what he has been taught. He is willing, positive in his approach, and extremely responsive to his master and his family. ¶Although the Soft-Coated Wheaten Terrier is a good working dog, he is a flawless companion animal as well and will settle down in the suburbs and city as long as his family is at hand. Wheatens should be exercised religiously so that they don't become "hyper" from confinement. They love to interact with other living things and should not be left for long periods of time without companionship, or else they will pine. Soft-Coated Wheaten Terriers need to belong and to share. ¶There should be nothing exaggerated about the Wheaten. His coat is a lovely shade of ripening wheat. It doesn't really settle down until the dog is almost two years old; then coat condition and color are final. Extreme clipping and trimming spoil the look of the dog. ¶It is likely that the Soft-Coated Wheaten Terrier will become popular in this country. (They weren't even known here until the late 1940s, and by 1961 there were only thirteen reported examples.) When purchasing, care must be taken to find examples that properly represent the fine qualities of this dog; mass-production should not be encouraged.

Staffordshire Bull Terrier

Land of origin: ENGLAND

Original purpose: Sport fighting

Recent popularity ranking by A.K.C. registration: 104th

Staffordshire Bull Terrier Club, Inc.
Marilyn Atwood, Corres. Secretary
24451 Dartmouth
Dearborn Heights, MI 48125

HEIGHT: Dogs to 16 inches   Bitches to 14 inches

WEIGHT: Dogs to 38 pounds   Bitches to 34 pounds

COAT
Smooth and short; close and not trimmed at all.

COLOR
Red, white, fawn, blue, or black, or any of these colors with white. Any shade of brindle with or without white. Black and tan or liver not allowed.

Amount of care coat requires: 1 2 3 4 5 6 7 8 9 10

Amount of exercise required: 1 2 3 4 5 6 7 8 9 10

*Suitability for urban/apartment life:**   1 2 3 4 5 6 7 8 9 10

*If given enough exercise.

In the England of Elizabeth I, bear and bull baiting were major pastimes. Large mastiff-like dogs were developed for these brutal contests, and from them have descended a variety of smaller breeds. One of these is the Staffordshire Bull Terrier, admitted to the American show scene by the American Kennel Club in 1975. He is descended from dogs known variously as Bulldog Terrier and Bull-and-Terrier, and he became known in time as the Old Pit Bull Terrier. He is probably ancestral to the English Bull Terrier we know today. ¶To say that the Staffordshire Bull Terrier has had all of his history bred out of him is wishful thinking. He is still a tough, tenacious, and intelligent dog who will probably continue to be aggressive toward other animals for many generations to come. In fact, aggression may never be bred out of him. ¶The Staffordshire Bull Terrier—he should not be confused with the nineteen-inch American Staffordshire Terrier or the much heavier (sixty-pound) Bull Terrier referred to above—has common ancestry with and was bred for the same purpose as these other fighting dogs, but he has not been used for that purpose for some time. He is now a companion animal who shows great affection toward his human family. He is said by his fanciers to have special fondness for children. ¶Because he is a robust, if not large, and certainly a powerful and athletic dog, he should be exercised regularly and well. He will keep his condition and certainly be less tense if allowed to work off steam every day on a reliable schedule. ¶The Staffordshire Bull Terrier is an easy dog to maintain because he is short-coated and clean. His ferocious background has not made him untrustworthy with people, but he is a potential fighter, and therefore is a dog who should be leashed and controlled at all times.

The Welsh is one of the oldest of terrier breeds and almost certainly figured
in the modeling of many of the other terriers we know today. He has had a number of
names down through history, including
Old English Terrier, Black and Tan Wirehaired Terrier, and various combinations of
those names with the designation *Welsh*.

The origin of the breed was undoubtedly
old England, but it was in Wales that the
Welsh Terrier evolved as a tough sporting
dog to hunt foxes, otters, badgers, and anything else that offered a chase and a fight.
He was bred to take on all comers and do
all the dirty work necessary. He can handle
any terrain and just about any tempera-

Welsh Terrier

Land of origin: WALES

Original purpose: Hunting and sporting

Recent popularity ranking by A.K.C. registration: 88th

Welsh Terrier Club of America, Inc.
Margie B. McClung, Corres. Secretary
200 Hazlemere Dr.
Richmond, VA 23236

HEIGHT: Dogs to 15 inches   Bitches to 13½ inches

WEIGHT: Dogs to 20 pounds   Bitches to 18 pounds

COAT
Wiry, hard, abundant, and very close.

COLOR
Black and tan or black grizzle and tan. No black marks (penciling) on toes.

Amount of care coat requires: 1 2 3 4 5 6 7 8 9 10

Amount of exercise required: 1 2 3 4 5 6 7 8 9 10

*Suitability for urban/apartment life:**   1 2 3 4 5 6 7 8 9 10

*If suitable exercise is provided every day.

ture—on land or in the water. Give him something to tackle, and nothing will deter him. ¶The first Welsh Terrier of record probably came here in 1888, but few were seen for a number of years. Even in 1901, when A.K.C. recognition allowed it to be shown at the Westminster Kennel Club show, only four dogs were presented. ¶This muscular, well-boned little roughneck needs plenty of exercise. Like all small terriers of his general styling, he has a fire inside, and is like spring steel. He is a dog that needs to run and needs to play and for that reason is great with children. He is good with his family but may be a little slow warming to strangers. He is a natural watchdog and can be relied upon to announce strangers day or night. He isn't yappy or silly, however, and serves well the family with whom he agrees to live. ¶These tough terriers vary in their adaptability to other animals. Some are just fine and never quarrel unless challenged. Others will be holy terrors wanting to dissect every four-footed creature they meet. One person's experience with the breed may not be a fair indication of what the next owner's will be. You have to watch and wait, and if you do have a scrapper, he must be controlled and trained to behave. ¶The Welsh Terrier is a first-rate family dog in the country or the city. He is half human most of the time and fun and games all of the time. It helps for you to be young and vigorous at the same time your Welsh Terrier is. He demands that you participate in his high-stepping style of life.

This marvelous little dog shares a common ancestry with the Scottie, the Cairn, and the Dandie Dinmont, as well as with the other rough-haired terriers of southern Scotland. Several of those breeds have never been seen in this country, and some of them, unfortunately, are now extinct. The West Highland White Terrier may have the best of all of them bred into his spirited little body. ¶This is a dog who is both an individual and a lover. He knows exactly who and what he is and never fails to exhibit the true terrier style and temperament. Never shy, he should not be really aggressive—assertive, certainly, but not snappy. He is courageous if a challenge is ever offered, and he is fine with strangers once he has done the usual terrier checkout. ¶West Highland White Terriers like games, toys, their own well-defined posi-

West Highland White Terrier

Land of origin: SCOTLAND

Original purpose: Companionship

Recent popularity ranking by A.K.C. registration: 36th

West Highland White Terrier Club of America
Ms. Anne Sanders, Corres. Secretary
33101 44th Ave. NW
Stanwood, WA 98292-7106

HEIGHT: Dogs to 11 inches   Bitches to 10 inches

WEIGHT: Dogs to 19 pounds   Bitches to 17 pounds

COAT
Double. Outer coat straight and hard, to 2 inches, shorter on neck and shoulders. Never silky or curly.

COLOR
Pure white with a jet black nose.

Amount of care coat requires: 1 2 3 4 5 6 7 8 9 10

Amount of exercise required: 1 2 3 4 5 6 7 8 9 10

Suitability for urban/apartment life: 1 2 3 4 5 6 7 8 9 10

tion in the house, treats, travel, and the undiluted attention of their master. They like to chase cats but usually for the chase and not with any real intention to do harm (they will live with a cat peacefully). They are adaptable and settle down in new situations as long as their family is with them. I have had friends visit us for weekends with their West Highland White Terrier without any problem, and that required the dog, a mature male, to settle down immediately into a household of six other dogs and ten cats. The Westy managed to check everybody out and get checked out by everybody in the first half hour. Relatively few dogs can handle that kind of situation so well. ¶Without giving the West Highland human qualities (which one is prone to do), it can be said that this breed has such a strong sense of himself that much of the nonsense some other breeds have to go through in order to establish identity is unnecessary. A West Highland White Terrier walks into a room with self-assur-

ance and an easy grace that seems to put other animals at ease. ¶West Highlands do shed and their white hair does show, but most owners don't complain. They feel it is worth it. I have known West Highland White Terriers to settle well into a family with children, but once again, if we were to seek a perfect situation, it would be where the West Highland White Terrier could be the child himself. He is certainly ideal for the couple without children or for the couple whose children have grown and left home. ¶A lot of poor-quality West Highlands are being bred and sold, and a prospective owner should proceed with caution. It is difficult to find an example with a perfect coat, and it is only with a coat at least near perfection that the true style of the West Highland White Terrier really shines through. People seeking this breed should stick with the specialty breeder and hold out for the ideal dog. It is a commitment that they will live with for a long, long time.

{Group 6}

The Toys

Affenpinscher

Brussels Griffon

Cavalier King Charles Spaniel

Chihuahua

Chinese Crested

English Toy Spaniel

Italian Greyhound

Japanese Chin

Maltese

Toy Manchester Terrier

Miniature Pinscher

Papillon

Pekingese

Pomeranian

Toy Poodle

Pug

Shih Tzu

Silky Terrier

Yorkshire Terrier

No one really knows where the Affenpinscher comes from, although it was somewhere in Europe. The breed dates back to at least the 1600s and probably is much, much older than that. The name translates from the German as "monkey terrier," an appropriate name for this strange, fiery little toy. ¶It was from the Affenpinscher, some people believe, that the now more popular Brussels Griffon was in part derived. The later breed all but eclipsed the older one, but there is some indication that interest in the Affenpinscher is reviving slightly. ¶Actually, this little dark dog is an ideal apartment animal. Although in need of some exercise, he

Affenpinscher

Land of origin: EUROPE

Original purpose: Companionship and ratting

Recent popularity ranking by A.K.C. registration: 118th

Affenpinscher Club of America
Kendall Davis, Secretary
3614 Luewan Dr.
Indianapolis, IN 46236

HEIGHT: Dogs to 10¼ inches   Bitches to 9 inches

WEIGHT: Dogs to 8 pounds   Bitches to 7 pounds

COAT
Very important in judging. Hard and wiry and varies from short and dense to shaggy and longer on different parts of body. Longer on face, legs, chest, and underparts.

COLOR
Black is considered best, but also black with tan markings, red, gray, and other mixtures allowed. Very light colors and white markings are faults.

Amount of care coat requires: 1 2 3 4 5 6 7 8 9 10

Amount of exercise required: 1 2 3 4 5 6 7 8 9 10

Suitability for urban/apartment life: 1 2 3 4 5 6 7 8 9 10

adapts easily to life in an apartment. Like a great many of the smaller dogs, the Affenpinscher will wait for an opening and then take over. He needs a firm hand, but he is smart enough to take any training necessary to make him into a suitable canine companion. Heaven help the careless owner; a monkeyish little dog will soon be running the household. ¶The Affenpinscher is tough, and he seems to take himself seriously. He is devoted and affectionate and usually quiet. He is, though, capable of real temper and will attack anything if seriously challenged. He can be moody and excitable if not given his own way. Until a real balance has been struck between man and dog, it may be a war of nerves; and it is funny to watch this smart little animal try to work things out to his own advantage. ¶The Affenpinscher requires little care. The coat is best trimmed slightly about every ten weeks, just often enough to maintain the round, wise facial expression. It is ten minutes' work and little more. An occasional brushing is all that is required beyond that. Although a toy, the Affenpinscher is reasonably hardy, but really bad weather and chills should be avoided. ¶It isn't easy to find a good Affenpinscher puppy when you want one. Anyone seriously considering this little character had better start the search early and stay with it until a good pup becomes available. Those people devoted to the breed say it is worth the hunt and the wait. Fewer than one hundred new Affenpinschers are registered with the American Kennel Club in any one year.

The Brussels Griffon has been around since at least the fifteenth century and possibly longer. He was a cross between the Affenpinscher and a Belgian street dog. Later the Pug and a breed known as the Ruby Spaniel were crossed in. At one time he was larger than the dog we know today and was used to control rats and mice around stables. It is believed that the Griffon was virtually a household fixture in French and Belgian homes. Long bred for companionship, it is in that capacity we know him today. ¶The Brussels Griffon is seen in two varieties: the rough and the smooth. The smooth, of course, harks back to the infusion of Pug blood. Both forms are delightful companions, intelligent, outgoing, and affectionate. They are not close

Brussels Griffon

Land of origin: BELGIUM

Original purpose: Companionship, and killing of stable vermin

Recent popularity ranking by A.K.C. registration: 94th

American Brussels Griffon Association
Terry J. Smith, Secretary
P.O. Box 56, 207 E. Jefferson
Grand Ledge, MI 48837

HEIGHT: Dogs to 8 inches   Bitches to 8 inches

WEIGHT: Dogs to 12 pounds   Bitches to 10 pounds

COAT

Rough style—wiry and dense, the harder the better. Never to look or feel woolly; never silky. Also not shaggy.

Smooth style—like a Boston Terrier, no sign of wiry hair.

COLOR

Reddish brown, black and reddish brown mixed, black and reddish brown markings, or solid black. Often dark mask or whiskers. Black not allowed in smooth form. White a serious fault in either variety except age frosting on muzzle.

Amount of care coat requires:

Rough: 1 2 3 4 5 6 7 8 9 10
         •••••••••

Smooth: 1 2 3 4 5 6 7 8 9 10
        •

Amount of exercise required: 1 2 3 4 5 6 7 8 9 10
                                 ••••••

Suitability for urban/apartment life: 1 2 3 4 5 6 7 8 9 10
                                          •••••••••••••••••••••

or mean in their dealings but open and willing. They are neat and take up little space. And they make good watchdogs. ¶Like many toys, the Brussels Griffon is quite capable of being a little mule, a bully, lording it over everyone in the house. How he behaves depends on how he is handled as a puppy. Without thwarting him or destroying his personality he can be made to behave—especially on a leash, which he generally hates—and his barking can be controlled. He will try tricks to avoid having to be well mannered, and he is smart enough to be challenging to anyone but the owner alert enough to know when he is being duped. ¶The pert, saucy little Brussels Griffon does well with or without outdoor exercise, although he enjoys a fair romp. Care must be taken around traffic because he cannot be depended upon to have good traffic sense. He travels well, like a great many toys, and prefers to be taken along rather than be left at home. He must not be left in a closed car during warm weather, since he can expire from heat exhaustion in minutes without ventilation. It is a tragic accident that happens more times than one would expect. ¶The Brussels Griffon is a toy lover's dog in all respects—sassy, assertive, lovingly responsive, and smart as a whip. A dog to admire and, sad to relate, to spoil absolutely rotten. Most owners of this breed do.

Cavalier King Charles Spaniel

Land of origin: ENGLAND (probably China or Japan, originally)

Original purpose: Companionship

Recent popularity ranking by A.K.C. registration: Too recently recognized

HEIGHT: 12 to 13 inches

WEIGHT: 13 to 18 pounds

COAT
Long, silky, very soft to touch. No curl but slight wave allowed. No trimming allowed.

COLOR
Bright chestnut on pearly white background; jet black on pearly white with rich tan markings; rich red overall; jet black and rich tan.

Amount of care coat requires: 1 2 3 4 5 6 7 8 9 10

Amount of exercise required: 1 2 3 4 5 6 7 8 9 10

Suitability for urban/apartment life: 1 2 3 4 5 6 7 8 9 10

The characteristics that are listed as "paramount" for the Cavalier are gay temperament, elegance, and a "royal" appearance. Bad temper and meanness are listed as intolerable for this breed and are considered faults that should disqualify the dog from the showring and certainly should disqualify a dog or bitch from a breeding program no matter what it looks like. This is a sweet, happy and very pleasant dog to have around and nothing should ever be done that takes away from those qualities. ¶This is a refinement of the English Toy Spaniel and although we think of England as its place of development it probably traces back to either China or Japan. Certainly the English Toy Spaniel and the Japanese Chin have a lot to do with the Cavalier although the latter is taller at the withers and several pounds heavier than either of the others. ¶There was considerable resistance by a great many Cavalier owners to AKC recognition. Like the Border Collie and the Jack Russell Terrier owners the Cavalier fanciers felt, and many still do feel, that their breed will suffer from popularity, which can lead to careless breeding by people hurrying to cash in on the fad value of so desirable a dog. Their concern is not without merit, but both the resisting Border Collie and Cavalier King Charles Spaniel owners have lost their battle to remain exclusive and apart. As the Cavalier gains in popularity, as it is sure to do, it can only be hoped that the people new to the breed will show the same concern for temperament and style as the owners of the past did with their "secret" dog.

The true origin of this smallest of all dogs (he may weigh as little as one pound) is unknown. Apparently the Toltecs had them in Mexico before they were conquered by the Aztecs, who took over the breed. This dog was apparently a status symbol among the ruling class, but there is reason to believe that the common people ate them. There is some tradition to suggest that a hairless or nearly hairless dog reached Mexico from China or some other Asian land in ancient times and that this animal figured in the ancestry of the dog we call the Chihuahua today. The original Toltec dog may have been the Techichi. The name *Chihuahua* comes from the Mexican state of that name, but the dog is no more common there than in any other part of Mexico. Actually, the breed as we know it is more an American creation, its popularity here being great and consistent year after year. ¶The Chihuahua, in the longhaired or smooth (shorthaired) variety (the latter is much better known), is the

Chihuahua

Land of origin: MEXICO in historical times, but probably ASIA originally

Original purpose: Probably status and companionship

Recent popularity ranking by A.K.C. registration: 15th

Chihuahua Club of America, Inc.
Lynnie Bunten, Corres. Secretary
5019 Village Trl.
San Antonio, TX 78218

HEIGHT: Dogs to 5 inches   Bitches to 5 inches

WEIGHT:* Dogs to 6 pounds   Bitches to 6 pounds

COAT

Smooth style—soft, close, and glossy, should be smooth and well placed over body. Undercoat permissible.

Longhaired style—soft, flat, or slightly curly, with undercoat desirable. Ears fringed; feathering on feet and legs. Large ruff on neck desired. Tail as plume.

COLOR
Any color; may be solid, marked, or splashed. No preferences.

Amount of care coat requires:

Smooth: 1 2 3 4 5 6 7 8 9 10

Longhaired: 1 2 3 4 5 6 7 8 9 10

Amount of exercise required: 1 2 3 4 5 6 7 8 9 10

Suitability for urban/apartment life: 1 2 3 4 5 6 7 8 9 10

*Weight range of 2 to 4 pounds preferred.

ultimate toy. This is a dog who need never go out, should not be exposed to weather extremes, and who really must be spoiled to be appreciated. He is companionable but highly temperamental, and he despairs if left out of anything that is going on. He does not like other breeds of dogs, and this is often referred to as clannishness. An important factor probably is that all other dogs are bigger than the Chihuahua and may seem challenging and dangerous. ¶The Chihuahua is an ideal dog for middle-aged and elderly people who want to fuss over and be fussed at by a tyrant of a toy. Chihuahuas are no trouble to keep, since they are neat and don't have to be walked. Although small eaters, as might be expected, they are fussy, and that generally pleases the people most interested in the companionship of the world's smallest dog. A bit of white-meat chicken will please the Chihuahua to get and the owner to give. That really is what the Chihuahua is all about. He has a job to do and a niche to fill. He accomplishes his mission with commendable skill. ¶The Chihuahua has long been popular and is variable in quality. Care should be taken in buying one of these fine little characters. The really serious fanciers and breeders are slow to part with a puppy. They want to know the kind of home he is going to get. You must be very reassuring if you want to own a really fine Chihuahua.

The happy and alert Chinese Crested is a fascinating if somewhat mysterious little dog. We don't know where he came from. China is a traditional source only. There is no real evidence to substantiate that idea. ¶The mysteries extend beyond place of origin. All Chinese Crested are expected to be people-oriented and al-though both styles, the powderpuff and the hairless, are shown as one breed, they differ in temperament. The powderpuffs are more anxious to please, perhaps even more trainable than the hairless. The hairless are more anxious for people contact, more cat-like. That could be because the hairless needs the warmth of other bodies more

Chinese Crested

Land of origin: Possibly CHINA

Original purpose: Companionship

Recent popularity ranking by A.K.C. registration: 80th

American Chinese Crested Club, Inc.
Janet Kiczek, Corres. Secretary
South New Boston Rd.
Francestown, NH 03043-0211

HEIGHT: Preferred but not limited to range of 11 to 13 inches

WEIGHT: Not specified but not robust

COAT
Two styles: *Powderpuff* Double, soft and silky. Straight or wavy, not standoffish. *Hairless* Hair on head, feet, and end of tail only. Single, soft and essentially straight.

COLOR
Any color or combination of colors is allowed. None is preferred.

Amount of care coat requires:
Hairless.　　1 2 3 4 5 6 7 8 9 10
　　　　　　•••••

Powderpuff:　1 2 3 4 5 6 7 8 9 10
　　　　　　••••••••••••••

Amount of exercise required:　1 2 3 4 5 6 7 8 9 10
　　　　　　　　　　　　•

Suitability for urban/apartment life:　1 2 3 4 5 6 7 8 9 10
　　　　　　　　　　　　　••••••••••••••••••••••••

than the powderpuff does. ¶The fact that the size of this dog, 11 to 13 inches, is "rough" and both larger and smaller examples are given equal consideration in judging is evidence that this breed is as yet unformed. In the future a size will be determined and variations will be faulted. And the fact that any and all colors and markings are allowed suggests a breed that has yet to be defined. It is interesting that this is so because the first Chinese Crested seen at a Westminster Kennel Club show was in 1885 in the Miscellaneous Class. it was dropped from the class in 1965 because of the vagaries of origin, standards and pedigree registration. It was placed back in the Miscellaneous Class in 1986 and in the Toy Group in 1991. ¶The Chinese Crested is an interesting little dog that is a bundle of mysteries on the one hand and a gay little companion on the other. It is a happy little participator in all family affairs and events.

The English Toy Spaniel has been known in England for several hundred years and has long been a favorite of royalty. Tradition has it that Mary, Queen of Scots, went to the block with her favorite at her side. The breed is certainly not English in origin, however. It may be an ancient Chinese breed that was exported to Japan and later to Spain and only then to England. That routing must always remain specula-tive. It is undoubtedly Asian though. ¶The English Toy Spaniel is lovable and good-natured. He gets along with children, bet-ter, in fact, than most other toys. He is emi-nently spoilable, and that is how he is most often encountered—eminent and spoiled absolutely rotten, which is when he is at his best. ¶Because he does not really require outdoor exercise and because he is a pretty little creature when properly fussed over

English Toy Spaniel

Land of origin: Probably CHINA or JAPAN

Original purpose: Companionship

Recent popularity ranking by A.K.C. registration: 120th

English Toy Spaniel Club of America
Ms. Susan Jackson, Corres. Secretary
18451 Sheffield Ln.
Briston, IN 46507-9455

HEIGHT: Dogs to 10 inches   Bitches to 9 inches

WEIGHT: Dogs to 12 pounds   Bitches to 11 pounds

COAT
Soft, long, silky, and wavy. Tendency to curl is a fault. Profuse mane down front of chest.
Feathering also profuse.

COLOR*

King Charles—rich black and glossy mahogany tan.

Ruby—whole colored, rich chestnut red.

Blenheim—red and white, broken colored.

Prince Charles—tricolor (white, tan, and black).

Amount of care coat requires: 1 2 3 4 5 6 7 8 9 10
                                    •••••••••

Amount of exercise required: 1 2 3 4 5 6 7 8 9 10
                                 •

Suitability for urban/apartment life: 1 2 3 4 5 6 7 8 9 10
                                          •••••••••••••••••••••••

---

*King Charles and Ruby are shown as the same variety. Blenheim and Prince Charles are shown
as the second variety.

and cared for, he is a favorite of a special kind of owner. He is equipped to fulfill many needs. The breed has never been popular in this country, although it is well known in England and on the Continent. None of the push-faced toys have ever really made it in America until recently, with the exception of the Pekingese and the Pug. A refined variety of the English Toy Spaniel, the Cavalier King Charles Spaniel, is gaining in popularity as a separate breed and may soon outstrip any fame this parent breed ever had. ¶Fine examples of this breed are not easily purchased in this country, and anyone really serious about it may have to use foreign sources. Anyone breeding this dog well here will be extremely careful about whom he sells to. As indicated, the interest being shown in the Cavalier King Charles Spaniel may change that considerably. ¶A word about spoiling as we use it here: a spoiled Weimaraner or Rhodesian Ridgeback is a crime against society, while a spoiled English Toy Spaniel is quite normal. The difference should be obvious to anyone. Spoiled, of course, refers strictly to the behavior and willfulness of an individual dog and has nothing whatever to do with standards and breeding. Spoiled in the sense of badly bred is intolerable in any breed, large or small.

This lovely little dog, who can be traced back to ancient times, has been the companion of kings and queens for almost as long as there has been written European history. He is nothing more than the ancient Greyhound bred down selectively and then refined. He differs little from the Greyhound except in size and personality.

¶The stories are legion about the roles this breed played in the lives of royal households. A king knelt weeping in the garden as he dug away the earth with his hands to lay to rest the dog who had sat on the throne with him. More than one king has been said to have gone to war with an Italian Greyhound on the saddle in front of

Italian Greyhound

Land of origin: ITALY, but very ancient

Original purpose: Companionship

Recent popularity ranking by A.K.C. registration: 58th

Italian Greyhound Club of America, Inc.
Lilian Barber, Corres. Secretary
35648 Menifee Rd.
Murrieta, CA 92563

HEIGHT: Dogs to 15 inches   Bitches to 13 inches

WEIGHT: Dogs to 15 pounds   Bitches to 9 pounds

COAT
Short, glossy like satin, soft.

COLOR
Any color and markings, except that dogs with tan markings where they would appear on black and tan dogs of other breeds cannot be shown.

Amount of care coat requires: 1 2 3 4 5 6 7 8 9 10

Amount of exercise required: 1 2 3 4 5 6 7 8 9 10

Suitability for urban/apartment life: 1 2 3 4 5 6 7 8 9 10

him. This dog was first seen in England about three hundred years ago and was an immediate favorite in England and Scotland. What lay behind this popularity, particularly among the privileged and super-privileged who could have owned any animal they chose? ¶The Italian Greyhound is one of the most pleasant of all dogs. Mild-mannered, sweet, and affectionate, he is never snappy or nasty, even though his size makes him exceedingly vulnerable. He is fine-boned, and like his relative, the Whippet, he is unable to assume an awkward pose. Often pictured in paintings by the masters and in fine china and porcelain, the Italian Greyhound always looks as if a work of art has suddenly come alive. It probably is the sweetness of his disposition and his beauty that has charmed the artistic and the discerning. ¶Owners of this breed insist that although one no longer has to be of noble blood to own an example, the owner is elevated to nobility, in a sense, by this dog. That is worth thinking about. ¶Italian Greyhounds do not like cold weather and should be protected from it. They are perfect home and apartment pets and are very easy to maintain with their short coats and natural good manners, manners naturally as good as the disposition that goes with them. They can be a little stubborn when it comes to housebreaking, though. ¶Graceful, elegant, refined, beautiful, and exceedingly pleasant, the Italian Greyhound is a dog to admire. His continuing popularity among the discerning is easy to understand.

The Japanese Chin, formerly the Japanese Spaniel, probably originated in China and only reached Japan after being established in his present form. Literally stolen from Japan by visiting sailors, these dogs came to be sold at high prices all over the world. Commodore Perry was presented with some legally, and he in turn presented a pair to Queen Victoria. The avenues of distribution of this breed were not recorded because they were so often contraband. ¶There are actually several different coat styles for these gay little dogs—the profuse coat, the shorter coat, and even a coarser textured coat—but all carry the high style and grand

Japanese Chin

Land of origin: Presumably CHINA

Original purpose: Probably companionship

Recent popularity ranking by A.K.C. registration: 77th

Japanese Chin Club of America
Lucien Collins, Secretary
470 Morse Ave.
Sunnyvale, CA 94086

HEIGHT: Dogs to 9 inches   Bitches to 9 inches

WEIGHT:* Dogs to 7 pounds   Bitches to 7 pounds

COAT
Profuse, silky, long, and straight preferred. Totally free from wave or curl. Tendency to stand out. Thick mane or ruff. Profuse feathering; very plumelike tail.

COLOR
Black and white or red and white. Reds range from sable, brindle, and lemon to orange. White to be clear. Good distribution required.

Amount of care coat requires: 1 2 3 4 5 6 7 8 9 10
•••••••••••••

Amount of exercise required: 1 2 3 4 5 6 7 8 9 10
•

Suitability for urban/apartment life: 1 2 3 4 5 6 7 8 9 10
••••••••••••••••••••••••

*There are classes for dogs under and over 7 pounds. Smaller animals very much preferred.

good looks of this ancient companion toy. ¶The Japanese Chin, still a relatively rare breed in this country, is a perfect apartment dog. He does shed, and his coat does require some brushing, but the dog himself is companionable, intelligent, and most affectionate and responsive. He does not require much exercise and is in general easily kept. A lively little animal, he wants very much to be a part of everything his family is involved in, including meals. He wants most of all to be spoiled, and many owners of this breed want them for just that purpose—spoiling. ¶Often, we must admit, this and other finely bred toys were created and are maintained along such elegant bloodlines expressly for spoiling. They never grow up and are what I refer to as *neotonous,* eternally childlike and perpetu-

ally naughty enough to serve their own purpose: to call attention to themselves. ¶Elderly people, single people, and couples without children may find these characteristics in a dog to be exactly what they have wanted all along, and they often are the ones to favor them. Like most toys, the Japanese Chin travels well and enjoys going along on house visits, to cocktail parties, and on other simple outings. The Japanese Chin is as fragile as most toys are and should not be exposed to extremes. Being locking in a closed car is very often a death sentence and must be avoided at all costs. It is far better to leave your Japanese Chin at home if you know you are going to be making stops where he cannot accompany you.

The Maltese, although often thought of as a terrier, is actually a form of tiny spaniel. He is one of the most ancient of purebred dogs and certainly one of the oldest of the toy breeds. For the romantic dog owner, the Maltese holds special attractions. He was a favorite of the upper classes in ancient Greece and Rome and was the beloved of titled ladies in the time of Elizabeth I. All through history, writers have spoken of this breed with reverence and a little awe. Five hundred years ago fine examples of the breed were selling for what even today would be considered enormous sums—the equivalent of the annual income for an entire village of working-

Maltese

Land of origin: MALTA

Original purpose: Companionship

Recent popularity ranking by A.K.C. registration: 22nd

American Maltese Association, Inc.
Pamela G. Rightmyer, Corres. Secretary
2211 S. Tioga Way
Las Vegas, NV 89117

HEIGHT: Dogs to 5 inches   Bitches to 5 inches

WEIGHT: Dogs to 7 pounds   Bitches to 4 pounds

COAT
Long, flat, and silky. No kinkiness, curls, or woolly texture allowed.

COLOR
Pure white. Some tan or lemon ears allowed but not desirable.

Amount of care coat requires: 1 2 3 4 5 6 7 8 9 10

Amount of exercise required: 1 2 3 4 5 6 7 8 9 10

Suitability for urban/apartment life: 1 2 3 4 5 6 7 8 9 10

class people. ¶The Maltese is a child, and no one should entertain the thought of buying this breed without that foremost in mind. The lovely flowing coat needs hours of care and constant attention, and the dog himself never really grows up. He is loving, even adoring, and loaded with personality, but he characteristically is a fussy eater with a tricky digestive system. He can be frail. The Maltese wants (and usually gets) his own way. He wants to be the center of attention and doesn't like sharing his love sources with anybody or anything else. He is, then, a nearly perfect dog for a single person or a couple who will not have children to compete with their dog. Because of his small size he is very appropriate in the apartment, although he is a dog who wants to be exercised a reasonable amount of time each day. Care should be taken in bad weather, though, and paper training as an emergency alternative is to be recommended. The Maltese prefers being warm and dry and makes no pretense of being a retriever or herding dog. This is a dog designed for the lap and the silken pillow almost thirty-five hundred years ago, and he seems to know it in every fiber of his body. ¶The Maltese generally will not treat strangers or even known outsiders the way he will treat his master. He can even be snappy with people he does not know, although that isn't much of a threat to human safety and well-being. It is, though, a reflection of the spirit and nature of this remarkable little animal with so much of the history of Western culture built into him.

Toy Manchester Terrier

Land of origin: ENGLAND

Original purpose: Ratting

Recent popularity ranking by A.K.C. registration: 95th

American Manchester Terrier Club
Ms. Diana Haywood, Secretary
52 Hampton Rd.
Pittstown, NJ 08867

HEIGHT: Dogs to 7 inches   Bitches to 6 inches

WEIGHT: Dogs to 12 pounds   Bitches to 10 pounds

COAT
Smooth, thick, short, close, glossy, and dense.

COLOR
Jet black and rich mahogany with clean breaks between the two.

Amount of care coat requires: 1 2 3 4 5 6 7 8 9 10

Amount of exercise required: 1 2 3 4 5 6 7 8 9 10

Suitability for urban/apartment life: 1 2 3 4 5 6 7 8 9 10

The standards for the Manchester Terrier, which is shown as a terrier, and the Toy Manchester Terrier, which is shown as a toy, are the same except for size and for the ears. The ears in the Manchester may be cropped, but they are never cut in the Toy variety. What has been said previously about the Manchester Terrier holds true for the Toy. On the subject of size: the Toy is up to but not exceeding twelve pounds, while the Manchester is from twelve to twenty-two pounds.

Miniature Pinscher

Land of origin: GERMANY

Original purpose: Probably companionship

Recent popularity ranking by A.K.C. registration: 23rd

Miniature Pinscher Club of America, Inc.
Vivian A. Hogan, Secretary
26915 Clarksburg Rd.
Damascus, MD 20872

HEIGHT: Dogs to 11¹/₂ inches   Bitches to 10¹/₂ inches

WEIGHT: Dogs to 10 pounds   Bitches to 9 pounds

COAT
Smooth, short, hard, straight, and lustrous; uniform over body.

COLOR
Red, lustrous black with sharply defined rust markings, solid brown, or chocolate with rust or yellow markings.

Amount of care coat requires: 1 2 3 4 5 6 7 8 9 10

Amount of exercise required: 1 2 3 4 5 6 7 8 9 10

Suitability for urban/apartment life: 1 2 3 4 5 6 7 8 9 10

Despite many statements to the contrary, the Miniature Pinscher undoubtedly has been around a few centuries longer than the Doberman Pinscher. He is not, as so many people believe, a bred-down version of the latter. ¶The breed was little known in the United States before 1928. From about 1929 on, the little toy has grown in popularity, and probably will continue to do so. ¶The Minpin, as he is often called, is a lively little devil with a high-stepping style that marks him everywhere he goes. He is a natural showman and is a favorite in the ring. He is a show-off and an assertive character. ¶The Miniature Pinscher is best owned by people who are at least as strong-willed as he is. He is affectionate and loyal and a real participator. He is also, given the chance, a bully and a brat. Having one of these handsome little dogs around is like having a gifted child: you have to know how to handle the situation or it quickly will get out of control. But the Minpin does respond well to authority. ¶Some people feel the Miniature Pinscher is better in a home without children, since he is clearly a child himself. Others have had quite different experiences and claim he is fine with children, indeed with any people as long as he considers them family. He is a perfect watchdog and will never let a stranger come near without giving voice. He is, in fact, a noisy little toy, always quick to express a point of view. ¶For the individual or family looking for a clean, compact, strong-willed little dog of character and high style, the Miniature Pinscher may be just about the perfect choice. There are more restful breeds, though, and more than a few easier to train and control. Here is a breed that should be matched to a personality need. When that is right, this is an outstanding breed of dog.

The Papillon probably acquired his present form in Spain, for he is, it is believed, truly a dwarf spaniel. These dogs were traded to wealthy fanciers, particularly in Italy and France, and became favorites with members of royalty. They were painted by some of the greatest artists—Rubens, Watteau, Fragonard, Boucher, and other fashionable portrait painters of the court. Madame de Pompadour and Marie Antoinette were fanciers, and in the early 1600s the future queen of Poland was known to own at least one dwarf spaniel. ¶The history of the Papillon is, then, one of elegance, privilege, and a certain élan that belongs only to the truly elite.

Papillon

Land of origin: Probably SPAIN

Original purpose: Companionship

Recent popularity ranking by A.K.C. registration: 53rd

Papillon Club of America, Inc.
Mrs. Janice Dougherty, Corres. Secretary
551 Birch Hill Rd.
Shoemakersville, PA 19555

HEIGHT: Dogs to 11 inches   Bitches to 10 inches

WEIGHT: Dogs to 10 pounds   Bitches to 8 pounds

COAT
Abundant, long and fine, silky and flowing, straight and resilient. No undercoat. Ears well fringed. Profuse on chest and tail.

COLOR
White predominates. Patches may be any other color except liver. Also tricolored. Color must cover both ears and extend over both eyes. No solid colors allowed, including white.

Amount of care coat requires: 1 2 3 4 5 6 7 8 9 10

Amount of exercise required: 1 2 3 4 5 6 7 8 9 10

Suitability for urban/apartment life: 1 2 3 4 5 6 7 8 9 10

Although he is the only working toy—he is still, they say, a good little ratter—his general use has been to weigh down silk cushions and help dispose of delicacies. He has been used consistently for adornment and rarely fails to make an elegant setting even more elegant, a regal person even more impressive. The little butterfly of dogdom was meant to be spoiled. ¶The Papillon, although not exactly a Labrador Retriever, is not as delicate as he may appear to some people. He can stand some weather and will do fine in an apartment, in a house, or on the farm. He does prefer to be comfortable, though, and people who fancy this breed will probably feel better themselves if their pet is indoors at night and not out hunting and fending for himself. ¶Anyone who purchases an example of this breed should make a firm commitment to his coat. It does require care if it is to look its elegant best. This is not something that happens by itself. The dog is small and the task isn't large, just regular and in need of a guarantee. ¶The Papillon likes exercise because he is an intelligent little busybody, but he does not require a great deal of it. The butterfly dog is affectionate and responsive to his family and is a very good little watchdog. He will not fail to announce strangers.

The Pekingese is second only to the Toy Poodle in popularity among the toy dogs in this country. He has long been a favorite with apartment dwellers who want a splendid little character to fuss over. ¶The Pekingese, the Little Lion Dog of China, dates back to ancient times, when they say it was a crime punishable by death to steal one. Slave girls were used as wet nurses to suckle these dogs, and special eunuchs were assigned to care for them. Whether they were actually sacred is not known, but they certainly were among the most spoiled dogs who ever lived. Specimens were stolen during the looting of China's imperial court in 1860, and some

Pekingese

Land of origin: CHINA

Original purpose: Ornamental companionship

Recent popularity ranking by A.K.C. registration: 27th

Pekingese Club of America, Inc.
Mrs. Leonie Marie Schultz, Secretary
Rt. #1, Box 321
Bergton, VA 22811

HEIGHT: Dogs to 9 inches   Bitches to 8 inches

WEIGHT:* Dogs to 14 pounds   Bitches to 10 pounds

COAT
Long, with thick undercoat; straight and flat, not curly or wavy, rather coarse but soft. Profuse ruff; very heavy on tail and legs.

COLOR
All colors allowed: red, fawn, black, black and tan, sable, brindle, white, and parti-colored. Well defined black mask and spectacles with lines to ears desired. White on feet and chest of otherwise solid colored dog is not a parti-color. Good distribution required.

Amount of care coat requires: 1 2 3 4 5 6 7 8 9 10
•••••••••••••••••••

Amount of exercise required: 1 2 3 4 5 6 7 8 9 10
••

Suitability for urban/apartment life: 1 2 3 4 5 6 7 8 9 10
•••••••••••••••••••••••

*The smaller the dog the better; 14 pounds is extreme and anything over this would be disqualified.

eventually reached Europe. But most were slaughtered by the Chinese, who did not want them to fall into the hands of Europeans. Out of all this romantic history comes the top push-faced toy in the world today. ¶Maintaining the coat of the Pekingese, his crowning glory, is a daily task, although not a big one. It must be seen to, however, or the Pekingese will soon look anything but elegant. This is an assertive, headstrong, willful, possessive, positive, brave, and forceful little character. He is not devoted to strangers and will make a good watchdog. Very often children are not adored, although this dog will accept his place in a family and work out all necessary relationships. There will be no problem as long as the Pekingese is where he feels he must be: at the center of the universe. ¶This is, of course, an ideal dog for the couple with limited space everywhere except in their hearts. This is a dog to cherish and share a life-style with. He is not to be left out or denied full recognition as a part of the family. He is the perfect animal to fuss over. He is a "sleeve-sized" dog, and most Pekingese owners like to carry their pets with them. The pets think that is just grand. ¶Owning a Pekingese is like having a human infant with an adult's wiles. It is quite an experience and one that many people simply will not deny themselves.

A very long time ago the diminutive toy we call the Pomeranian was a sled dog, one of the group known as the spitz dogs, essentially northern, full-coated dogs with a curled tail. Later, the breed was used for sheepherding, although its exact history remains uncertain. Somehow the center for breeding the spitz seemed to be in Pomerania on the Baltic Sea, although possibly the ancestral dogs may have come from Iceland and Lapland. It was probably in Pomerania that breeding down started, although it is difficult to understand what may have originally motivated that development. ¶By the time the breed reached England in the middle of the last century,

Pomeranian

Land of origin: POMERANIA (Baltic Sea)

Original purpose: Pulling sleds, then sheepherding, then companionship

Recent popularity ranking by A.K.C. registration: 10th

American Pomeranian Club, Inc.
Tim Goddard, Corres. Secretary
Rt. #2, Box 540
Opelousas, LA 70570-0540

HEIGHT: Dogs to 7 inches   Bitches to 6½ inches

WEIGHT: Dogs to 7 pounds   Bitches to 5 pounds

COAT
Double—short, soft, thick undercoat with a long, coarse, glistening outer coat. Off-standing and profuse. Always straight.

COLOR
Red, orange, cream and sable, black, brown and blue, white, sable, chocolate, plus others.

Amount of care coat requires: 1 2 3 4 5 6 7 8 9 10

Amount of exercise required: 1 2 3 4 5 6 7 8 9 10

Suitability for urban/apartment life: 1 2 3 4 5 6 7 8 9 10

It was down considerably in size, although specimens probably weighed five or six times as much as they do now. It is said that some were still in the thirty-pound class. That is a far cry from the four- to five-pound toys we see today. ¶The Pomeranian now is strictly a companion dog. He is a spirited, brash, proud little strutter with some of that old northern spitz fire still evident. He is a dog who is made to be spoiled, and both owner and dog, apparently, are happiest when that is the situation. The Pomeranian tries to take over; that appears to be his chief motivation in life. Many Pomeranian owners, amused by the brashness of this little charmer, seem pleased to relinquish command. ¶Some Pomeranians are fine with children, but as a general rule they are best when they are the children of the household. They have a short temper when someone tries roughing them up and are ideal for single people and elderly couples. They are fiercely loyal and are good little watchdogs. ¶The Pomeranian is an ideal apartment dog. He requires little exercise, since even a brief walk with his short legs seems like miles to him. He likes to be comfortable and neat and will use a paper in a plastic pan, making walks in bad weather unnecessary. That is particularly important for some people who are limited in their outdoor activities and who do not like to go out in the city at night. ¶The Pomeranian's coat is glorious. The dog should not be bathed very often because that does soften his coat, which needs some care. Brushing is important to keep the coat off-standing and glistening. ¶Pretty as a picture, sassy as a bumblebee, the little Pomeranian is just about the perfect dog for the right kind of home. He is demanding but rewarding to own, assertive yet loving and protective.

Toy Poodle

Land of origin: Possibly GERMANY, but not really known

Original purpose: Probably water retrieving

Recent popularity ranking by A.K.C. registration: 5th

Poodle Club of America, Inc.
Mr. Charles Thomasson, Corres. Secretary
503 Martineau Dr.
Chester, VA 23831-5753

HEIGHT: Dogs and bitches under 10 inches

WEIGHT: Dogs to 7 pounds   Bitches to 6 pounds

COAT
Naturally harsh in texture, extremely profuse and dense. Seen in a variety of clips.

COLOR
Solid only, never parti-colored. Colors seen include blue, gray, silver, brown, café au lait, apricot, cream, black, and white.

Amount of care coat requires:*   1 2 3 4 5 6 7 8 9 10
•••••••••••••••••••••

Amount of exercise required: 1 2 3 4 5 6 7 8 9 10
•••••••••••••

Suitability for urban/apartment life:†   1 2 3 4 5 6 7 8 9 10
••••••••••••••••••••••

*Varies somewhat with style of clip and age of dog.
†If appropriate exercise is provided.

The standard, history, and origin of the Toy Poodle is the same in all respects as that of the Standard and Miniature Poodles. ¶The Toy Poodle is to be ten inches or under and should weigh between five and seven pounds. There is a much smaller Toy now called the Teacup Poodle, who is the size of a small Yorkshire Terrier, probably not much over two pounds. ¶All poodles combined (Standard, Miniature, and Toy) rank third in popularity among purebred dogs in America. The Toy is the most popular of the three and makes a splendid apartment pet because of his size. His coat, of course, requires a great deal of care if he is to look his best. All in all, the Toy Poodle is a companion or "sleeve dog" without peer.

We assume several things when we take up the Pug. First, we assume the breed originated in China a long time ago. This animal has the pushed-face and curled-tail look of a Chinese dog. We also assume the Pug was never intended for any task except loving, for that is where the Pug fits into human society. The Pug is a child who never grows up. ¶The Pug doesn't have a particularly strong odor, although like all push-faced dogs he does tend to gulp air, and that has predictable results in a closed room. He doesn't shed much, and he doesn't drool. This is altogether a pleasant little dog to have around. He is another of those dogs who make absolute prisoners

Pug

Land of origin: CHINA

Original purpose: Companionship

Recent popularity ranking by A.K.C. registration: 26th

Pug Dog Club of America, Inc.
Mr. James P. Cavallaro, Secretary
1820 Shadowlawn St.
Jacksonville, FL 32205

HEIGHT: Dogs to 11 inches   Bitches to 10 or 11 inches

WEIGHT: Dogs to 18 pounds   Bitches to 17 pounds

COAT
Fine, smooth, short, glossy, and soft to the touch. Neither hard nor woolly.

COLOR
Black, silver, or apricot fawn. The light-colored dogs have black masks and ears and a dark line or trace on back.

Amount of care coat requires: 1 2 3 4 5 6 7 8 9 10

Amount of exercise required: 1 2 3 4 5 6 7 8 9 10

Suitability for urban/apartment life: 1 2 3 4 5 6 7 8 9 10

of their owner. Pug owners tend to be Pug owners all their lives once they have tried the breed. ¶A Pug is good with children, although a small child might seem something of a challenge to him. Children, when they get a little older, from five or six on, seem to do better with this breed than in their earlier years. The Pug is jealous of other dogs, and small children seem to get lumped in there. A disgruntled Pug may decide to punish his owner by neglecting previously well understood rules about toilet habits. Pugs, in fact, train well and easily and, once they catch on to the idea of reward at the far end, are not difficult. This dog, however, is always looking for an opening and will quickly take over and run the show if indecision and lack of assertiveness become apparent. For example, a Pug is not a picky eater as a rule, but let an owner start with the diced chicken breast and bonbon routine, and he will have a first-rate food brat on his hands. In brief, some Pugs, like some children, are a lot smarter than some parents, and it really isn't reaching too far out to suggest that people who avail themselves of a Pug come closer to parenthood than dog ownership. ¶The character of the Pug—smart, tidy, willing, and loving—should be viewed in light of the breed's development. He does exactly what he was designed to do perhaps a thousand or more years ago. He is only playing the role for which he was cast. ¶The Pug owner of today is joining a long line of famous and royal men and women who have preferred this breed. Many Pugs have sat beside the throne, and the trick with the Pug is to convince him that he doesn't belong *on* the throne. If you want to love with the absolute certainty of being loved back, you might want to think about the Pug, this dog of ancient China.

The Shih Tzu (pronounced *sheed-zoo*) is a legendary creature who also just happens to exist as a flesh-and-blood companion animal in our own time. We do not know where he came from originally, although the Byzantine Empire, Tibet, and other areas of Asia and the Middle East have been proposed. What we do know is that by the seventh century A.D. the breed was the rage in the royal courts of China. The breed does have the typical Asian-dog pushed face and curled tail, but it is clear his true origins will never be known, so the legends do nicely and add to the character of the beast. ¶The Shih Tzu probably always was bred for exactly what he is used

Shih Tzu

Land of origin: CHINA since the seventh century; unknown before that

Original purpose: Companionship

Recent popularity ranking by A.K.C. registration: 12th

American Shih Tzu Club, Inc.
Ms. Jo Ann Regelman, Corres. Secretary
837 Auburn Ave.
Ridgewood, NJ 07450

HEIGHT: Dogs to 10½ inches   Bitches to 10 inches

WEIGHT: Dogs to 18 pounds   Bitches to 16 pounds

COAT
Luxurious, long, and dense. May be slightly wavy but never curly. Woolly undercoat.

COLOR
All colors allowed.

Amount of care coat requires: 1 2 3 4 5 6 7 8 9 10

Amount of exercise required: 1 2 3 4 5 6 7 8 9 10

Suitability for urban/apartment life: 1 2 3 4 5 6 7 8 9 10

for today: companionship. It is unlikely that he was ever a guard dog or a hunting animal, although he most likely was once a little larger than his present nine to eighteen pounds. His popularity as a companion of kings and queens a thousand years ago is easy to understand when you get to know a few good examples of the breed today. ¶The Shih Tzu, whose name means "lion" in Chinese, is a perfect companion animal for the city dweller who enjoys having something to fuss over. A sprightly little character with great charm and personality, the little chrysanthemum-faced dog prefers the quiet dignity of a well-appointed apartment to the longest dog run in the world. If you gave an adult Shih Tzu an entire national park for a playground, he wouldn't use an acre. For the Shih Tzu, home is where his human family is and where the goodies, the comfort, and the security he demands are. ¶Enormously appealing to fanciers of the toy breeds, the Shih Tzu stands twelfth in popularity of all breeds in America, although he has been known here only since the end of World War II. Although not even accepted by the A.K.C. stud registry until 1969, the breed is already among the top five toys in popularity. ¶The Shih Tzu, needless to say, has a coat that demands attention. This is a dog to cherish and fuss over and enjoy for his great charm, his unfaltering loyalty, his beauty, and his exotic and romantic past.

The Silky Terrier is apparently a cross between the Australian Terrier and the Yorkshire Terrier. Like the latter, he is shown as a toy today, although he is clearly terrier all the way through. ¶The lovely little eight- to ten-pound Silky is more active than some of the other toy breeds and should get plenty of exercise. He can be an exhausting little creature with his endless demands for attention and action, but most people who have known the breed have felt it was worth the effort. ¶There are stories of Silky Terriers being used in Australia as ratters and snakers on poultry farms, but knowing something of the character of Australian snakes, I tend to doubt

Silky Terrier

Land of origin: AUSTRALIA

Original purpose: Companionship, and to some extent ratting

Recent popularity ranking by A.K.C. registration: 61st

Silky Terrier Club of America, Inc.
Ms. Louise Rosewell, Secretary
2783 S. Saulsbury St.
Denver, CO 80227

HEIGHT: Dogs to 10 inches   Bitches to 10 inches

WEIGHT: Dogs to 10 pounds   Bitches to 9 pounds

COAT
Flat, very fine in texture, glossy; decidedly silky; 5 to 6 inches long on mature dog. Pronounced topknot.

COLOR
Various blues and tan.

Amount of care coat requires: 1 2 3 4 5 6 7 8 9 10
•••••••••••••••••••••••

Amount of exercise required: 1 2 3 4 5 6 7 8 9 10
•••••••••••

Suitability for urban/apartment life: 1 2 3 4 5 6 7 8 9 10
••••••••••••••••••••••••

most of those tales. The Silky Terrier is essentially a companion animal, like all toys, and at that task he excels. He is bright to a fault, responsive, demanding, and even, at times, aggressive. Apparently no one has bothered to tell the Silky just how small he is. He makes a great little watchdog, for he does tend to be vocal. In fact, when you add up all of the Silky Terrier's qualities, what you have is a perpetual-motion machine. He is seldom still. ¶A great many people live fairly active lives, even though they are essentially city dwellers. The space available to them may necessitate a small dog, while they may crave an active animal of forceful character. The Silky Terrier is the answer for those people, for he is really the largest dog in the world pushed down into a very small body. ¶The Silky Terrier is one of those breeds with a crowning-glory type coat, and it does require care. That lovely silky look will last *only* as long as the dog is bathed and brushed and combed and his coat kept from getting stringy and matted looking. It does take all that and some judicious trimming to have a Silky Terrier look like a Silky Terrier is supposed to look. It is important to keep that in mind when considering this breed. ¶There are signs of rising favor for this breed in the United States, and it will be wise to be wary of poorly bred or mass-produced puppies. Some are passed off as Yorkshire Terriers and vice versa. It is wise to stick with an established specialty breeder and avoid all risk.

The Yorkshire Terrier is a fantastic bundle of assertiveness. This cross of perhaps several different terriers with a few toys is a creature of dignity and character. In our household we have a Bloodhound that weighs well over a hundred pounds, a large male Golden Retriever, an English Bulldog bitch, a bitch Siberian Husky, a random-bred shepherd bitch, a Yorkshire Terrier, and several cats. The Yorkie is without question not only the dominant male but the dominant animal. None of the other dogs challenges him or fails to back off when he gives warning of temper. ¶The Yorkie is a delightful little animal, ideally suited for an apartment and unstint-

Yorkshire Terrier

Land of origin: ENGLAND

Original purpose: Companionship

Recent popularity ranking by A.K.C. registration: 11th

Yorkshire Terrier Club of America, Inc.
Mrs. Shirley A. Patterson, Secretary
2 Chestnut Ct., Star Rt.
Pottstown, PA 19464

HEIGHT: Dogs to 9 inches   Bitches to 9 inches

WEIGHT: Dogs to 7 pounds   Bitches to 6 pounds

COAT
Very important—glossy, fine, silky, and long; straight, highly styled.

COLOR
Steel blue and golden tan.

Amount of care coat requires: 1 2 3 4 5 6 7 8 9 10

Amount of exercise required: 1 2 3 4 5 6 7 8 9 10

Suitability for urban/apartment life: 1 2 3 4 5 6 7 8 9 10

ing in his display of affection. He is a participator and expects to be taken along, even if only in a handbag. He couldn't care less about walks and exercise, and many city people simply train him to a cat litter box with fresh newspapers several times a day. ¶What the Yorkshire Terrier saves the owner in long walks in bad weather he makes up in the care his coat demands. It must be seen to, preferably at least once a day. The marvelous little Yorkshire becomes, then, a perfect dog for people who want to fuss. As it happens, many Yorkshire Terrier owners do not brush their pets once a week, much less once or twice a day. Their pets look it. Because his hair does hang to the floor when in its full splendor, the Yorkie quickly is in a first-class mess in the country. Most people keep their Yorkshire Terriers at home. ¶No matter what the owner does, the Yorkshire Terrier is going to run the show. People and animals all get in line, and the little tyrant of the dog world, the marvelously well-organized Yorkshire Terrier, takes over. He spends his every waking hour seeing to the matter of his household. He is a fussbudget, busybody, watchdog, and knockabout dictator. He is among the most lovable and most clever of all dogs. Beware of mass-producers and retailers, for there are *many* poor examples of the breed around. Some are passed off as Silky Terriers, and vice versa. Fine examples of the Yorkshire Terrier are a work of art, and they will both look and act the part.

{Group 7}

The Nonsporting Dogs

American Eskimo Dog
Bichon Frise
Boston Terrier
Bulldog
Chinese Shar-Pei
Chow Chow
Dalmation
Finnish Spitz

French Bulldog
Keeshond
Lhasa Apso
Poodle
Schipperke
Shiba Inu
Tibetan Spaniel
Tibetan Terrier

The history of the American Eskimo Dog is something of a mystery, or at least a muddle. The Eskie, as he is commonly known, is clearly a Nordic or spitz dog and contains German, Dutch and probably Italian spitz blood. Certainly the Keeshond and Pomeranian are in there somewhere. What Scandinavian blood is included is not known or at least cannot be quantified. It is entirely possible that Japanese spitz bloodlines were incorporated by West Coast breeders forty years ago. ¶Whatever his background, today's smart little Eskie is all his own dog. He is not a Pomeranian, a Keeshond or any of the other foundation breeds—he is all Eskie

American Eskimo Dog

Land of origin: EUROPE and possibly ASIA (Japan)

Original purpose: Companionship

Recent popularity ranking by A.K.C. registration: 92nd

American Eskimo Dog Club of America
Barbara E. Beynon, Corres. Secretary
1107B Northcape Dr.
Austin, TX 78753

HEIGHT: Standard: Over 15 inches—but not over 19 inches
Miniature: Over 12 inches—including 15 inches
Toy: Not under 9 inches—including 12 inches

WEIGHT: Not specified but appropriate to height.

COAT
Stand-off, double. Dense undercoat with guard hairs showing through to form outer coat. Body coat never trimmed. Males may show good ruff.

COLOR
Sparkling white with some biscuit cream allowed. Any other color disqualifies. Pure white preferred.

Amount of care coat requires: 1 2 3 4 5 6 7 8 9 10
•••••••••••

Amount of exercise required: 1 2 3 4 5 6 7 8 9 10
•••••••••••••

Suitability for urban/apartment life: 1 2 3 4 5 6 7 8 9 10
••••••••••••••••••••••••

and very beautiful to boot. Snow white (he isn't a mini-Samoyed, either) or white with biscuit, he is a smart little enthusiast of all endeavors. He is spectacularly trainable and became widely known in this country as a stage and circus performer. He was known as the American spitz back then and was one of the most readily recognized of all dogs in America before World War II. It wasn't until 1995 that he was placed in the Non-Sporting Group by the AKC. ¶The Eskie is intelligent, alert, an excellent watch dog, and exceptionally eager to please. He should be friendly if somewhat conservative. If he is overly shy or in any way aggressive he is off the mark and those undesirable characteristics are severely penalized in the show ring. Except for size (never under 9 inches, never over 19 inches) the three sizes (toy, miniature and standard) are all judged by the same standard and are shown in the same ring today. All are expected to display the same beauty, same style, and same intelligence and willingness to "belong."

The Bichon Frise is a small French toy-like companion dog whose derivation is cloaked in mystery. The breed has been known by many names, we think, and among them may be Tenerife Dog, Curlycoated Poodle, and Bichon à Poil Frise. In all likelihood any number of old French toy breeds went into the makeup of this little white bundle of charm. ¶The Bichon Frise was bred to be a companion animal. If he fails at that, he fails at everything. He should be gay, playful, affectionate, and lively. The whole attitude should be one of involvement, participation, and willingness. Shy, snappy, or overly moody specimens were probably poorly bred or badly

Bichon Frise

Land of origin: FRANCE

Original purpose: Companionship

Recent popularity ranking by A.K.C. registration: 32nd

Bichon Frise Club of America, Inc.
Mrs. Bernice D. Richardson, Corres. Secretary
186 Ash St. N.
Twin Falls, ID 83301

HEIGHT: Dogs to 12 inches   Bitches to 12 inches

WEIGHT: Not specified in breed standards

COAT
Double—outer coat is profuse, silky, loosely curled; 2 inches or longer

COLOR
Pure white; sometimes with cream, apricot, or gray on ears.

Amount of care coat requires: 1 2 3 4 5 6 7 8 9 10

Amount of exercise required: 1 2 3 4 5 6 7 8 9 10

Suitability for urban/apartment life. 1 2 3 4 5 6 7 8 9 10

raised. The Bichon Frise should give the impression that he is smiling. When he is serious, he is even more endearing. He is an ideal apartment dog and requires little exercise, although a chase around the coffee table after a rubber toy will be appreciated, perhaps more for the pleasure of interacting with a human being than for the exercise obtained. ¶Anyone contemplating this breed should keep that coat in mind. It does require care, and the dog you so admire in the show-ring or in photographs will not be the dog you have at home unless you are prepared to give it some time each day. A Bichon Frise can be a matted, ropy mess or a picture-book white muff of a dog. The difference is the time spent allowing the one or achieving the other. ¶The Bichon Frise is one of the most recent breeds to gain recognition in the United States, and it is attracting a great deal of attention because of the continual demand for ideal urban pets. Its small size and predictable popularity are going to bring a great many unscrupulous backyard breeders into the field. Bichon Frises should be purchased with care. They are enough like other European toys and nonsporting dogs to tempt less-than-honest breeders to use what they can find—the Maltese and other breeds as well. Stick with the professional breeder who is devoted to perfecting and perpetuating this delightful breed. Any would-be owner of this new breed to America's shores may well be in the vanguard with what could be one of the most popular dogs in the country ten to fifteen years from now.

The Boston Terrier, the descendant of the crossing of an English Bulldog and a white English Terrier, is an American breed, one of the few. He is also one of the most delightful of canine companions. Naturally bright and high-spirited, this is a consummate pet dog for any setting; farm, suburban home, and city apartment are all equally his natural turf. ¶The Boston has only one use: love. He is certainly not a hunting dog and not a working or herding animal, and although he will bark when strangers approach, he isn't much of a guard dog either. He was bred for loving, and that is what he does best, first, and always. ¶There is great need for city dogs, dogs

Boston Terrier

Land of origin: UNITED STATES

Original purpose: Companionship

Recent popularity ranking by A.K.C. registration: 24th

Boston Terrier Club of America, Inc.
Marian Sheehan, Corres. Secretary
8537 E. San Burno Dr.
Scottsdale, AZ 85258

HEIGHT: Dogs to 17 inches   Bitches to 16 inches

WEIGHT: Dogs to 25 pounds   Bitches to 19 pounds

COAT
Short, smooth, bright, and fine. Must be shiny and alive.

COLOR

Brindle and white or black and white. Brindle and white with nicely balanced distribution considered best.

Amount of care coat requires: 1 2 3 4 5 6 7 8 9 10

Amount of exercise required: 1 2 3 4 5 6 7 8 9 10

Suitability for urban/apartment life: 1 2 3 4 5 6 7 8 9 10

that, although they like exercise and should get their share, are not demanding and do not require long walks in foul weather. The Boston Terrier may fit the bill of the perfect city dog. Any Boston will be grateful for the chance to chase a ball (the breed seems addicted to this sport), but he is content to sit and be quiet or fuss with a rubber toy on the kitchen floor. He wants to be in on everything in the family, but he gives as good as he gets. This is one of the most affectionate of all breeds. The Boston is also intelligent and takes to training with enthusiasm. To a Boston it is all part of the lovely game of living. Fortunately, he tends to be very long-lived, often making it into the upper teens. ¶Bostons hardly shed at all, and they do not have a "doggy" odor. They seldom need bathing, and a minute or two a week with a brush does it all. They are shiny, clean little animals. ¶Like the other short-nosed dogs, Bostons snort and gulp enough air to make them gassy. They may vomit when upset, but none of these things are bad enough to be a problem. Counter them with the fact that you can housebreak a Boston Terrier in a matter of hours, or days. ¶Fortunately or unfortunately, depending on how you view it, the Boston Terrier has long been one of the most popular dogs in America. Examples are registered now at the rate of ten to twelve thousand a year, and so many Bostons are bred for the pet trade that at least as many are not even registered. So be careful when you buy a Boston and avoid the buck-takers. If you buy from the wrong line, you may not get a superb companion but an idiotic, neurotic, snappy monster. Buy *only* from a recognized specialty breeder and when you have a chance to meet your puppy's parents and see what manner of dog they are. When you set out to buy this superb little dog, you have every right to expect the best in performance and character.

The Bulldog was designed to fight bulls, and that, simply, is how he got his name. He probably also was used to fight bears and other pit animals in a much more cruel era of England's history. Despite all of that nasty background, the English Bulldog of today is a gentle, companionable animal. ¶The Bulldog is adoring and wants to be adored back. He can do well with other animals as long as they will recognize who is at the top of the order. Bulldogs do not like being challenged or insulted. When a fight does start, all hell breaks loose, and the other dog may be dead before anything effective can be done. Bulldogs should definitely be on leashes when they are apt to encounter strange dogs. ¶Curiously, bulldogs and cats get along very well together

Bulldog

Land of origin: ENGLAND

Original purpose: Bullbaiting

Recent popularity ranking by A.K.C. registration: 33rd

Bulldog Club of America
Dennis Quinn, Secretary
9443 Chapel Green Rd.
King George, VA 22485

HEIGHT: Dogs to 15 inches   Bitches to 14½ inches

WEIGHT: Dogs to 50 pounds   Bitches to 40 pounds

COAT
Straight, short, flat, close lying, fine, smooth, and glossy.

COLOR
Brindle or red brindle, solid white, solid red or fawn, piebald; colors should be bright and clearly defined.

Amount of care coat requires: 1 2 3 4 5 6 7 8 9 10

Amount of exercise required: 1 2 3 4 5 6 7 8 9 10

Suitability for urban/apartment life: 1 2 3 4 5 6 7 8 9 10

as long as the cats understand the position Bulldogs take over a food dish—total possessiveness. There can be unfortunate accidents involving otherwise extremely sweet Bulldogs if this fact is overlooked. if the household contains other animals, Bulldogs are best fed by themselves, and food dishes should not be left around. ¶With children Bulldogs are another story. They seem to have a built-in sense of manners, and even the smallest child is unlikely to be knocked over. Bulldogs approach babies as if they really did understand their own weight and power. They are flawless pets, giving and getting love endlessly and never tiring of the opportunity to interact with human beings. ¶There has to be a debit side, and in that column can go snoring. Bulldogs seem to sleep more contentedly than most any other breed, and they certainly let you know it. The variety of snorts, wheezes, grunts, huffs, and snores that can come from a sleeping Bulldog is nothing less than astounding. ¶Bulldogs are immensely appealing with their marvelous shoulders-out attitude, and they tend to enslave their owners. They are like superpowered tanks when faced with a challenge, charging forward even when in doubt because of their poor eyesight. Much of that is bluff, however, and a harsh word will turn most Bulldogs off. ¶Bulldogs like a walk and can be downright frisky pups, but as they mature, they need little strenuous activity. They are fine on the farm, in the suburbs, or in an apartment. They are not long-lived dogs, and ten years would be an old and perhaps even unusual Bulldog. They should *never* be locked in a car, for they mind the heat terribly. More than one Bulldog standing in the sun at a dog show has ended up with an oxygen mask over his face. Their health generally requires careful watching under all circumstances.

The first Chinese Shar-Pei were seen in the United States in 1966. There were breeders in Hong Kong and Taiwan but the dog was touted as "extremely rare" and interest was high. An importation in 1973 again raised great interest. By the time the breed was placed in the Miscellaneous Class by the AKC in 1988 there were well over 29,000 of them in this country. There are many breeds on the AKC roster with fewer dogs than that. Still, the word "rare" continued to be associated with the breed. it was placed in the Non-Sporting group in 1993. ¶The Chinese Shar-Pei continues to generate interest whenever they appear although it is not unusual to see them in

Chinese Shar-Pei

Land of origin: CHINA

Original purpose: Possibly dog-fighting

Recent popularity ranking by A.K.C. registration: 25th

Chinese SharPei Club of America, Inc.
Jocelyn Barker, Secretary
P.O. Box 113809
Anchorage, AK 99511-3809

HEIGHT: 18 to 20 inches

WEIGHT: 40 to 55 pounds

COAT
Extremely harsh—feels somewhat like sandpaper. Straight, short, offstanding on body, flatter on limbs.

COLOR
Only solid colors with some shading of the same ground color on back and ears. No albino, brindle, or parti-colors allowed, no spots, no "points."

Amount of care coat requires: 1 2 3 4 5 6 7 0 9 10
                ••

Amount of exercise required: 1 2 3 4 5 6 7 8 9 10
               •••••••••

Suitability for urban/apartment life: 1 2 3 4 5 6 7 8 9 10
             •••••••••••••••••••••••

any American city or town. Their wrinkled skin, the rough sand-papery feel of their coat, their alert, dignified demeanor all attract attention. They have one characteristic that they share with only one other dog, the Chow Chow. The tongue, roof of mouth and flews are bluish-black. In lighter colored dogs that color may be lavender, but never pink or spotted. Whether or not the Chinese Shar-Pei and the Chow Chow are related would be difficult to prove. ¶The standards call for the Chinese Shar-Pei to be regal, alert, intelligent, dignified, lordly, sober, snobbish, independent, devoted to family members, stand-offish with strangers. It is also described as calm and confident. That line-up of requirements, if met, could explain the devotion the owners in turn offer their pets. The Shar-Pei is now strictly a companion animal although we may assume it was once used in more ferocious pursuits, fighting in dog pits in southern Chinese village squares.

This dog of China is at least two thousand years old. There are endless suggestions as to what animals were ancestor to this breed and to which breeds it in turn gave rise. No one knows, and the mystery is compounded by the fact that the Chow Chow is the only breed of dog left on earth with a black mouth. Because the polar bear also has a black mouth, there are absurd stories about a direct line of descent from the great white bear of the North. It may in fact be the ancestral breed to many of the sled and spitz-type dogs we know today—for example, the Akita. It is generally agreed that it did not come from any familiar Western breeds. ¶The Chow

Chow Chow

Land of origin: CHINA

Original purpose: Probably hunting and some guard work

Recent popularity ranking by A.K.C. registration: 17th

Chow Chow Club, Inc.
Irene Cartabio, Corres. Secretary
3580 Plover Pl.
Seaford, NY 11783

HEIGHT: Dogs to 20 inches   Bitches to 19 inches

WEIGHT: Dogs to 60 pounds   Bitches to 55 pounds

COAT
Dense, abundant, straight, and off-standing. It is rather coarse in texture, and there is a woolly, much softer undercoat.

COLOR
Any clear color, solid throughout. There are generally lighter shadings on ruff, tail, and breechings.

Amount of care coat requires: 1 2 3 4 5 6 7 8 9 10
••••••••••••••••••••

Amount of exercise required: 1 2 3 4 5 6 7 8 9 10
•••••••••••••••

*Suitability for urban/apartment life:** 1 2 3 4 5 6 7 8 9 10
•••••

*If properly exercised.

Chow (very often just referred to simply as the Chow) is an aloof and dignified dog. He was used extensively for hunting in China and also, apparently, for guard work. He is not at all demonstrative and can be very hardheaded. He is a massive-looking animal, handsome and powerful, and to some people he appears to be ferocious. The heavy head and ruff and the thick muzzle may give that impression. In fact this dog is not ferocious, he is just very self-contained. He should not be expected to act like a romping hound or a terrier looking for a game; that is not his style. He is loyal, may be affectionate toward his owner, and can be an excellent watchdog. Because he can be a little on the tough side, he should be watched around other animals. This is not always the best breed for a household with children. The Chow may be fine with an owner's kids, but friends of the kids are another matter. ¶That magnificent Chow Chow coat does require a lot of care. Bathing tends to soften it, so it is not recommended any more often than necessary. Constant brushing is essential if mats are to be avoided. There is considerable shedding in the summertime. ¶People looking for a cuddly pet should not look to a Chow Chow. This is an animal of high style; he is both decorative to the discerning and formidable to the uninvited. He is a stunning dog in the showring and should be obedience-trained simply because he is powerful and is a bit on the stubborn side. Strangers should not expect much in the way of a greeting. In fact, they should expect to be ignored as long as they do not appear to be threatening toward the household.

The Dalmatian, wherever he came from (the point has been argued in print for more than a century), is a charmer with more ways to please an owner than we can probably record. In their long and varied careers these dogs have been shepherds, guard dogs on border patrol, war dogs as couriers and sentinels, ratters, bird dogs, retrievers, draft dogs, coach dogs, general farm dogs, and household pets. You ask it, and a Dalmatian will do it with élan. We know he was very popular in Dalmatia, part of former Austria-Hungary, in the last century, and hence the name. ¶The Dalmatian is an active animal—a spirited and willing animal who takes training more

Dalmatian

Land of origin: Ancient and unknown, but later AUSTRIA

Original purpose: Hunting, ratting, guard patrol, war, draft dog, shepherd, and coach dog

Recent popularity ranking by A.K.C. registration: 9th

Dalmatian Club of America, Inc.
Mrs. Anne T. Fleming, Corres. Secretary
4390 Chickasaw Road
Memphis, TN 38117

HEIGHT: Dogs to 23 inches   Bitches to 23 inches

WEIGHT: Not specified in breed standards

COAT
Short, hard, dense, fine, sleek, and glossy. Never woolly or silky.

COLOR
Very important in standards. Ground color pure white. Black or liver spots as near uniform in size as possible. Patched a fault. Puppies born pure white.

Amount of care coat requires: 1 2 3 4 5 6 7 8 9 10

Amount of exercise required: 1 2 3 4 5 6 7 8 9 10

Suitability for urban/apartment life:*   1 2 3 4 5 6 7 8 9 10

*But not all unless given a great deal of exercise.

readily than many other breeds. He loves to run with horses (and horses seem to love being with Dalmatians), and he is a historical necessity in the firehouse. ¶Wherever the action is, there the Dalmatian wants to be. He isn't yappy, but he will bark with excitement as he runs back and forth along the ladders of fire apparatus rushing into action. He is a good watchdog and is fine with children. ¶The Dalmatian is devoted to his master above all else and is good within the family circle. While not a particularly suspicious and certainly not a shy dog, he does like to get his facts straight when it comes to strangers. He takes his time and then generally makes a wise decision. ¶This is a clean dog, easily housetrained and requiring little care. He is hardy and solid, and he loves to be in motion. For that reason he is a questionable choice for city life. Of course, there are city dwellers who lead active lives, taking long walks in the streets and heading out to a country place on weekends and holidays. A Dalmatian can enjoy that kind of life as long as he gets his workouts on schedule. People leading a sedentary life should resist the perfectly understandable temptation to own one of these splendid animals and should look elsewhere for a pet to share their quiet life-style. ¶There is an inherited tendency for deafness among Dalmatians, and the prospective owner should be cautious before confirming a purchase. The spots are extremely important in judging this breed and in the ideal those on the body should not be smaller than a dime or larger than a half-dollar. The spots on the head and face should be smaller than on the body and should be separate and distinct with as little running together as possible. A well-put-together Dalmatian is a beautiful animal. People have apparently thought so since ancient times.

This active, spry busy-body is the national dog of Finland where it is known by the virtually unpronounceable name of *Suomenpystykorva*. Very little was done to establish standards for the breed until the end of the 19th Century, when a few enthusiasts travelled through northern Lapland looking for outstanding examples of a dog that had been known in the region for several thousand years. It was already the most popular and frequently encountered dog in both cities and on farms. It was known as an absolutely fierce hunter despite its relatively small size. ¶The ori-

gins of the Finnish Spitz remain a mystery in part because of its antiquity. It is said to have derived from the ubiquitous pariah dog that is found near human settlements around the world yet it is a typical northern spitz-type dog, a group that includes the Norwegian Elkhound, the Keeshond, and all of the sled dogs including the Samoyed and Husky from Siberia and the Malamute from Alaska. In any case, there is surely a good deal of wolf in the genes of this breed as there is in the genes of all of the northern dogs. That means more than the genes of their original wolf ancestor, but includes

Finnish Spitz

Land of origin: Ancient and not really known. Reportedly in FINLAND and LAPLAND for thousands of years.

Original purpose: Hunting—everything from squirrel to bear.

Recent popularity ranking by A.K.C. registration: 131st

Finnish Spitz Club of America
Richard A. Yates, Secretary
110 Knots Landing
Macon, GA 31210

HEIGHT: Dogs to 20 inches   Bitches to 18 inches

WEIGHT: Not in published standards

COAT
Double, short, soft, dense undercoat (which sheds out in warm weather) and long, harsh straight guard hairs measuring one to two inches on the body. Coat very important in judging. No trimming except for feet is allowed.

COLOR
Bright and clear, pale honey to deep auburn. Undercoat paler. Only white allowed is on tips of toes and quarter-sized spot or half inch wide white stripe on chest. Sparse, individual black hairs on tail and back allowed, the fewer the better.

Amount of care coat requires: 1 2 3 4 5 6 7 8 9 10
                                   •••••••••••••

Amount of exercise required: 1 2 3 4 5 6 7 8 9 10
                                 •••••••••••••

Suitability for urban/apartment life: 1 2 3 4 5 6 7 8 9 10
                                          •••••••••••••••••••••••

input along the way as the breed evolved in high northern latitudes. ¶It wasn't until 1927 that the first pair of the reconstructed Finnish Spitz was brought to Great Britain and seven years later that the Kennel Club accorded the breed recognition. By the early 1970s the breed began showing up in Canada and by 1974 it was recognized by the Canadian Kennel Club. It made its way south and is now recognized in the United States. It was well known here well before the time recognition came. It has been a long trip for a breed dearly beloved by all who own them. ¶The overall look of the Finnish Spitz is best described as foxy and very alert. It is a compact, solid little dog that should never be either coarse or snipey. It is a dog of balance and style. ¶On the first encounter with a stranger, a Finnish Spitz is likely to be cautious, but that should not mean shy. Shyness is a fault. When the ice has been broken the Finnish Spitz is typically friendly, active, very lively, and willing to engage in any game or activity. It is a brave little dog and faithfulness is to be expected and that means a good watchdog with a sharp alarm bark. ¶The Finnish Spitz makes a fine house pet as long as it gets a reasonable amount of exercise. Owners who are willing to give some care to that glorious reddish coat with the handsome neck and tail display, and who are able to attend a basic obedience course with their dog are certain to have a first class pet that is at once very well mannered and a splendid display piece. The affection part of the contract comes naturally to any healthy dog that is treated well.

If there is such a thing as a perfect apartment dog, the French Bulldog could be it. He certainly would be in the finals when the choice was made. This is a neat, clean, compact dog who sheds hardly at all, is easily trained, has nice manageable habits, and doesn't need or really want too much exercise. ¶The French Bulldog has nearly caused international incidents: the English laugh at the name, recognizing in the breed a miniature of the English Bulldog that didn't suit the English fancy and was exported to France; the French, in a kind of desperate thrashing around, claim him as an original. The English are undoubtedly right, but that's history, and it doesn't much

French Bulldog

Land of origin: ENGLAND and FRANCE

Original purpose: Companionship

Recent popularity ranking by A.K.C. registration: 81st

French Bulldog Club of America
Diana H. Young, Corres. Secretary
5451 Vance Jackson Rd.
San Antonio, TX 78230

HEIGHT: Dogs to 12 inches   Bitches to 12 inches

WEIGHT: Dogs to 28 pounds   Bitches to 22 pounds

COAT
Moderately fine, short, and smooth. Skin soft and loose.

COLOR
Solid brindle, fawn, white, brindle and white, and any colors except black and white, black and tan, liver, mouse, or solid black.

Amount of care coat requires: 1 2 3 4 5 6 7 8 9 10
                                       •

Amount of exercise required: 1 2 3 4 5 6 7 8 9 10
                                     • • • • •

Suitability for urban/apartment life: 1 2 3 4 5 6 7 8 9 10
                                              • •

matter. What does matter is that the French Bulldog is an outstanding companion animal under the right circumstances. ¶The ideal situation for this breed is an apartment or house with a single person. The French Bulldog does not like to share and is not keen on strangers. This breed is also less than perfect with children. That is not to say that a French Bulldog would not settle down and become a good family dog—the family including a parcel of youngsters—because a great many have. It is just that if one were to seek the ideal setting, it would be with one person in need of getting and giving boundless affection and one French Bulldog in the same situation. ¶The overall impression one gets from one of these little companions is of a muscular, alert animal of good substance and intelligence. And all of that is true. Size is important, and dogs over twenty-eight pounds in weight are disqualified from showing. ¶If a person wants to show a dog, this is a good breed to consider. There aren't too many of them around, so the competition is not overwhelming, and the dog is easy to transport because of his small size. His coat requires virtually no care, so there is not a lot of get-ready time. Pick up your dog and walk into the ring ready to go. ¶A single person seeking both love and involvement might find owning and showing a French Bulldog just about a perfect outlet. None of this should discourage other categories of owners, though, for this dog also will be happy on a farm. He may not do a heck of a lot of work, but he will be happy as long as he has access to his special person. And there is always a special person in the life of a French Bulldog.

The Keeshond (the plural form is *Kees-honden*) has a complex and colorful history. In the period just before the French Revolution, the followers of the Prince of Orange, known as the Partisans, were vying with a group known as the Patriots to become the dominant political force in Holland. The leader of the Patriots was a man called Kees de Gyselaer of Dordrecht. He owned a dog, also called Kees, an example of a breed we know today as the Kees-hond. The dog became the symbol of the Patriots, a part of working-class people. ¶In time the Prince of Orange prevailed, and a lot of people apparently felt it best not to have living symbols of the opposition around the house. The Keeshond did not so much fall from favor as vanish for safety reasons. Once seen on all the small barges moving along the canals and in almost every farmhouse, the Keeshond soon became something of a rarity. About 1920 the

Keeshond

Land of origin: HOLLAND

Original purpose: Companionship and as watchdog

Recent popularity ranking by A.K.C. registration: 47th

Keeshond Club of America, Inc.
Tawn Sinclair, Corres. Secretary
11782 Pacific Coast Hwy.
Malibu, CA 90265

HEIGHT: Dogs to 18 inches   Bitches to 17 inches

WEIGHT: Dogs to 40 pounds   Bitches to 36 pounds

COAT
Abundant, long, straight, harsh, and off-standing. Thick downy undercoat. On legs, smooth and short except for feathering. On tail, profuse and plumelike. Never silky, wavy, or curly and not parting on back.

COLOR
Mixture of gray and black. Undercoat pale gray or cream. Outer-coat hairs black tipped. White markings not allowed. Dark spectacle markings on face typical and desirable.

Amount of care coat requires: 1 2 3 4 5 6 7 8 9 10

Amount of exercise required: 1 2 3 4 5 6 7 8 9 10

*Suitability for urban/apartment life:**   1 2 3 4 5 6 7 8 9 10

†As long as proper exercise is provided.

Baroness van Hardenbroek took an interest in the breed and found enough good examples still left to re-establish it in Holland and, since then, around the world. ¶The Keeshond is another perfect house dog. Handsome, small, and companionable, he is generally quieter and perhaps more sensible than the other spitzlike breeds to which he is related. All the relationships have not been worked out, but it is likely the Keeshond has common ancestry with the Pomeranian, Samoyed, Norwegian Elkhound, and Finnish Spitz. ¶The splendid little Hollander depends a great deal on his handsome coat for his high style, and there is daily work involved in keeping it in good condition. The hair is brushed against the grain to keep it off-standing. Since washing tends to soften hair and make it floppy, the Keeshond is seldom, if ever, bathed. ¶The Keeshond is a loyal, loving family dog and a good watchdog, and he is easygoing with other animals. He does not take immediately to strangers but will accept those who do not appear to be threatening to his home and family. He should be walked regularly, of course, but the Keeshond does well in the suburban home and the apartment. This dog has an engaging personality and a lot of style. Mass-producers and retailers have tended to make something of a mess of this breed, producing outsized and unpleasant-looking specimens, so the prospective Keeshond owner should head for the specialty breeder. The Keeshond seldom disappoints the new owner who has taken the time and trouble to learn about the breed and to seek a fine specimen. Charming in the show-ring and never failing to attract attention, they are equally desirable as family pets.

The Lhasa Apso, one of the four breeds that we know came from the mountains of Tibet, was the small companion animal kept inside the house to warn of intruders. Outside was the fierce Tibetan Mastiff. The Lhasa Apso, because he was the inside dog, naturally became a pet. He is bred for that role today and is rapidly increasing in popularity. Aiding his rise in favor is the fact that he is a perfect city companion and has high style and charm. ¶Lhasa Apsos are devoted to their masters and mistresses and to their families. They are forever suspicious of strangers, a characteristic that harks back to their early role as watchdogs. Strangers coming into the

Lhasa Apso

Land of origin: TIBET

Original purpose: Companionship and as inside watchdog

Recent popularity ranking by A.K.C. registration: 28th

American Lhasa Apso Club, Inc.
Amy Andrews, Secretary
18105 Kirkshire
Beverly Hills, MI 48025

HEIGHT: Dogs to 11 inches   Bitches to 10½ inches

WEIGHT: Dogs to 15 pounds   Bitches to 14 pounds

COAT
Heavy, straight, hard, and dense. Not woolly or silky. Long.

COLOR
Golden, sandy, honey, dark grizzle, slate, smoke, parti-color, black, white, or brown. Golden or lionlike colors are considered best. Dark tips to ears and beard very good.

Amount of care coat requires: 1 2 3 4 5 6 7 8 9 10

Amount of exercise required: 1 2 3 4 5 6 7 8 9 10

Suitability for urban/apartment life: 1 2 3 4 5 6 7 8 9 10

home should let them be, and allow them to make any overtures. Pushing yourself on a strange Lhasa Apso is one way of forcing an issue and making him snappy. ¶ Because the Lhasa Apso is such a demanding pet, this is not always the best breed to have around young children. He will be in direct competition for the role of baby of the house and will tend to be jealous and resentful. This is a strong-minded, purposeful little animal, not a pushover in any category. The owner should establish at the start who is to be master of the house. The Lhasa Apso is perfectly willing to take over and become a splendid despot, and if that happens only the owner is to blame. ¶ The coat of the Lhasa Apso, one of his shining highlights, does require care, considerable care, and enough time should be left each day to bring it up to full glory and keep it there. The Lhasa Apso will compensate for the time you spend on his coat by not demanding long walks in nasty weather. Although his typical Tibetan coat (all Tibetan dogs apparently have that heavy coat and the upcurled tail seen in this breed) will enable him to withstand any weather you are likely to encounter, the dog does not crave long walks and is happy around the house. ¶ The Lhasa will take training readily and will always strive to please family members. He is playful and affectionate and loyal. He has risen so suddenly in popularity in the last few years that it is wise to be careful when making a purchase. Make sure you are getting a really good puppy from a truly good line or you will inherit a bundle of bad manners and disappointing conformation.

No one really knows where the Poodle originally came from. It almost certainly is not France, despite the fact that he is so often referred to as the French Poodle. It may have been Germany, although even that is doubtful. The breed is probably of great antiquity. ¶Almost everywhere in the world that the breed is known it is at the top of the popularity chart. In the United States it is consistently in first place. Many reasons are put forward for this phenomenon, but the answer probably lies in intelligence. The Poodle is one of the most intelligent of all dogs. He seems able to learn anything, he makes a fine watchdog, and he is an excellent water retriever. We are told that the exaggerated clips we see today are outgrowths of clips that facilitated the retrieving Poodle in water. The name *Poodle* is derived from the German slang word *pudelin*, which means, roughly, to splash around in the water.

Poodle

Land of origin: Possibly GERMANY but not really known

Original purpose: Probably water retrieving

Recent popularity ranking by A.K.C. registration: 5th

Poodle Club of America, Inc.
Mr. Charles Thomasson, Corres. Secretary
503 Martineau Dr.
Chester, VA 23831-5753

HEIGHT:

Standard—dogs and bitches over 15 inches

Miniature—dogs and bitches between 10 and 15 inches

WEIGHT:

Standard—Dogs to 55 pounds   Bitches to 50 pounds

Miniature—*Dogs to 16 pounds   Bitches to 15 pounds

COAT
Naturally harsh in texture, extremely profuse and dense. Seen in a variety of clips.

COLOR
Solid only, never parti-colored. Colors seen include blue, gray, silver, brown, café au lait, apricot, cream, black, and white.

Amount of care coat requires:† 1 2 3 4 5 6 7 8 9 10

Amount of exercise required:‡ 1 2 3 4 5 6 7 8 9 10

Suitability for urban/apartment life:§ 1 2 3 4 5 6 7 8 9 10

*See Toy Poodle for specifications of that variety.
†Varies somewhat with style of clip and age of dog.
‡Larger varieties require more
§If appropriate exercise is provided.

¶The Poodle in his magnificent show clip is the brunt of many jokes, and the uninformed sometimes see it as an effete kind of status symbol. Were they to know! The Poodle in any clip is a superb dog—assertive, extremely responsive, loyal, and intelligent beyond belief. ¶Because Poodles come in such a variety of colors and can be clipped in so many ways, they serve any taste. That, too, no doubt, has added to their popularity. They do not shed, although their hair is fast growing and has no apparent maximum length. It keeps right on growing as long as you let it. It does need regular clip-ping and styling—every four to six weeks—and that is a chore many people prefer to leave to the experts. It is not inexpensive, but the Poodle, owners feel, are worth the investment. ¶Poodles get along well with children, and with other dogs and cats. They fit in and respond to the people around them in an almost uncanny way. A Poodle in the family is truly like having an extra person on hand. There is nothing Poodles do not seem to understand. They are, as a result, immensely popular and probably will be for a long time to come.

The Schipperke, a dog from the Flemish areas of Belgium and to some extent northern France, is not of spitz derivation, although this has been suggested. He is bred down from the Belgian Sheepdog and is a version of the sheepdog known as the Leauvenaar. The name *Schipperke* (pronounced *skip-er-key*) is Flemish for "little captain" and refers to his use as a watchdog on barges that plied the rivers and canals of norther Europe. ¶Generally an outstanding pet, the Schipperke is a born watchdog. Though not argumentative or snappy, he is very curious about everything that is going on around him. He checks out things and people and will be quick to let you know if

Schipperke

Land of origin: FLEMISH BELGIUM

Original purpose: House companionship and as watchdog

Recent popularity ranking by A.K.C. registration: 50th

Schipperke Club of America, Inc.
Bonnie Lou Baker, Secretary
22955 West 244th St.
Paola, KS 66071-9232

HEIGHT: Dogs to 13 inches   Bitches to 12 inches

WEIGHT: Dogs to 18 pounds   Bitches to 16 pounds

COAT
Abundant, longer on neck, forming ruff or cape. Undercoat short and dense. Outer coat somewhat harsh to touch.

COLOR
Solid black only.

Amount of care coat requires: 1 2 3 4 5 6 7 8 9 10
                        ••••

Amount of exercise required: 1 2 3 4 5 6 7 8 9 10
                     ••••••••••••••••

Suitability for urban/apartment life:*   1 2 3 4 5 6 7 8 9 10
                     •••••••••••••••••••••••

*If properly exercised.

he finds anything amiss. He is a vivacious dog, intelligent, loyal, and very responsive to his own family and their likes and needs. He has one outstanding specialty, though: children. He is naturally drawn to them and watches them constantly. He is not only their companion but also their guardian. His small size makes him an ideal house pet. ¶The bobbed tail and foxy face of this lively little outdoor dog is most distinctive, and the breed just can't be confused with any other. He does well on the farm, where he makes a good ratter, and he has been used to hunt small game; he will be equally fine in the suburbs and the city. In an apartment there is an obligation to provide exercise. The Schipperke needs walks several times a day, and in the country a good romp is deeply appreciated. ¶The Schipperke's coat is deep and sheds water. It will take any weather and does shed out in the summer. It is easy to care for, and a good brushing a couple of times a week will keep it in order. ¶The Schipperke, while never a fad dog in this country, has a devoted following. People who get to know the many fine qualities of this breed tend to stick with it. It is a long-lived breed, and more than a few individual dogs have been known to reach seventeen or eighteen years. Schipperkes are strong, durable, healthy, and easy to keep.

Shiba Inu

Land of origin: JAPAN

Original purpose: Hunting

Recent popularity ranking by A.K.C. registration: 75th

National Shiba Club of America
Jacey Holden, Secretary
3991 W. Peltier Rd.
Lodi, CA 95242

HEIGHT: Dogs to 16½ inches   Bitches to 15½ inches

WEIGHT: ". . . in proportion to height"

COAT
Double, natural, outer coat strong and straight. Ruff permitted but no trimming allowed. Long, woolly or wavy coats are faults.

COLOR
Important in judging: red, red sesame (red with a light black overlay), black and tan with markings that give a foxy look—"vague" white (not snow white) on sides of muzzle (not over it) and on the cheeks, lower jaw, neck, chest, and stomach. Some white allowed underneath.

Amount of care coat requires: 1 2 3 4 5 6 7 8 9 10
••••••••••

Amount of exercise required: 1 2 3 4 5 6 7 8 9 10
••••••••••••••••

Suitability for urban/apartment life: 1 2 3 4 5 6 7 8 9 10
••••••••••••••••••••••••

The Shiba Inu was designated a "precious natural product" by authority of the Cultural Properties Act of Japan in 1936, so highly regarded is this foxy little hunting dog in his native land. He is, as well, a very good watch dog and a smart little companion. In Japan, in his native mountainous terrain, he was used on big game, once upon a time. But he is now considered a dog for small game as he himself has been kept as small in size as he is smart in appearance. ¶The Shiba Inu has something special to offer dog fanciers, the opportunity to get in on the ground floor. There are still relatively few in this country and the breed's popularity seems certain. The first ones ever seen on this side of the Pacific, as far as we know, appeared in 1954 when returning U.S. servicemen brought some back with them. The first litter born in the United States was whelped in 1979. It is a very new breed to America and there is the chance to help define its future. ¶The Shiba Inu is smart, compact, well-boned, well-muscled and very well proportioned. He is a neat, active little dog and a perfect size for house or apartment living. He should be spirited but never sharp in temperament. Personality does not require temper and the Shiba Inu should not display it. Ideally he does not. ¶Whether for show or companionship—or both—the Shiba Inu has a lot to offer experienced dog fanciers as well as newcomers to the field.

The *exact* origin of this ancient breed cannot be established. It was almost certainly somewhere in or near Tibet or China, however. This gay little sprite is related to the Pekingese, Pug, and Japanese Chin but is distinctly not a spaniel anymore than the Tibetan Terrier is a terrier. It is believed that the breed did finally evolve in closely-guarded kennels in Tibetan monasteries. It has been called the Tibetan prayer dog because one of its duties is said to have been to turn the prayer wheels. It was probably more heavily relied upon as a companion, good luck charm, and watch dog. It is still doing those jobs today although the good luck part is really a matter of personal faith. ¶The first Tibetan Spaniels in the U.K. arrived in 1920. In the mid-60's they began appearing in North America. The breed is now recognized in the United

Tibetan Spaniel

Land of origin: TIBET/CHINA

Recent popularity ranking by A.K.C. registration: 105th

Tibetan Spaniel Club of America
Valerie Robinson, Corres. Secretary
103 Old Colony Dr.
Mashpee, MA 02649

HEIGHT: About 10 inches

WEIGHT: 9 to 15 pounds

COAT
Double, silky, smooth on face and front of legs, moderate on body but lies rather flat. Ears and back of legs well feathered.

COLOR
All colors and mixture of colors allowed.

Amount of care coat requires: 1 2 3 4 5 6 7 8 9 10

Amount of exercise required: 1 2 3 4 5 6 7 8 9 10

Suitability for urban/apartment life: 1 2 3 4 5 6 7 8 9 10

States and Canada. This little dog is typically gay and very assertive. It is active and alert and is extremely intelligent, enough so to be overtly manipulative. Although it tends to be aloof with strangers it is deeply involved in everything that goes on within its family circle. It likes to initiate as much of that activity as possible but will be happy playing by your game plan as long as it is in the thick of things. It is not a passive animal. You can't be when you believe the world was invented for your personal enjoyment. ¶Despite its obvious antiquity the Tibetan Spaniel is a "new breed" to the West and therefore offers an opportunity to get in on the formation years where the Western version of the breed is developed. It will probably become one of those very popular breeds, well suited to relatively small living quarters. It has a quality badly needed by millions of people, it gives humans the sense of being needed. A great many people do need to be needed and that kind of situation suits the Tibetan Spaniel just fine. ¶This breed requires enough coat care to keep the owner-pet interaction regular and ideally routine. That is good for both man and beast. It is a pretty little dog and that provides a sense of pride. Tibetan Spaniels take very readily to being spoiled and that works well in the relationship between dog and owner, too. For many kinds of people the Tibetan Spaniel is a breed made in heaven. It is supposed by many that that is where the monasteries of the Himalayas are. ¶When a dog so perfectly fits so many human personality types and needs it must be reckoned a welcome addition to our national canine picture. One thing is certain, the Tibetan Spaniel, vain little commander that he is, is sure that that is the case.

Tibetan Terrier

Land of origin: TIBET

Original purpose: As mascot and watchdog; was held sacred

Recent popularity ranking by A.K.C. registration: 87th

Tibetan Terrier Club of America, Inc.
Ms. Brenda Brown, Secretary
127 Springlea Dr.
Winfield, WV 25213

HEIGHT: Dogs to 16 inches   Bitches to 16 inches

WEIGHT: Dogs to 23 pounds   Bitches to 22 pounds

COAT
Double—undercoat is a fine wool; outer coat profuse and fine but not silky or woolly, long and either straight or waved.

COLOR
Any color, including white, or any combination of colors. Nose must be black.

Amount of care coat requires: 1 2 3 4 5 6 7 8 9 10

Amount of exercise required: 1 2 3 4 5 6 7 8 9 10

Suitability for urban/apartment life:*   1 2 3 4 5 6 7 8 9 10

*If properly exercised.

The Tibetan Terrier is another of those Asian breeds that comes down to us from ancient times loaded with legend, romance, and tradition. The Tibetan Terrier was said to have been bred exclusively by monks in a hidden valley and only given as gifts to honored friends (usually visiting monks), never sold. Only males were ever given, and these sometimes were crossed with the so-called Tibetan Spaniels. The dog was slow in reaching the outside world and is now attracting a great deal of attention. ¶The Tibetan Terrier is distinctly *not* a terrier. He was named that years ago when all large dogs were called *guard dogs,* all medium-sized dogs *hunting dogs,* and all small breeds *terriers.* It is doubtful that there is a trace of terrier in the breed; a more likely choice would be a spaniel-like dog and some small form of mastiff. Misnamed or not, the Tibetan Terrier is a fine, solid little character and one treasured by those lucky enough to own examples.

They are good watchdogs, being slow to take up with strangers. They are busybodies and participators. In the city they can tolerate limited exercise, but they love a good romp, particularly in the country. ¶The look of the Tibetan terrier is solid and square. He moves well, and although not "hyper" and silly, he is active and playful. He is fetching as a puppy and should become popular fairly quickly now that he is here and has American Kennel Club recognition (approved in 1973). Tibetan Terriers still vary in size, and no doubt a preference will be shown in the years ahead and the standards altered accordingly. ¶There is a studied ragamuffin look about the Tibetan Terrier, but the coat does require some attention every day or it can become tangled. ¶This breed is bound to become a super niche fitter. The real popularity days of the Tibetan Terrier may be just ahead.

Afterword

If you have this book, it is reasonable to assume you have an interest in dogs, or at least *a* dog. There are some matters that transcend breed, however, and have a great deal to do with all dog owners.

Don't breed your own pet, except in truly exceptional cases. The individual dogs photographed by Alton Anderson for this book are outstanding representatives of their kind. Many of them are the best examples in the United States today, or at least they have won more Best-of-Breed, Group 1's, and Best-in-Show ribbons than nearly all other members of their breed now alive. The chances are your pet will not look quite as much like the idealized dog as these specimens do. Unless you pay a considerable amount of money for your pet, and then are very lucky, your dog will be a lovable example of what we call *pet quality*. No pet-quality dog should ever be bred, for the following simple reason: There are already far too many puppies. The shelters, pounds, and humane societies in this country destroy between thirteen and fifteen million puppies and kittens every year—many of which are pure-bred (not that it matters if a homeless puppy is pure-bred or random-bred). Or perhaps there are far too few suitable homes. Either way, the tragedy can be reduced in dimensions only if fewer puppies are born.

What dogs should be bred? Only those that are such outstanding examples of their breed that their individual genetic potential is really needed for the continuation and even the improvement of the breed. These finest dogs will produce more than enough pet-quality puppies in time to fulfill most people's desire to own an example of one breed or another.

So again, unless you have invested heavily in a dog and have shown it all the way through to champion status, do not allow it to produce puppies that will add to that already tragic surplus. Even if you find homes, good homes, for each of the puppies you allow to come into this world, you will be killing another puppy. For each one you place, another will sit unadopted in a cage until its time runs out. You will have used up a home. *One puppy placed is another puppy killed.* Sad, but it is the truth.

What about random-bred dogs, so called mutts or mongrels? All dog breeds were mixed at some stage in their development. The histories of those breeds that came into being in recent enough times for records to survive show a blending of several and sometimes many breeds to achieve a desired result. With the mixed-breed dog found today by the millions in shelters, the mix is admittedly random and the result that will be produced—what the puppy will look like when it matures, for example—is not easily predictable. But an interest in pure-bred dogs should not be an exercise in snobbery. Random-bred dogs can make magnificent pets and fit in very well in a multi-dog household. Nevertheless, all random-bred animals, males as well as females, should be neutered as soon as your veterinarian says it is safe to do so. No random-bred animal should ever be bred, again because of the staggering surplus.

I have stressed time and again in the breed descriptions that certain dogs should be obedience trained professionally, or that the dog in question will make a much better pet if a professional guides you in your training regimen. That advice can be misleading only in that I did not stress it in every breed description. I should have. All dogs are better for obedience training; all kinds of problems with housebreaking, chewing, barking, car chasing, wandering, and a good many more irksome traits, can generally be solved by basic obedience training. Just *Come, Sit, Stay, Down, Heel*, and most especially *No* are usually enough to turn a monster of a dog into a mature and stable friend.

Somewhere near where you live there is a humane society struggling to stay alive and carry out its mission of mercy and humane education. If you care enough about dogs to own one, care enough to help out. Locate the humane society nearest you and pitch in. If you can't spare time, perhaps you can spare dollars. If pet owners don't care to help other pets in trouble, who will? On the national level I think the American Society for the Prevention of Cruelty to Animals (ASPCA, 424 East 92nd St., New York, N.Y. 10128) is the one to join. Why not write to them and find out what they are doing to help solve the seemingly endless array of humane problems this country faces.

When you accept the responsibility of a dog you should give careful consideration to your friends and neighbors. Their affection for, even toler-ance of dogs may be limited in some cases. Don't let your dog become a nuisance, and never let it become a menace. Your neighbor's shrubs are not for wetting, and no one wants to hear your dog bark and yowl. No one, cer-tainly, wants to have their kid thrown from a bicycle or their car charged by an ill-mannered dog. All of those matters must be under your firm control. Your dogs must fit in and be good citizens.

Man apparently began keeping dogs about twenty thousand years ago. There were pure-bred dogs almost ten thousand years ago. There must be something to it. Of course, there is. It is a fine idea, one of the most durable man has ever had. And since it is such a good idea, it is worth doing right. Congratulations on your decision to get a dog; once that decision has been made, pick wisely and love a lot. You will be rewarded with ten to fifteen years of enormous pleasure.

Roger Caras

Photographer's Note

In photographing the dogs for this book I have often felt I was hobnobbing with royalty—the dog's aristocracy deriving not only from their distinguished ancestry, the result of great breeding, but also from their crowns earned in ring competition. Many of the dogs are at the very top of their breed. Even included is the number one champion of all breeds in the country—the white poodle.

The great ones have usually been the easiest to photograph. Their ring presence carries over into their photographs. Consider the Irish Setter: When I asked the professional handler to have him turn his head "a little bit this way," the dog understood and did it!

Any camera can take good dog pictures. All it requires is some knowledge of the breed you're photographing and, most important, patience and practice. Try to photograph only in bright sunlight. You need the brilliant light to give the coat sparkle and "aliveness."

Although I usually shoot about fifty pictures at a dog sitting, I consider myself fortunate if I end up with one outstanding portrait. On rare occasions almost every exposure results in a good picture, but some breeds, notably terriers, are such bundles of motion that a good picture requires great patience.

You may have noticed that the full-dog photos in this book are without a handler holding up a tail or head. What I was trying to do was to portray these champion dogs the way most of us see our dogs: outdoors and around the house, sitting and lying down, in relaxed attitudes.

In photographing the many breeds (some of them very rare), professional handlers were most helpful, and I appreciate their kindness. Among area people I thank Ele (Eleanor) Wilson; Roger Cornell, who owns a fictitious guard dog and has dire warnings posted on his exterior doors; Bob and Sylvia Sherman, color processors who were often baffled by dog coat colors, since they have been conditioned to human flesh tones; and, finally, Allen and Mara Borack, conversion (color-to-black-and-white, panalure) experts, whose love of dogs was so evident. What wonderful people!

Alton Anderson

Index

SOCCER
FUNDAMENTALS

SOCCER
FUNDAMENTALS

Basic Techniques and Training for
Beginning Players

by John Learmouth

Artwork by Bob Hogarth
Photographs by Brian Raven

St. Martin's Press, New York

By the same author
THE YOUNG GYMNAST

Library of Congress Cataloging in Publication Data

Learmouth, John.
  Soccer fundamentals.

  1. Soccer.   I. Title.
GV943.L394   796.33'4   78-19415
ISBN 0-312-73132-9
ISBN 0-312-73133-7 pbk.

Contents

This book is dedicated to all those American young-sters who are in the process of discovering the joys of soccer—the activity that Pelé describes as "the beau-tiful game."

Acknowledgments

My grateful thanks are due to my wife Gwen, who, as my coauthor, has done all the research and all the other unglamorous but vital work that kept me supplied with working material. They are also due to Brian Raven for the photographs, to Bob Hogarth for the artwork, and to Joyce Braithwaite for producing the manuscript in record time. My especial thanks go to:

John Dunne
Craig Halstead   of Warley Road Junior School,
Neil Jepson   Halifax
Richard Smith

Simon Bairstow
Paul Dunn   of Holy Trinity (C.E.) Junior School,
Andrew Ingle   Halifax
Philip Orrell

Anthony Lewis
Nicholas Richardson   of St. Mary's (R.C.) Junior School,
Jeremy Starsmore   Halifax

Rainford Bowley   of J.H. Whitleu Secondary School,
                     Halifax
Gary Hughes   of Sowerby Bridge Grammar School,
                     Halifax
who endured the discomforts of several very cold winter
days when we had the photographs taken.

Thanks also to Mitre Sports Ltd. of Huddersfield,
England, for supplying the Multiplex and Mouldmaster
balls and the soccer shoes for the boys.

J. K. L.
Huddersfield
England

APRIL 1978

SOCCER FUNDAMENTALS

About the Game

"Soccer" is a funny word, and certainly a strange name for a game. The names of other games usually tell you something about the game. For instance, basketball suggests that the game has something to do with a ball and a basket; baseball tells you that the game is concerned with bases and a ball. But "soccer" tells you nothing about the game. The word "soccer" is English schoolboy slang, from the last century. This is how the game came to be known by that name.

In England, a school which is called a public school is, in fact, a private school—usually a boarding school—and parents pay high fees to enable their children to attend such schools. In the middle of the last century, team ball games formed the entire physical education program in the public schools, and during the winter, they all played football. Each school had its own type of football: some played a kind of football where the ball was an oval sort of shape, and was mostly *handled* rather than kicked. Others used a ball which was nearer in shape to being round, and which was *kicked* most of the time, but sometimes handled. Some schools had rules concerning how many players should play in each team, while others allowed a team to field as many players as it could find.

Many of the boys from these schools went on to college, Oxford or Cambridge, and they wanted to continue playing football as a pastime. However, since they all came from different schools, they could not agree on how the game should be played. They all wanted to play according to the rules of their former schools. Eventually, a group of students from schools where football had been a game where the ball was mainly kicked agreed to a set of rules so that they could form teams and play matches. This happened at Cambridge, and, shortly afterward, in 1863, a meeting of followers of the kicking game got together in

London and formed the Football Association, which became the ruling body of the game in England, and the model for other national associations.

An interesting side effect of this was that, at the time the Football Association was formed, those who preferred the handling type of football found themselves outside the Association, and with no fixed set of rules under which they could play. They then got together and formed a "union" of those who wished to play the handling game in a manner similar to the way it was played at Rugby School. Thus was formed The Rugby Football Union, which became the governing body for the handling game as it was, and still is, played in England and other parts of the world.

At that time, a favorite form of slang among public schoolboys and the alumni of these public schools was to shorten a word and then add "er" to the end of it. Using this slang, they called breakfast "brekker," a preparatory school was a "prepper," and so on. And so, quite naturally, Rugby Football became "rugger" and Association Football became known as "Assocc" and then "soccer."

If you think of all the different forms of football that you may know—American Football, Association Football, Gaelic Football, Rugby Football, Australian Rules Football, and so on-you might think it rather strange that they are all called football, when, in fact, Association Football, or soccer, is the only one where the game mainly involves kicking a ball with the foot. All the others concentrate more on running with the ball in the hands and passing it from hand to hand. In many countries, particularly on the continent of Europe, soccer is called football, but that is probably because the countries concerned have not got another form of football game of their own.

The organization which controls soccer throughout the world is the *Fédération Internationale de Football Association*, generally known as FIFA. Any country may have its own rules for soccer, but if a team from one country wishes to play against a team from another country, then both teams must play under FIFA rules. What FIFA has done is exactly the same as what that first Association did in England, in 1863: it has made sure everyone plays under the same rules, throughout the world.

The rules of soccer are simple, and there are not many of them. This is one of the reasons why so many people all over the world play soccer, or watch it, as spectators. Because there are not too many rules, the referee is not continually blowing his whistle to stop play, and so the game flows, and this makes it fun to watch. Of course, there used to be all sorts of rules saying things like, "players must remove their hats before heading the ball"—necessary in the early days because all the players would wear hats of different kinds when playing. Nowadays, however, the rules are easy to understand and remember. When you start playing, all you really need to know is that:

1. When play is going on, no player except the goalkeeper is allowed to touch the ball with his hand or arm;
2. No player may hit, kick, trip, push, or jump at another player;
3. The playing area should be marked like this:

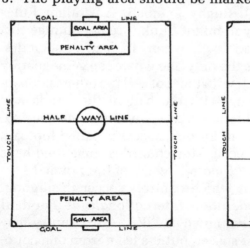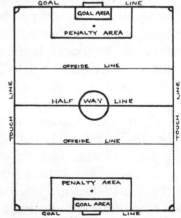

PLAYING PITCH F·I·F·A· REGULATIONS   PLAYING PITCH N·A·S·L· REGULATIONS

The rules of the North American Soccer League require the inclusion of an extra line in each half of the field,
thirty-five yards from the goal line. These are "offside
lines" and an attacking player can only be offside, under
NASL rules, if he is between the offside line and the goal
he is attacking when the ball is played. This is different
from the FIFA offside rule, which says that a player is
offside if he is between the center line and the goal he is
attacking when the ball is played.

Also, the NASL rules call for a "shoot out" to decide
the result of a game which is tied at the end of the normal
period of playing time. FIFA rules do not allow the "shoot
out." Thus, the final result of a game under NASL rules
cannot be a tie, while under FIFA rules it can. There are
eleven players on a full team. I use the term "full team"
because there is nothing to prevent playing the game with
a smaller number of players on each team. Seven, six, or five
on a team are very popular numbers for boys' games.

A full team may adopt any one of several playing
formations. The position of the goalkeeper is fixed, because he has to guard the goal, but the other ten players
may be positioned either in a 4−2−4 formation, like this:

Goalkeeper

Right Fullback   Right Center Back   Left Center Back   Left Fullback

Right Midfield   Left Midfield

Right Winger   Striker   Striker   Left Winger

or a 4−3−3 formation, like this:

Goalkeeper

Right Fullback   Right Center Back   Left Center Back   Left Fullback

Right Midfield   Center Midfield   Left Midfield

Striker   Striker   Striker

or a 4−4−2 formation, like this:

Goalkeeper

Right Fullback   Right Center Back   Left Center Back   Left Fullback

Right Midfield 1   Right Midfield 2   Left Midfield 1   Left Midfield 2

Striker   Striker

The formation that a team adopts is decided according to the strengths and weaknesses of its players, the strengths and weaknesses of its opponents, and the overall policy for the match—that is, mainly attacking or mainly defensive. There is no magic about any system. No single system can make a poor team good. Any system can be only as good as the players using it. You will see many variations of these systems—and some that are totally different.

Any system that any team uses or invents, however, is built on the various players:

1. A goalkeeper;
2. Players who have special defensive skills. (These are the "backs" and they form the line of defense in front of the goal. Many of them also possess first-class attacking skills, which they use as the situation demands.);
3. Players who have both attacking and defending skills. (These midfield players must have the stamina to assist in an attack at one minute, and be a hundred yards back the next minute, helping out with the defense. They must also be very skilled in setting up attacking situations, because most attacks start from the midfield.);
4. Players with special attacking skills. (These are the front line of attack, and may be known as "strikers," or sometimes as "wingers" if they operate mainly along the sides of the field. The strikers and wingers are expected to score most of the goals.)

The only true specialist, however, is the goalkeeper. The rules of the game fix his position so that he really cannot do anything other than use his goalkeeping skills, while the other ten players have to consider themselves as interchangeable, no matter what special skills they have. A back who cannot set up, take part in, and sometimes finish off an attack is only half a player. The same is true of a striker who cannot play an effective defensive role when necessary. It is often said in soccer that the team that controls the middle of the playing field wins. This means that the midfield players have got to be able both to win the ball in the tackle and then make good use of it to set up an attack.

It is a great mistake for any young player to tie a label on himself as, say, a striker or a center back. Many of the greatest players started their careers in a different position from the one in which they achieved real success. Aim to become a good soccer player first, and try out for different positions. Never be afraid to try a new one. Pele, Bobby Moore, and Franz Beckenbauer would all have been great players in *any* position.

PLAYING EQUIPMENT

Fortunately, the clothing and equipment needed for soccer is not expensive—or perhaps I should say that it need not be expensive. If you are playing for a team it is probable that your jersey, at least, will be supplied. For practice, a T-shirt makes a very acceptable jersey and any shorts will do, but whether you are practicing or playing "for real," you do need a good, well-fitting, and comfortable pair of football boots, or shoes. That is not to say that you cannot practice in a pair of tennis shoes—many professionals do so when the ground is hard—but you need a good pair of boots for match play and you need to wear them in practice so that they become as comfortable as a glove.

For a boy, I would always recommend boots, which are made slightly higher in the ankle than are the low-cut shoes. Any footballer has four joints which are constantly under strain during play—his knees and his ankles. There is not a lot that anyone can do to protect the knee from strain when playing games (knee injuries tend to be the result of bad luck as much as anything), but while the bones are still growing, ankles should be supported as much as possible to help prevent injury. A boot that gives some support to the ankle is therefore much better for boys than is the low-cut shoe. A bad ankle injury to a boy can finish him as a games player for the rest of his life, and so it is simply foolish to take unnecessary risks.

Much the same reasoning applies to the wearing of shin guards. Why risk a bad bruising, or worse, when there is a perfectly good and simple piece of equipment designed to protect you? Shin guards, these days, are light and comfortable to wear, and they are designed to protect you. If you want to be a soccer player, or a footballer of any kind, your legs are your most valuable asset—so look after them.

Soccer balls are obtainable in different materials, including leather, various plastics and laminates. For practice, it does not really matter which type of ball you use, provided it is the correct size and weight. For players up to the age of ten years, size three is recommended, and the ball should weigh eleven and one-half ounces. Players over the age of ten should use a size four ball, weighing twelve and one-half ounces. Any practice, done with any ball, is good practice, however, and many of today's star players learned most of their individual skills as youngsters, using old tennis balls, or, indeed, any ball they could find.

The Practice Grid

In Britain, where soccer is on the curriculum of almost all schools with pupils over the age of seven years, many schools and soccer clubs use a practice grid. This is sometimes marked out on grass, but more often on a hard surface—an asphalted school yard or something similar. The hard surface is more popular since the lines can be painted and will remain visible and usable for long periods, and since the surface is unaffected by weather, except for snow and ice. The great benefit of a practice grid is that a large number of players can practice the same, or different, skills within a limited area. This makes it easier for the teacher or coach to keep contact with the whole group while being able to give help to individuals where needed. As far as the players are concerned, each small group is working within a small area (10 yds x 10 yds) with clearly defined boundary lines, and this makes it necessary to use greater control, which makes them better players. The whole grid can be subdivided to make fields for small games, such as four against four.

Typical layouts for a practice grid are:

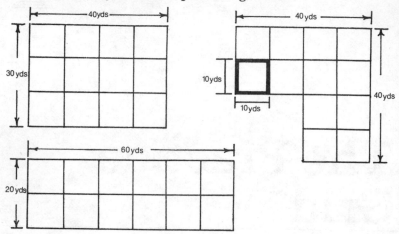

Each contains twelve squares, 10 yds x 10 yds, and the type of layout depends upon the shape of the space available. Each square is large enough for use by three or four players engaged in the type of game which helps them to master the basic skills, such as "Two on one," "Three on one," "Poison!" "Number passing," and numerous others.

It might be difficult to find such a grid in which to practice, but it is always a good idea to use a marked space of about eighty-five square yards in area. It need not be square—an oblong or even a circle will do—provided it has clearly marked boundaries. Although soccer is played on a fairly large field, you will find that, in a game, when you have got the ball, the area within which you have to do what you want to do is fairly small—you haven't got a lot of space to work in, because opponents are trying to crowd in on you. It is, therefore, very wise to learn to work in the sort of restricted area that a practice square provides, and it does not really matter what shape it is. The practice grid uses squares only because it is more convenient to site and easier to mark that way.

3

Passing and Dribbling

One of the special points to remember about soccer is that, except for the goalkeeper, everybody has to be able to do everything. There are no specialist kickers, specialist headers, or specialist runners—every player must be master of all the skills. The most frequently used skill is kicking, and so that is the one to start with. When kicking a ball, the object is to make it do exactly what you want it to do, to go where you want it to go. Not approximately where you want it to go, but *exactly* where you want it to go. Until you can make the ball do this, there is no point in thinking about how far you can kick it or how hard. Accuracy is everything. I was once told that a good games player (of any game) was one who "does the right thing quickly," and that seems to be a very good definition. In soccer no player can do the right thing, either quickly or slowly, until he can make the ball go where he wants it to go.

It is unfortunate that the English language does not

Fig. 1

have another word for the action of propelling a soccer ball with the foot, because the word "kicking" suggests a hard, sharp, leg-swinging action. Indeed, in all other types of football, such as American or Rugby, the ball *is* kicked with a hard, sharp, leg-swinging action, but this is not the most commonly used kick in soccer. In soccer the ball is *pushed* with the foot or *rolled* with the foot most of the time, because absolute accuracy is necessary. By pushing the ball with the foot, rather than kicking it in the normal way, we can learn to make it go where we want it to go.

PASSING WITH THE INSIDE OF THE FOOT

The ball can be pushed with either the inside of the foot as shown in figure 2, or with the outside border, but since the inside border is more often used and is easier to manipulate, we'll look at that first.

Whenever you are going to push a soccer ball, you use one foot to push it and the other foot to aim. Notice in figure 3 how the player's right foot is pointing at the other player, which is where he wants the ball to go. He is using the right foot as an aiming foot while he pushes the ball with the left.

Remember that you should practice pushing the ball with either foot. You must become as good a passer with your left foot as with your right.

To learn to pass with the inside of the foot, play the following game with a partner.

Fig. 2

Fig. 3

Poison!

This should be played by two boys. Later, the number of participants can be increased to three.

Boy No. 1 pushes the ball to boy No. 2. As soon as the ball leaves his foot, the ground he is standing on becomes POISON! He must *quickly* move at least five paces away from it. It doesn't matter whether he goes forward, backward, or sideways—as long as he moves quickly. Boy No. 2 receives the ball and pushes it to No. 1. As the ball leaves

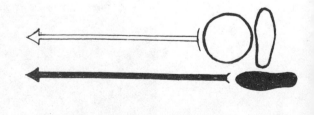

No. 2's foot the ground he is standing on becomes POISON! and he must in turn move away quickly. Both players must pass and move, pass and move, pass and move, until they have made twenty consecutive passes. Remember, every time the ball leaves your foot, the ground you are standing on becomes POISON! (See fig. 4.)

Points to remember:

1. Before pushing the ball to your partner, take aim by pointing the other foot at him (fig. 3).
2. As the ball comes to you, you must do two things. First, stop the ball with your foot, and then *look* for your partner before trying to push it back to him. Remember—as soon as you have the ball under your control, *look*.

Now that you are starting to push the ball around, let us look at the way you should be doing it.

When pushing with the inside of the foot you should:

1. Look at the ball all the time, which means that you must keep your head down while you are making the push. If you know anyone who plays golf, ask that person to explain about why it is important to keep the head down when striking the ball.
2. Point your nonkicking foot at the exact spot where you want the ball to go.

Fig. 4 Playing "Poison."—*both players on the move*

3. Turn your kicking foot fully sideways so that the whole of the inside border of the foot is presented to the ball.
4. Use a pushing action with the foot, to roll the ball where you want it to go.
5. As the ball goes away from you, keep the kicking foot moving after the ball. This is called "follow-through" and the same action is used in all games where a ball is struck, such as golf, tennis, baseball, hockey, and so on.

Each time you play the ball this way you should say to yourself, "Head down, push, follow through," until it becomes such a habit that you cannot do it any other way (figs. 5, 6, and 7).

Fig. 5 Passing with the inside of the foot—a last look at where he wants the ball to go

Fig. 6 Passing with the inside of the foot—head down

Fig. 7 Passing with the inside of the foot—follow through with the kicking leg—and the head still down!

6. Throughout the whole action, you should hold your arms out to the side to assist your balance. This is very important because, if you think about it, whenever you kick anything you are standing on one foot to do so. Therefore, whenever you kick, you are in a very delicate balancing situation, and need all the assistance you are able to get. Holding your arms out sideways helps a great deal.

PASSING WITH THE OUTSIDE OF THE FOOT

There will be times (and as you have gone through the practices, you will have noticed this) when, for one reason

or another, it is not possible to play the ball with the inside
of the foot. Sometimes it will take too long to get yourself
into the right position to do so. On these occasions, you
can play the ball with the outside border of the foot. Let us
look at the technique of pushing with the outside of the
foot.

The foot is held fairly rigidly and extended (pointed)
so that it is firm when contact with the ball is made. The
action is still a firm push, not a flick. It is a great temptation
to flick the ball with the outside of the foot, but you must
not do it, because a flick cannot be well directed and will
not send the ball very far. The ball must be pushed firmly,
and to do so requires that you make contact with the ball,
using the base of the small toe, with a firm and rigid foot.
Do not forget to follow through after the ball has left the
foot (fig. 8).

Fig. 8

Remember, keep your head down so that you can watch the ball throughout the movement. Push the ball firmly with the outside edge of the foot and let the leg follow through as the ball moves.

Every soccer player should practice until he is an accurate passer of the ball with both the inside and the outside of the foot, either "first time" (as it comes to you, without stopping it first) or after having stopped the ball. Sometimes, however, it is necessary to move with the ball in your possession before passing. In soccer, this is called "dribbling," as it is in basketball, hockey, and other games.

DRIBBLING

One of the things coaches often say about a young soccer player is: "As soon as he gets the ball he becomes blind." What they mean is that the youngster has not learned to control a ball with confidence and consequently, when he has the ball at his feet, he dare not take his eyes off it. He drops his head to watch the ball closely, and then has no idea what is going on around him. There might be a teammate well placed to receive a pass, or there might be a good opportunity to shoot at goal, but he will not see it; he is "blind."

A good soccer player dribbles in the same way as a good basketball player, looking around him all the time (fig. 9). He can see the ball all right; he has trained himself to keep his eye on the ball while looking more or less straight ahead, keeping much of the game scene within the range of his vision. The really great players are able to do this even when they are under great pressure—with an opponent about to tackle.

The young soccer player must practice hard in order to perfect this ability, which can make the difference between a good player and a great player. When you are

Fig. 9 Dribbling with the insides of the feet and looking around

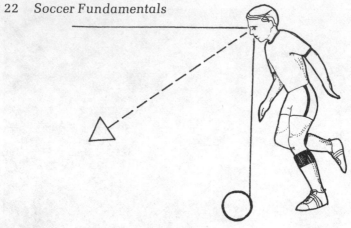

practicing, then, keep saying to yourself, "Look around, look around, look around." When you are practicing with others, say it to one another, and every teacher or coach should be urging his players to look around constantly.

The easiest, most basic way to dribble a soccer ball is to walk along pushing the ball from one foot to the other, using the inside of the foot all the time (fig. 9). If you do this, the path of the ball will be as below. As you can see,

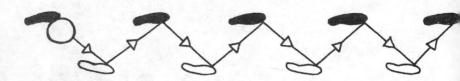

this is a fairly slow way of going forward because the ball is constantly going back and forth across the player's line of progress. Sometimes you need to dribble slowly, and in that case you would move at a walk or slow run, but more often the player will need to move a bit faster with the ball. To move more quickly he will be pushing the ball *forward* with the inside of his foot, rather than *across* the line to his other foot. When he makes his next contact he will again push the ball forward with the inside of whichever foot is more convenient, as shown in the following illustration.

Dribbling in this way, with the inside of the foot, requires a lot of practice. This is the method of dribbling that gives you the most control over the moving ball, and at the same time allows you the greatest opportunity to look around. It cannot be said too often that the skill of *looking* while dribbling is as much a habit as anything else, and it is a habit you must acquire.

Unfortunately, once you start trying to move fast with the ball at your feet, you will find that you cannot be sure of making contact every time with the inside of the foot. You might wish to change direction, or your position might make it difficult to get the inside of your foot to the ball and still be able to do what you want to do. This means that sometimes you will have to play the ball with the outside of your foot. Every young player must be able to dribble by occasionally alternating between the inside and the outside of the foot—and that means the right and left foot, not just one—while keeping his head up to look around him (fig. 10).

The golden rule of all dribbling is to keep the ball close to the foot—to pretend that the ball is attached to your toes by a piece of elastic. If you let it get too far away from your foot a defender can come in and take it from you. On the other hand, the best way to fool a defender is to make him *think* that you have allowed the ball to get too far away from you when in fact you can play it with your foot at any time you choose. The defender, thinking that you have lost control, will come lunging in at the ball, and you will simply reach out a foot and pull it away from him, leaving him floundering, waving his leg at nothing.

While you are practicing, learn to judge how far ahead you can allow the ball to go and still be able to play it with

Fig. 10 *Dribbling fast—and still looking around!*

good control. This does not mean a distance at which you are still able to push a foot forward and stab the ball in any direction; it means to play the ball with *control*, either to continue the dribble or to make a good pass, or shot, or even to put your foot on it and stop it or pull it back.

Practice drills that are useful for learning dribbling are:

1. On your own, just dribbling the ball—anywhere. Concentrate on (a) keeping the ball close to your feet, and (b) keeping your head up so that you can look around you. You do not necessarily need a soccer ball to do this—almost any round ball will do. In Europe, many boys teach

themselves to dribble well by using an old tennis ball.
2. Set up a slalom course and dribble around it—either on
your own, or as a member of a group of two or more.

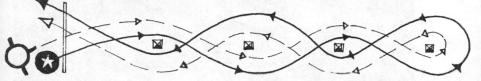

3. Relay races. In teams. From a starting line, dribble the
ball up the course, around the marker and return. Stop the
ball on the line; the next player carries on. A relay race
could also be organized along a slalom course.

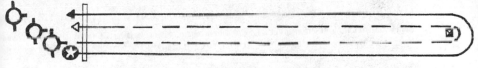

DRIBBLING AND PASSING GAMES

These games are ideal for small groups and fit well into the
squares of a practice grid. They provide plenty of practice
in the two types of push pass and they also give you the
opportunity to use other passing techniques—the prod
with the toe end (fig. 11) and even the back of the heel (fig.
12). These are not skills that you need to use very often, but
you can learn how to use them in these games, as the
opportunities arise.

Number Passing—Stage 1

*Played by any number from three to six. It's easier to learn
to play this game with four players, increasing the number
of players as you become more familiar with the game.*
     Each player has a number, i.e. "Two," "Three,"
"Four," and "Five" (fig. 13). There is no No. 1 since, in
soccer, 1 is the goalkeeper's number.

Fig. 11

Fig. 12

Fig. 13 Number Passing, No. 2 has called for the ball and is moving in toward the passer (No. 5). No. 3 is changing direction to be ready to call for a pass from No. 2.

No. 2 starts dribbling the ball, keeping on the move and in possession of the ball until No. 3 calls out his own number, "Three!" As soon as No. 3 does so, No. 2 passes the ball to him. No. 3 continues to dribble until No. 4 calls his own number, "Four!" Then No. 3 passes the ball to No. 4. No. 4 continues to dribble until No. 5 calls his own number, i.e. "Five!", when No. 4 passes the ball to No. 5. The game goes on with each player calling his own number when it is his turn to receive the ball and he is ready to receive it. No. 5 would pass to No. 2 and the sequence would start over.

Points to remember:

1. Do not pass the ball until the next number calls for it. Just keep dribbling if he doesn't call. Keep it—he'll soon get the message! By keeping the ball you are forcing him to move into a position to receive a pass.

2. As soon as you get the ball and start dribbling, *look* for the next number so that you are ready to push the ball to him as soon as he calls his number.

3. When it is your turn to call your number, start moving toward the boy with the ball as you call, so that you can receive the ball from a short pass rather than from a long one.

4. Watch the play so that you are ready to receive the ball as soon as the number before you gets it. As he calls his number, you should be moving toward him and calling your own number. This will keep the ball moving around quickly and teach everyone to react at a moment's notice.

Number Passing — Stage 2

Next, the same game is played in silence. The player who has the ball must watch for the next number moving into position to receive the ball, and then push it to him. Similarly the next number after him must move into position to receive the next pass. By now, having practiced Number Passing by calling numbers, every player will know who gives him the ball, and to whom he passes; for example, "Gary always gives me the ball and I always pass it to Chuck."

These two little games are very good for encouraging players to pass the ball quickly and accurately. The important things to learn from both these games are, first, that you must pass accurately. In a real match, if you pass well, your teammate will get the ball and your team will keep possession. If you do not pass accurately, your teammate will not get the ball—an opponent will nip in and take it, and then your team will have lost possession—and it will be your fault. The golden rule is that if you are in any doubt at all about whether your pass will reach a teammate, then don't make it—keep the ball at your feet until you *are* certain. The second thing you learn is that as soon as you have passed, you must move in order to keep yourself in the game. If you pass and then just stand where you are, you have taken yourself out of the game because the play has moved forward and you have not gone with it. Whenever you make a pass you must be sure that you are in position to have the ball passed back to you, and in order to be there, you've got to *move* as soon as you have made the pass.

We must now go on to learn how to use the push pass to beat an opponent.

Two Against One

Always remember this: In any team game, two must always beat one. If there are two of you against only one from the other team, the two of you *must* win. There is just no way that one has any chance of success against two, *provided that the two know what they are doing.* Once you understand this, you are well on the way to becoming a good team player, so we must now learn how to work a "two on one" situation to ensure success. Basically, there are four ways of working the situation, and they are:

1. the pass which goes "inside" the defender
2. the pass which goes "outside" the defender
3. the "wall" (or "1—2") pass
4. the continuous dribble, with the partner running as a decoy

It is absolutely necessary that every young soccer player learn to work the "two on one" situation almost automatically, so that as soon as he sees himself and a teammate in a "two against one" position he does the right thing quickly.

You set up practices for this by using an object as an opponent: a post, a chair, a barrel—almost anything (fig. 14).

Fig. 11 *Two against one—using a chair as an opponent*

You also have a goal of some sort—only about one yard wide—behind the object which is acting as the opponent, to allow you to finish the movement by scoring a goal, or by not scoring if you cannot push the ball accurately.

Note: In all the following practices, A1 and A2 are teammates trying to score a goal against 0, who is their opponent. Remember that, at this stage, 0 is an object, not a person.

> shows the path of the player
> shows the path of the ball
> shows path of player with ball

SET MOVE No. 1

A1 dribbles the ball forward, going slightly to the right of 0. While still about 1.5 yards from 0, he pushes the ball across to A2, who dribbles on to score. Having passed the ball, A1 goes on past 0 and keeps level with A2, in case A2 needs to pass the ball back to him.

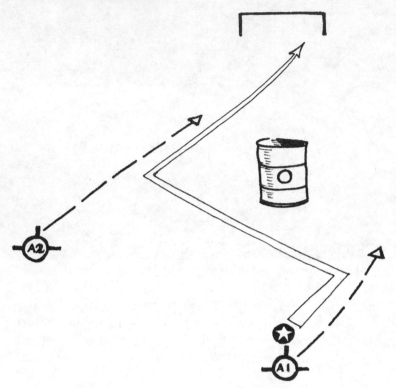

SET MOVE No. 2

A1 dribbles the ball forward, going slightly to the right of 0. While still 1.5 yards from 0, he pushes the ball behind the back of 0. As he does so, A2 runs behind the back of 0 to meet the ball, dribbles on and scores. As soon as he has passed the ball A1 cuts left, across the front of 0 and then runs for goal, to support A2, as he did in No. 1.

Note: In both the set moves, 1 and 2, it is important that A2 not start to move forward until A1 pushes the ball. He must not go past 0 until A1 has made the pass. This means that A1 has got to push the ball at just the right speed, and that A2 has got to move like a blue streak as soon as A1 makes the push pass.

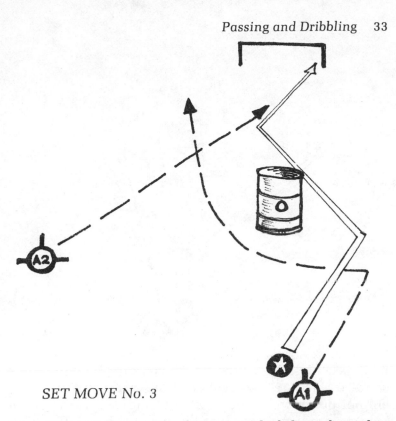

SET MOVE No. 3

A1 dribbles the ball toward 0, going slightly to the right a little faster than before. While still 1.5 yards from 0, A1 pushes the ball to A2 who, without any dribbling at all, immediately pushes it back into the space behind 0. As soon as A2 pushes the pass, A1 runs past 0 to receive the ball from A2, dribble on, and score. A2, having made the pass, runs toward goal to support A1. This move is called the "wall pass."

These three set moves should be practiced over and over. A2 should sometimes be on the left, as shown in the diagrams, and sometimes on the right, to make the move go in the other direction. A1 and A2 should swap places regularly. These drills should be continued until a score results every time a move is played. At that point we can introduce a live opponent. When a team is practicing these "two on one" moves, the coach will often act as the oppo-

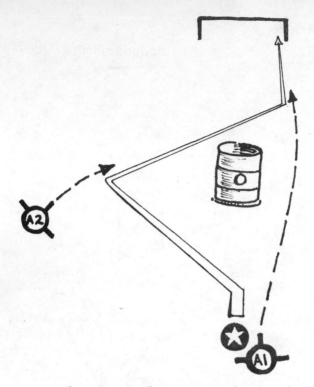

nent, because in this position he can direct the plays. He can also see what his players are doing well, and what they are not doing well, and correct where necessary. So we now put another player into the game, to be 0—the opponent.

You might have wondered why, at the beginning of each move, A1 goes to the right of 0. The reason is to make 0 move sideways, away from A2. 0 has to move, whether he wants to or not, since he must cover the man with the ball (A1), and try to keep between him and the goal. Once A1 has got 0 moving sideways, he can push the ball across to A2, knowing that 0 cannot stop, turn, run and get to A2. A1 has in fact, done two good things. He has first "pulled" the opponent away from A2 by making him go sideways, and then he has given A2 a good pass with plenty of room to work in.

Let us now see what to do if 0 decides that he is tired of being "pulled" sideways and that, instead, he will stay between A1 and A2 to try to cover both of them.

MOVE No. 4

Note: This is not a *set* move, since you cannot *make* it
happen. You make this move *when* 0 refuses to be
"pulled" and stays between you and your partner.

A1 dribbles the ball forward and to the right of 0. 0
thinks, "He is trying to pull me away from A2 again, so that
he can make a pass to him. I'm staying where I am, between
the two of them." Seeing that 0 will not come to him, A1
pushes the ball past 0, runs on, and scores.

A2 can help by running on and getting ahead of 0,
which will probably make 0 half turn toward A2 to see
what he is doing, thus giving A1 a clearer run to the ball. In
this case, A2 is acting as a decoy runner.

While playing in all these practices, you should try
hard to push the ball with either foot. Everybody has a

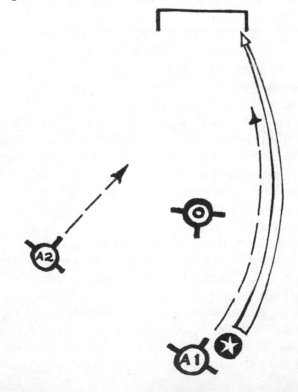

strong foot and a weak one, and if you want to be a good soccer player, you must educate your weak foot along with your strong one. It will be very difficult at first—the weak foot will just not do what you want it to—but if you keep practicing it will get better and better, until you are the complete "two-footed" player.

Two Against One, With A Live Opponent

One of the really important things that you must understand, and must learn to do when you are playing, either in practice or in games, is to make the defender commit himself. This is sometimes called "attacking" the defender.

When you have the ball, and there is a defender in a position to stop your progress, there are really only two choices open to you.

You may either beat him with a pass, or beat him yourself by taking the ball past him. Whichever you choose to do, you first have to make the defender think that you are going to do something else, and make him move to stop your doing it. If a player with the ball allows a defender to stand and wait for him to arrive with the ball, he is giving all the advantage to the defender. The defender can wait, perfectly balanced and ready to move either way. Consequently, the attacker must try to make the defender move in the way he wants him to move. Using the same set plays as before, with a live "0" (opponent), let us see how we can force him to move.

As an example, in this diagram, the attacker, A1, is going forward with the ball but is also moving to the right. This makes the defender 0 move across to the right in order to keep between A1 and the goal. A1 has now forced 0 to move—he has made him commit himself to going across to the right. 0 probably does not want to go to the right. He has probably seen A2 on the other side of him and would much rather stay in the middle to keep an eye on both of

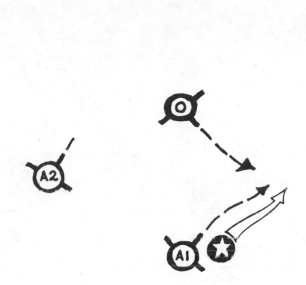

them, but he *cannot*. A1, who has the ball and is therefore
the danger man, has started on a run which will take him
around the outside of 0 to the goal. Whether he wants to or
not, 0 has got to move across to cut A1 off from the goal.

A1 has now:

1. "pulled" 0 right away from A2, so that if he wants to
push the ball into the space in front of A2, 0 cannot stop A2
going in on goal with the ball, and;
2. got 0 moving to the right, so that if A1 decides to cut
back to the left with the ball, 0 now has to stop and turn and
start moving the other way in order to try to stop him. By
the time 0 has done all this, A1 and the ball should be long
gone!

In short, what A1 has done is to force 0 into a bad
defensive position by making him move out to the right.

If, on the other hand, A1 merely came straight forward
with the ball, all 0 would have to do would be to let him
come to within about 2 yards of him and then start backing away, keeping between A1 and the goal, and, at the
same time, keeping an eye on A2. As he backs away, 0 is

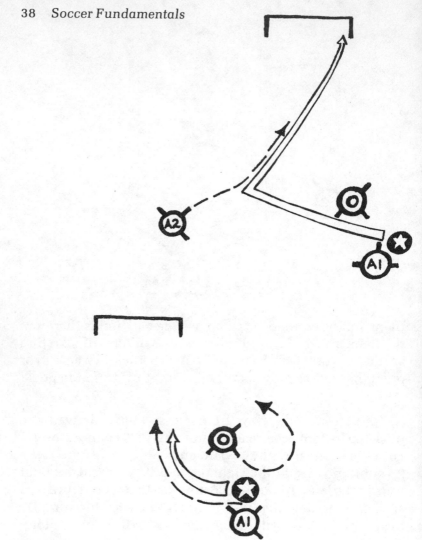

well balanced on both feet and ready to move either way, so it would be very difficult for A1 to take the ball past 0. If he should try to pass to A2, 0 could probably intercept the pass, but even if 0 did not, he could easily keep between A2 and the goal.

Three Against One

When you are playing "two on one" games and you have the ball, decisions about what to do are fairly easy, because there is only one person you can pass the ball to, and that is your partner. All you have to do is watch what the opponent is doing, and as soon as your partner has moved clear of him, push the ball to your partner. If, however, there are three of you against one, you not only have to make the opponent commit himself, you also have to decide which of your two teammates is better placed to receive a pass. Again, you should start playing three against one in a square or some other marked space, where all you are trying to do is to keep the ball moving about between the three of you, without the opponent's getting it. (See fig. 15, where player No. 6 is the opponent.) Now that the boy with the ball must choose which of his partners to push the ball to, it becomes more difficult for him, especially if the opponent is close to him. It is at this point that young players should learn to call for the ball. Professional soccer players talk to one another all the time they are playing,

Fig. 15 *Three against one. The defender, No. 6, is going in very aggressively on No. 2, who is already playing an easy pass off to No. 4. Nos. 2, 4, and 5 have all moved well to keep in a triangular formation and make life difficult for No. 6.*

but it is a very disciplined sort of talking. Nobody says anything unless it is helpful to a teammate. When playing small games like "three on one" it does help the boy with the ball if his teammates let him know when they are ready to receive the ball (remember "number passing"). Sometimes the opponent will be guarding the boy with the ball so closely that the boy might not see the teammate who is best placed to receive the ball. In such a case the teammate must call for the ball. There are two golden rules in calling for the ball.

1. If you are in a good position to receive the ball, let the boy with the ball know this by calling *his* name—just the name, nothing else. If Chuck has the ball and you want it, you just call "Chuck." You don't say, "Over here, Chuck" or "Gimme the ball, Chuck"—you just call his name. And you call only *once*. When you've called, Chuck knows you are there and ready for the ball. If he doesn't give it to you, it is because he has other plans for it, and he doesn't want you yelling "Chuck, Chuck, Chuck, Chuck," at him. So, remember, just his name, and just once, and only when you are in a good position to receive the ball (fig. 16).

Fig. 16 The player is calling for the ball—letting his teammate
know he is there, ready for a pass, and where he wants the
ball delivered.

2. When you have the ball, if a teammate calls your name
to let you know that he is in a good position to receive the
ball, he means now. In five or ten seconds' time the position
may have changed entirely and by that time he may not
want the ball. So, when a teammate calls for the ball,
unless you have positive plans to do something else, give it
to him quickly. Pause only long enough to see where he
wants the ball and then push it there.

When you are playing "three on one," it is best if the
three players who are playing together try to form a
triangle (and retain it) all the time they are playing. The
general dimensions of the triangle will change, and so will

Fig. 17 Because they have not moved, 2 and 5 are close together, behind the defender (6) and 4 cannot get a pass to either of them.

the positions of the players in it, but the triangular shape should be kept. If it is kept, no matter where the defender positions himself, someone is in a position to receive a pass. (Look again at fig. 16.)

You should also remember what we did right at the start; pass and *move* still applies. As soon as you push the ball to a teammate, *move*. If all three of you move *every* time you make a pass, life becomes absolutely impossible for 0. If, however, you do not move when you've passed, all 0 has to do is to keep himself roughly in the middle of the triangle and wait for one of you to make a slightly bad pass, which he can then intercept (fig. 17). It is just like the situation in "two on one"—you must make the defender commit himself. You must not let him stay where he is, comfortable and balanced. He will not move unless you force him to do so.

Kicking

There will be occasions when you need to kick the ball with rather more force and speed than the push will produce. Shooting for goal might well be one such occasion. Hitting a long pass for defensive reasons might be another. In these situations a different type of kick must be used. You have perhaps noticed that I have used the term "hitting" in connection with this type of kick. It is a crisp, explosive type of action, in the same way that hitting a ball with a bat is a crisp, explosive action.

Keeping the ball on the ground when hitting it in this way is a lot more difficult than when using a push—first because you will be using more force that you did with the pushing action, and then because kicking is a more difficult technique to master. There are four points to remember (fig. 18):

1. Put your nonkicking foot right next to the ball. If it is placed slightly behind the ball you will kick the ball into

Fig. 18

the air, because you will be leaning back as you make contact, allowing your kicking foot to slide under the ball. If your nonkicking foot is placed too far forward you will hit the ball downward into the ground, and it will rebound upward into the air.

2. The knee of the kicking leg should be immediately above the ball as contact is made.

3. The ball is struck with the upper surface of the foot—it is often said that the ball is kicked with the player's shoelaces—and this is a fairly accurate description of the point of contact. The toe of the boot is scraping the ground as the ball is hit.

4. Use a good, long follow-through of the kicking leg as the ball goes away. This makes for accuracy, always provided that the follow-through is in the direction of the target!

When hitting a ball in this way, bearing in mind that you want to keep the ball on the ground, you must remember to direct the kicking force into the middle or the upper half of the ball. This will help you avoid "getting under the ball" which always causes the ball to go into the air.

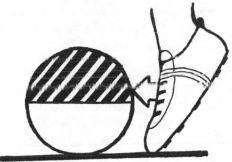

If, on the other hand, you *want* the ball to go into the air—maybe to make a long, defensive clearance kick or to pass the ball to a teammate's head—then a slightly different technique is used. Goalkeepers use this technique when making a goal kick; wingers use it when making corner kicks, and almost every player who makes a free kick uses it. This is, then, the type of kick that every member of the team should practice.

1. The nonkicking foot is placed beside and slightly behind of the ball.
2. The contact point is the top of the foot, but slightly to the inside—that is, the inner line of lace holes on your boot or shoe.
3. The foot should make contact with the ball at a point slightly below the midline. This in itself will cause the ball to rise.

4. Again, a good, long follow-through with the kicking foot in the direction of the target is important. Because your body is leaning slightly back as you hit the ball, the follow-through can and should be fuller than it was when you were hitting the low ball.

If you use this technique, but aim to stab the foot under the ball and stop the foot as soon as contact is made—no follow-through—you will "chip" the ball. The ball will go high, but only for a short distance, and as it drops to the ground will almost stop instead of bouncing and rolling on as it normally would. As the foot goes under the ball to make contact, it puts a backspin on it—in the same way that a similar action would apply backspin in tennis, table tennis, or golf. The chip is a very useful skill to acquire and is used for putting the ball over the head of an advancing goalkeeper to score, or for passing over the head of a player to a teammate.

THE VOLLEY

Sometimes it will be necessary to move in and kick a ball that is in the air. As in tennis, this is called a volley, and the difficult thing about it is that you cannot choose either the position of the ball or the position of your body when such a kick has to be made. If you had any choice you would probably wait for the ball to drop to the ground and then push it or hit it as you have done up to now. When an

Fig. 19

Fig. 20

opponent is moving in on you, however, he will get to the ball first and steal it, if you don't move in and play the ball. You have no choice—you must move in and kick the ball while it is still in the air, before he does. Again, you might want to make a quick pass or a shot at goal, and you cannot wait for the ball to drop before making your move. Under these circumstances you should go in and volley the ball. You should let the ball drop as low as possible before kicking it—the higher it is the more difficult the kick— and you must, as always, watch the ball constantly. You should meet the ball with the top of your foot (your shoelace) if you want a strong kick that will travel a long way (fig. 19), or with the inside border of the foot if you want to make a short pass (fig. 20). The body should be leaning back slightly as you make contact with the ball.

The overhead volley, known as the "bicycle kick," is a very useful skill to possess. It is especially valuable to a striker who often has half a chance to volley the ball while standing with his back to the goal. The ability to shoot at goal using an overhead volley will often bring a score, if only because none of the defenders is expecting it to happen. Use the following technique:

1. Watch the ball carefully as it comes to you, lean back and allow yourself to start to fall backward.
2. As you start to fall, still watching the ball, swing the kicking leg up to "hook" the ball back over the head.

It is possible to do this, as described, and keep the non-kicking foot on the ground, which allows you to break your fall (fig. 21). Done this way, however, the resulting volley will not be powerful and the ball will tend to rise. To hit a powerful overhead volley which will not rise, the player must jump in order to lift his hips high. Since he is falling backward as he jumps, he must "scissor kick" his legs, kicking the ball with the "second" leg. Once the player has jumped, both feet are off the ground and he has no means of breaking his fall. Consequently, this is one skill that should not be practiced too frequently.

Fig. 21

BENDING OR SWERVING THE BALL ("THE BANANA KICK")

Strangely enough, kicks which result in the ball's swerving in flight more often occur accidentally than deliberately. For this reason, the ball frequently misses its mark. In order to kick the ball along a straight line, which is what we want to do most of the time, the foot should touch the ball at the vertical center line of the ball.

If contact is made to one side of the center line, the ball will spin and swerve, whether on the ground or in flight. This is exactly what happens when a ball is sliced or pulled in golf or tennis—it has been struck off center. A good player, however, learns to make the ball swerve deliberately. Any player who takes a corner kick should be able to make the ball swerve, either inward toward the goal (the inswinger) or outward, away from the goal (the outswinger). A player taking a free kick within scoring distance of the goal always finds a wall of opponents lined up 10 yards in front of him, almost completely blocking the goal. The goalie will have the rest of the goal covered. It is, therefore, very useful to be able to "bend" the ball around the end of the "wall." Many goals are scored this way. Basically, the technique is one of hitting the ball to the side of the center line of the ball. If the contact is to the left of center, the ball will swerve to the right, and if the contact is to the right of center the ball will swerve to the left. If the foot is traveling across the face of the ball as contact is made, the swerve will be more pronounced.

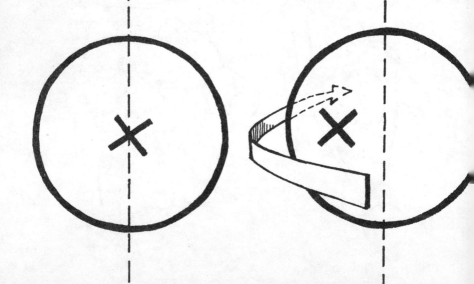

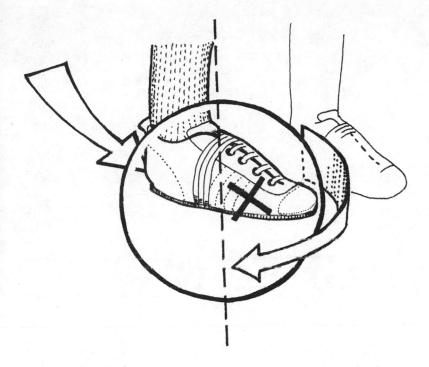

Ball Control

Every soccer player needs to be able to bring the ball quickly under his control as it comes to him and then to be able to move efficiently. Controlling the ball as you receive it is generally known as "trapping" because you are making a trap out of some part of your body (other than your hands) and catching the ball in it.

On many occasions you will want to bring the ball under control, slowing its pace, without "killing" or stopping it. This can be done with the foot, when the ball is coming along the ground to you, by executing the reverse action of the push pass with the inside of the foot. You must position yourself so that the ball is coming straight at you, making sure that the other foot—the one that you are not going to use to meet the ball—is pointed straight at the ball. Turn the foot outward and push it forward so that you meet the ball with the inside border of the foot. As contact is made, start to withdraw the foot straight back, with the

Fig. 22

leg relaxed. This cushions the impact, absorbing the ball's force. By the time the ball is level with the other foot, it should be almost stationary, fully under your control and ready for you to play in whichever way you choose (fig. 22).

A similar technique is used to deal with a ball that is coming toward you but is bouncing at about knee height. You prepare to meet the ball in the same way, except that you lift the foot and do not extend it so far forward—you do not reach out for the ball. Instead, you plan to meet the ball when it is level with the other leg, or thereabouts. You then withdraw the foot, as before, to take the pace off the ball (fig. 23).

Fi

WITH THE CHEST

A ball which is bouncing high, or coming straight toward you at chest height, or which is dropping from a low height, can be controlled by letting it come onto your chest. As contact is made, the chest and stomach are pulled back, the arms lifted sideways and the upper body bent forward, so that a curved surface is presented to the ball. When the ball hits this curved surface, it will drop straight down to the feet, where it can be played off, or further controlled with the feet (fig. 24).

Fig. 24

If the ball is dropping from a height, it is often better to use the chest as a platform on which the ball can bounce before it drops to the feet. As the ball drops, the whole of the upper part of the body is arched sharply backward. At the same time, the arms are raised sideways, both for balance and to flatten the platform formed by the chest (fig. 25). The ball is allowed to drop onto the chest and the upper body gives slightly as contact is made. The ball then bounces gently on the chest and rolls down the front of the body to the feet.

Fig. 25

WITH THE THIGH

A steeply dropping ball may also be brought under control by using the thigh in much the same way as the chest was used in the platform method. The thigh should be lifted until it is parallel with the ground. As the ball drops onto it, the thigh is lowered slightly to take the speed off the ball (fig. 26). The ball is then allowed to drop to the ground.

One of the best practices to help you to acquire this kind of ball control is an individual drill where you merely try to keep the ball in the air. You toss the ball up and then play it with your head, chest, thighs and feet, trying to keep it off the ground as long as possible. If it does drop to the ground, then flick it up with your foot and continue. This can also be done against a wall, keeping the ball off the ground while using rebounds off the wall.

Remember that you have *two* feet and *two* thighs and you must learn to use both. You should spend more time practicing with your weak foot than with your strong one. Professional soccer players or coaches will often say of a poor player, "The only thing his left foot is good for is standing on."

SHIELDING

A very important skill that all young players should acquire and practice as they learn to control and dribble a ball is shielding. You will read elsewhere in this book that the best time for a defender to make a tackle is at the moment that the attacker is trying to get the ball under control. The attacker cannot really concentrate on both controlling the ball and avoiding a tackle at the same time, and is an easy target for the tackler.

To avoid losing the ball before you've really got it, shield the ball with your body by placing your body be-

Fig. 26

tween the ball and the opponent who wants to take it from you. The defender will not be able to reach the ball because your legs will be in his way—between him and the ball. As you can see in figure 27, if a player is shielding the ball with his body, it is impossible for the defender to make a tackle without committing a foul.

As a general rule, then, try to keep your body between your opponent and the ball when an opponent is in a position to challenge for it.

Fig. 27

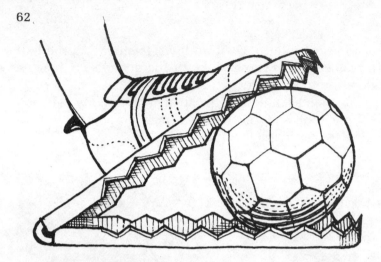

TRAPPING

Catching the ball between your foot and the ground is the only true "trap." This may be done with the sole of the foot, with the inside, or the outside of the foot. Once the ball is in the trap, the top jaw—your foot—closes gently, but firmly, and holds it. As soon as the ball is in the trap, however, the foot must draw back very, very slightly. This ensures that the ball stays in the trap and does not bounce out again, as it will if the foot is held too rigidly.

With The Sole Of The Foot

Watch the ball carefully as it comes toward you. Lift your foot off the ground and point your toes upward. You should now have positioned yourself so that the ball will hit the ground under your trapping foot. As it does so, press the foot down onto it (fig. 28). Having trapped the ball, *look up* and move away with the ball. Trapping the ball under the sole of the foot "kills" it absolutely and you will be left with a "dead ball" under your foot, unless you begin moving away with the ball immediately. This is why

Fig. 28

you should always make sure that there are no opponents
running toward you before you go about trapping a ball in
this way. During the time it takes you to trap the ball and
then get on the move again, you are a sitting target for an
opponent.

With The Inside Of The Foot

This is used when you are standing sideways along the
line of the ball's trajectory. The trap is made between the
ground and the inside border of the foot—along most of its

Fig. 29

length and nearly as far up as the ankle. Once again, watch the ball as it comes to you. The ball hits the ground and the trapping part of the foot at the same time (fig. 29). The foot is pressed onto the ball and then relaxed to avoid presenting a rigid surface, which would cause the ball to bounce out of the trap. Although the ball is held in the trap, this action does not "kill" it absolutely. It can be pushed forward with the inside of the foot to make a pass or start a dribble. Thus, when trapping with the inside of the foot, you can capture the ball and start to move away with it almost in one continuous action. Don't forget to *look up* as you start to move away.

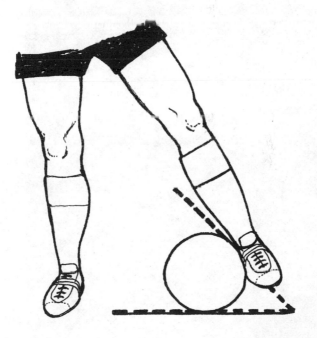

With The Outside Of The Foot

This is used when you want to move away from your position *immediately* after trapping the ball. It may be that you have an opponent coming at you; it may be that you want to turn and go in a different direction; whatever the reason, you need to trap the ball and be on your way immediately. Watch the ball as it comes toward you and make the trap between the outside border of the foot and ankle, and the ground. The trapping foot is turned well outward and, as before, is pressed down onto the ball as the ball hits the ground (fig. 30). As the trap is made, the foot is

Fig. 30

relaxed to prevent its rebounding away from you, but the ball can now be pushed with the outside of the foot so that you move away with the ball *as* you trap it. As soon as you feel that you have successfully trapped the ball, lift your head and *look around* as you push the ball to start moving away.

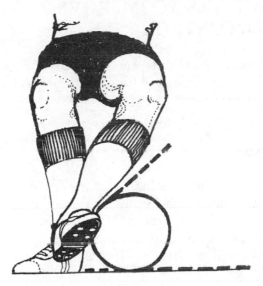

Basically, then, there are three important things which must be practiced until they become automatic:

1. Watch the ball right into the trap. (This will cause you to lower your head.)
2. Capture the ball in the trap. (Your head will stay down as you make sure that you've got it.)
3. Lift your head to look around you, and make your next move—pass, dribble, shoot, or whatever.

Every other player knows that you are a sitting target while you are trapping a ball, because you've got to stop—even if only momentarily—in order to do it, and because you have to concentrate on watching the ball. For that moment you are stationary *and* blind, which is just how an opponent wants you. Therefore, you should practice until you can trap smoothly and quickly, no matter how the ball comes to you.

PRACTICES TO IMPROVE BALL CONTROL

There are many excellent practice drills for ball control which are done in groups of two and three, and which can be varied as necessary.

In Pairs

1. No. 1 passes with the inside of his foot to No. 2, who takes the pace off the ball with the inside of this foot and passes it back to No. 1, who does the same.
2. No. 1 throws the ball to No. 2 at knee height. No. 2 takes the pace off it and returns it to No. 1 using the outside of his foot.
3. No. 1 throws the ball to No. 2 at chest height. No. 2 controls it with his chest and then passes it back to No. 1, who takes the pace off it with the inside of his foot.
4. No. 1 throws the ball high to No. 2, who lets it drop onto his chest and roll down. As it hits the ground he passes it back to No. 1 with the outside of his foot.
5. No. 1 throws the ball up and, as it drops, controls it with his thigh. He then passes it to No. 2, who passes it back to him, using a first-time pass with the inside of the foot.

In Triangular Formation

1. No. 1 passes to No. 2, who controls the ball with his foot, at the same time turning to shield the ball from No. 1.

No. 2 then passes to No. 3, who shields from No. 2 and passes to No. 1, who shields from No. 3 and passes to No. 2, and so on.

2. No. 1 throws the ball to No. 2, who traps it with the sole of his foot and then passes it off to No. 3, who takes the pace off the ball with his foot and passes it to No. 1, who stops it with the inside of his foot, picks it up and starts again.

3. No. 1 throws the ball to No. 2, who traps it with the outside of his foot and then passes it off to No. 3, who hits it for the first time to No. 1, using the outside of his foot.

4. No. 1 throws the ball to No. 2, varying the type of throw he uses. No. 2 traps the ball with either the sole, the inside, or the outside of the foot and then passes it off to No. 3, who hits a first-time pass to No. 1, using either the inside or the outside of the foot.

All these drills can be adapted to any skill that you want to work on. The important thing is to have every player doing something useful and not merely serving the ball to someone else.

Heading

FROM A STANDING POSITION

Heading is the part of soccer that is most frequently done badly. Some world-famous players readily admit that they cannot head a ball well. It is true that when playing in games, players in some positions—notably defenders and strikers—have to head the ball more frequently than players in other positions—for instance, wingers—but every player ought to be able to make the ball do what he wants it to do with his head as well as with his feet. Like every other skill, this is a matter of learning to do it properly, and then practicing until you can do it perfectly every time. The first thing you must learn is to "meet" the ball correctly, with your forehead. There is only a very small area on your head which is almost flat—and that is the central lower part of your forehead, the part used in heading.

If you imagine a rectangle drawn on your forehead, like this,

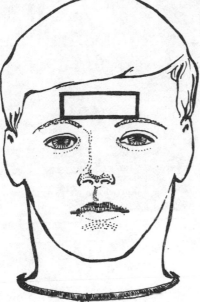

you have described the flat area of your forehead that should make contact with the ball.

Take a soccer ball in both hands, and hold it in front of your face, as shown in figure 31. The ball should be about six to eight inches away from your forehead. At the same time, push your forehead forward fast, simultaneously pulling the ball back toward your forehead. The ball will be headed forward out of your hands. Make sure that it is the contact area of the forehead that meets the ball, and make sure that you are watching the ball throughout— before you start the action, as you pull it toward you and move your head forward, and as it goes away.

When you first start heading, it is very tempting to close your eyes as your forehead makes contact with the ball. You, no doubt, expect hitting a ball with your head to be uncomfortable. This is a natural reflex—but there is no

Fig. 31

need! To head a ball well gives you one of those really nice feelings that you get from time to time in sport. When you hit a baseball just right, with that lovely crack of bat on ball, the feeling in your hands is marvelous. A really good smash in tennis gives you a similar sort of feeling, and so does heading a ball well. It is in no way uncomfortable— in fact, it feels great!

Now try heading the ball out of your hands by moving only your head. Do not pull the ball toward your head, just push your head. This will mean holding the ball closer to your head when you start—only four or five inches away. Again, keep watching that ball! You will be surprised how much force you can put into a header when you are holding the ball this way and meeting the ball correctly with the contact area of the forehead.

Now try throwing the ball up and heading it as it comes down. Don't throw it too high—a foot above head level is about right. This time, you should try to head the ball downward. When playing in a game, you will need to be able to head the ball upward, downward, and sideways, but the downward header is the one you will use most. Soccer is a game which is played mainly with the feet, and the feet are usually on the ground, so that is where the ball needs to be. Occasionally it gets up in the air and you have to head it, but most of the time you head it to get it back onto the ground, so you must practice that downward header.

Practice heading with a partner. Throw the ball up and head it to his feet. He then throws it up and heads it to your feet, and so on (fig. 32).

Practice against a wall. Throw the ball up, and head it down against the wall. Make a mark low down on the wall and try to hit it with the ball every time.

Fig. 32

You will notice, both from the photographs and from doing it yourself, that to add some force to your headers you will need to lean the whole top part of your body backward and then bring it forward as your head meets the ball. You are, in fact, using the whole of your body from the waist upward to get a good, forceful header (fig. 33).

You will need to watch the ball very carefully to ensure that it is in exactly the right place as you meet it

Fig. 33

with your forehead. If it is slightly too high, the round part of your head, above the contact area, will meet it, and it will go upward.

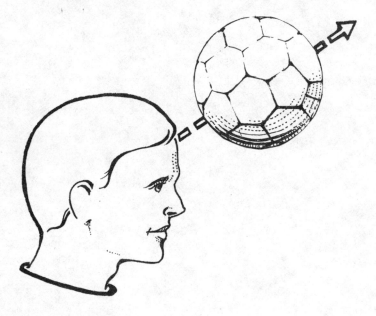

If it is slightly too low, some part of your face below the contact area (probably your nose!) will meet it, and the ball could go anywhere (and I promise you that you will not enjoy it very much!).

If, however, the correct contact area meets the ball, it will go exactly where you want it to go—in this case forward and downward.

You will also need to pay some attention to the positioning of your feet. In the first place, for the type of heading you are practicing now, both feet need to be firmly on the ground. This provides a solid base, and you need a solid base in order to get some force behind your heading.

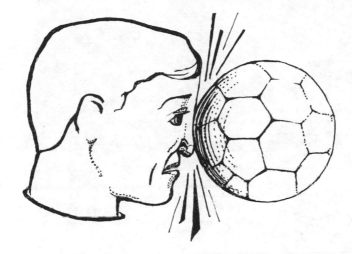

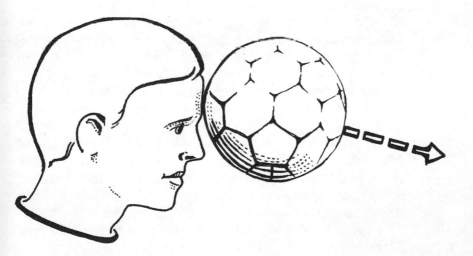

Fig. 34

It also puts you in a well-balanced position. Look again at the photographs and notice first how one foot is always ahead of the other. You need this for balance, because you are going to bring the top half of the body forward pretty forcefully. If you did this with the feet side by side, you would probably topple forward. Notice, also, that although the boy comes up onto his toes as he meets the ball and heads it forward, his feet do not leave the ground (fig. 34).

Once you have mastered the art of heading the ball downward, you should practice heading it straight forward, and heading it upward. Heading it straight forward is simple. You began your heading drills by heading a ball straight forward, out of your hands. All you have to do is to move your head straight forward and meet the middle part of the ball with the contact area (fig. 35).

Fig. 35

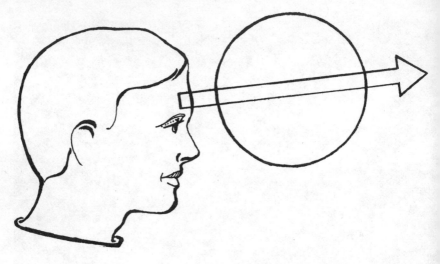

When you were heading it downward, you waited for the ball to drop slightly below forehead level and then moved your head forward and downward and met the ball with the contact area.

In order to head it upward, you meet the ball when it is still slightly above forehead level. Because the ball is above eye level, you will be holding your head back

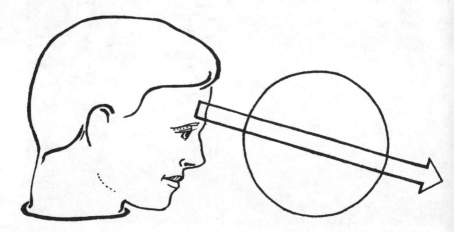

slightly in order to see it properly. The head, held slightly back, is moved forward to meet the ball with the contact area (fig. 36).

Fig. 36

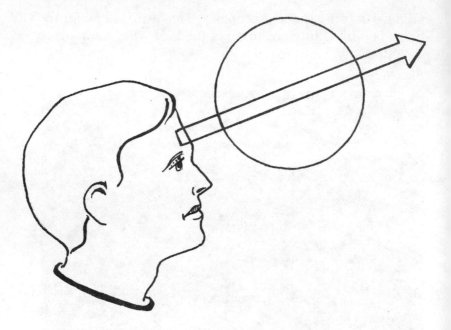

Practice this by throwing the ball up and heading it as it drops. Do this against a wall, or with a partner throwing the ball to you. Try to head it over something—a volleyball net or even a string stretched between two upright objects will do.

Until now, all the heading practice drills have been concerned with sending the ball forward, either straight forward, or upward or downward and forward. We must now learn to head the ball sideways. The ball needs to be coming at you from the front, and so it is better to have two or three in a group to practice this skill. What you are trying to do, when you first start on this drill, is merely to change the direction of a ball which is coming toward you. It is coming straight at you, and you are going to make it go to one side or the other. Accuracy is all important, but force does not matter at all here.

As you stand facing the ball, feet slightly apart, nicely balanced, you must follow the procedure below.

Assuming you wish to head the ball away to your right,

1. Sway your upper body to the left so that the ball is now going to pass to the right of your head.
2. Turn your head and upper body to the right and lean back so that the contact area of your forehead is aimed at the place you want the ball to go.
3. Push the upper part of the body and head at the ball as it comes level with the contact area (fig. 37).

Fig. 37

If there are three of you, No. 1 can throw the ball to No. 2, and No. 3 can collect it after No. 2 heads it; then No. 3 can throw it back to No. 2, who will head to No. 1.

You must be sure to watch the ball constantly until it touches your forehead, and keep watching it as it goes away to your target—in this case, another boy. You must also be sure that you meet the ball with the contact area, and not with the side of your head. If you do meet it with the side of your head, you have either not turned your head quickly enough, or far enough, or both. As a result, the ball will skid off the head. As you become more used to heading sideways, you will probably start moving your back foot around as you turn the upper part of your body, in order to bring your whole body around to face the target. This is perfectly natural, and will allow you to put more force behind your header because you've made your base more solid and you are better balanced.

It is important that you practice heading sideways both to the right and left. Once you are doing it well, practice the downward, upward, and forward motions. It is probable that more goals are scored by a sideways—downward header than with any other kind, and so this technique is very well worth a lot of practice time.

JUMPING TO HEAD THE BALL

It would be very nice if all heading could be done with both feet firmly on the ground, because, as you have found out, this is a well-balanced position. From such a solid base you can bring some real power to the header by using the whole of the upper body in the heading action. However, in a game of soccer, the ball sometimes reaches a height where a player has to jump in order to head it, and heading the ball in the air is a little different than heading with the feet on the ground. The main difference is that you cannot draw your trunk back while you are in the air without hopelessly disturbing your balance. When you are heading a ball in mid-jump it becomes mainly a matter of neck power rather than trunk power. The other techniques are exactly the same as they are for heading from a standing position. Obviously, the timing of the jump is very important. You want to meet the ball at the peak of your jump—not on your way up or down. Just as some of the great basketball players seem to have the ability to "hang in the air" at the top of their jump—to get up there

and then stay there while they take a leisurely shot at the basket—some soccer players seem to develop the same ability. This gives them plenty of time to direct their headers. The ability to do this—in either basketball or soccer—is no magical gift; it's all a matter of perfect timing. It is knowing how to do what you have to do—shoot or head a ball—right at the peak of the jump, plus the knowledge that if you push your trunk forward when you are at the top of the jump, it will give you more time at the top. When you jump upward, you bend at the ankles, knees, and hips as you take off, and, unless you make a real effort to do so, you never really straighten out at the hips as you go upward. If, at the top of your jump, you do make a real effort to push your hips forward, this effectively gives you another split second at the peak of your jump. It's well worth practicing.

When you come to think about it, in all the team running games—basketball, football of any description, field hockey and the like—about eighty percent of the qualities required to be a good player have nothing to do with the object you play with—the ball—but involve the most basic skills of human movement—the ability to run fast, start, stop, and turn quickly, jump high with good timing, and so on. Only twenty percent of the skills necessary to the athlete have to do with how well you can kick, dribble, shoot, or head a ball.

You should practice heading while in the air much as you did when you had your feet on the ground—with a partner to throw the ball up so that you can jump and head it sideways, downward, upward, or straight forward. Once you are up there, you need only to:

1. keep watching that ball, all the way to your forehead and then to its target, and
2. meet the ball with the contact area every time (fig. 38). If you meet it with the top or side of your head, you've timed your jump badly.

Fig. 38

When you jump to head a ball, think about your balance. With both feet off the ground this really *is* balance — the hard way! As soon as you are off the ground, try to straighten your legs and get them and your feet together. You have a fairly complicated movement to perform at the top of your jump if you are going to head that ball well, so you need to be well balanced, and you will not be well balanced if your legs are sticking out at odd angles.

PRACTICE DRILLS AND GAMES WHICH WILL IMPROVE HEADING

With A Partner

1. Hold the ball with two hands, and head it out of the hands to the partner (see page 72).
2. Throw the ball up and head it (a) straight to your partner, (b) to his feet, and (c) over him (heading upward).
3. Your partner throws the ball to your head; you head it (a) straight to him, (b) to his feet, and (c) over him.
4. Against a wall, first on your own, see how many consecutive headers you can make. Next, with your partner, alternate heading the ball against the wall, to see how many consecutive headers you can make between you.
5. Keep the ball up (a) on your own, and (b) with a partner, to see how many consecutive headers you can make.
6. Heading in the air, practice drills 2 and 3 with the ball thrown, so that a jump is necessary.

With A Larger Group

Practice sideways headings in a triangular formation. Player No. 1 throws the ball to No. 2, who heads it sideways to No. 3. Repeat with No. 3 throwing the ball to No. 2, who heads it sideways to No. 1.

Tackling

Tackling is one of the most difficult soccer skills to perform well. It is not only a matter of keeping an opponent from gaining ground with the ball, as it often is in football or basketball, but it is also a matter of taking the ball from him while obeying some fairly strict rules—the most important of which is to play the ball, not the opponent's body. Quite often, in playing the ball, you will make some contact with the opponent, but the referee must be satisfied that this contact was made as part of an attempt to play the ball. If he thinks that you intended to make bodily contact without bothering about the ball—or even if you make accidental contact during a failed attempt to play the ball—the referee must call a foul on you if your contact hinders the opponent in any way.

Certain deliberate contacts are permitted, provided that both the players involved are close enough to the ball to be able to play it. The shoulder charge, where one player does little more than nudge the shoulder of an opponent to shove him off balance, is often used in conjunction with a tackle and is perfectly fair. The important thing to understand about tackling is that you must not try to stop the man with the ball by attacking the man—your attack must be on the ball. A good tackle is one where the tackler emerges with the ball well under control at his feet.

Sometimes, a desperate tackle is necessary to take the ball from an opponent who would otherwise certainly score. At such times, you cannot afford to be too particular about what will happen to you or to the ball. You will probably end up on your back and the ball might go off the field altogether, but it does not matter; your tackle has stopped a score. These occasions are very rare, however. The first important thing to learn is how to tackle firmly, successfully, and with full control so that you come out of the tackle with the ball at your feet.

BLOCK TACKLE FROM THE FRONT

This is probably the most common form of tackle used in soccer. An opponent dribbling the ball is coming more or less straight at you, or you are moving straight toward him. Either way, you are going to meet face to face, so your tackle will be delivered to his front.

The first thing you must do is to watch the hips and thighs of the opponent as he comes toward you. If you are looking at this part of him you will keep the ball within your range of sight. More importantly, in the split seconds before you actually go into the tackle, any hip movement he makes will give you early warning that he is going to try to change direction. A smart opponent will always try to tempt you into the tackle, so that he can fool you by some unexpected move.

Once you've made up your mind to tackle, then proceed as follows:

1. Go in with knees slightly bent and body slightly crouched. Keep your arms by your side to avoid being accused of pushing or elbowing your opponent.

2. Get your nontackling foot down right beside the ball.

3. Turn your tackling foot outward so that you can force the whole of the inside edge of your foot against the middle of the ball to block it and then stop its forward progress by leaning into the tackle (fig. 39).

Fig. 39 Block tackle i. The block.

At this point in the tackle, the ball is wedged between your foot and your opponent's foot, and you now have to go through with the tackle to ensure that you get the ball. The advantage is normally with the tackler because he is already powering forward, while his opponent's forward movement has either slowed very considerably, or stopped altogether, as he attempts to keep control of the ball. You, then, must continue to apply maximum force to complete your tackle in one of the following ways:

1. Push the ball through the gap between your opponent's feet (fig. 40).
2. Nudge the opponent's shoulder with your own shoulder so that he falls away from the tackle, leaving you in possession of the ball.
3. Bring the ball sideways out of the tackle. The ball must be pushed over the opponent's foot or rebounded off his foot or shin, so that it comes away sideways, in your possession.

Whichever way it happens, you are on your feet, and you have now got the ball—the two results of a successful tackle.

Summing up those points, you must,

1. watch the opponent's hips and legs as he comes toward you;
2. get your nontackling foot beside the ball and block the ball with the inside of your tackling foot; and
3. go right through with the tackle, i.e., keep forcing your tackling foot forward, using all your body weight to do so, until you come out of the tackle with the ball at your feet.

ALWAYS go into a tackle intending to come out of it with the ball and act as if you are going to do so. Determination is fifty percent of the secret of success in tackling. Tackle with your whole body's weight so that your opponent knows that he's being tackled by something. It has been said of many of the really great tacklers in soccer,

Fig. 40 Block tackle ii. Forcing the ball through between the opponent's feet.

"When he tackles you, you stay tackled," and "When he tackles you, it's like colliding with a bulldozer," or, "He comes into the tackle like a ton of bricks." These players all played very clean soccer, but they played it hard in the tackle, because that's the way to do it and win.

BLOCK TACKLE FROM THE SIDE

Sometimes an opponent with the ball will be on the move and you will be unable to get in front of him, but must approach from the side. In such cases you use the *block tackle from the side* (fig. 41).

Fig. 41

For this tackle you must approach your opponent from the side, getting the nontackling foot in close to the ball and then pivoting on that foot to bring yourself into a front block tackling position. This probably sounds very complicated if you've never tried it, but if you get someone to stand still with a ball at his feet while you walk in from either side, you will soon see how it works. The diagram shows the tackler approaching from the opponent's right side. He edges his left foot in close to the ball, and pivots on it to bring himself around until he is more or less facing the opponent. He then brings his right foot in to make a front block tackle.

The main points to remember about this tackle are, first, the importance of timing. Seeing you coming, the opponent might put on a burst of speed to take him out of the range of your tackle. So judge the exact moment carefully! Also, get close to your opponent before actually making the tackle. This will help you judge the right moment for your tackle and allow you to get some body weight behind it. If you do not get in close enough, you will be merely stretching out a leg and pushing a foot into the tackle. The tackle will not be firm and will be easily "ridden" by the opponent without disturbing his control of the ball.

THE SLIDING TACKLE

There comes a time, now and again, when an opponent is moving into a position to score, and you just cannot get near enough to use a block tackle. To rob the opponent of the ball on such an occasion you would have to use the sliding tackle (fig. 42).

This is a tackle of a desperate man. You know before you go into it that you are going to end up on the ground, without any hope of controlling the ball. Often, too, you will graze or bruise your skin. This tackle was developed in Europe—mainly in England—where for two-thirds of the soccer season the fields are very wet, soft, and slippery. Under such conditions you can slide into tackles all through the game and the worst that happens is that you get very muddy. On hard, dry fields, however, bare thighs and arms are more readily hurt. What you are trying to do in a sliding tackle is to slide on the knee of the nontackling leg across the front of the opponent in the hope that the foot of the outstretched tackling leg will push the ball away from him. Since most of the outstretched tackling leg is in contact with the ground from start to finish, and since

Fig. 42 Sliding tackle. The tackler has taken the ball right off the foot of the dribbler. He has not secured the ball for himself but he has dispossessed his opponent.

the slide must cover two to four yards, it is easy to understand why hard, dry surfaces present special risks.

Once again, timing is crucial. If the tackler goes in too
early, he will glide across the front of his opponent, who
will then collide with the tackler's upper body. This would
sweep the opponent's legs from under him and cause a
very heavy fall. If the tackler goes in fractionally late, the
sole of the foot, with all his cleats exposed, will go behind
the ball and straight into the opponent's legs, making
contact somewhere around the ankle, or lower shin—and
that is a real leg breaker! Sliding tackles should be left to
really experienced players whose timing is good enough
to ensure that they do not injure their opponents.

TACKLING FROM THE REAR

If you are chasing after an opponent who has the ball and if
there is no one in front or to the side of him to make a
tackle, you might try to tackle him from the rear. Tackling
from the rear is a matter over which there is much difference of opinion. In the English soccer leagues several rear
tackles occur in every match that is played. In some other
countries, referees automatically call foul on any attempt
to tackle from the rear. They do so because they consider
that the mechanics of a rear tackle make it impossible for
the tackler to get a foot into a position where it can contact
the ball without tripping the opponent. In Britain, a different view is taken: if the tackler's foot plays the ball, any
other contact is accidental and therefore not a foul. This
may be so. But some very bad fouls occur in British football
because tackling from the rear is *not* an automatic foul.
Tacklers who have no chance at all of playing the ball
come in from the rear and slam their foot, or both feet, into
the back of the legs of the opponent. They know full well
that there is no chance of playing the ball, but they pretend
that they think there is a chance and that they have only

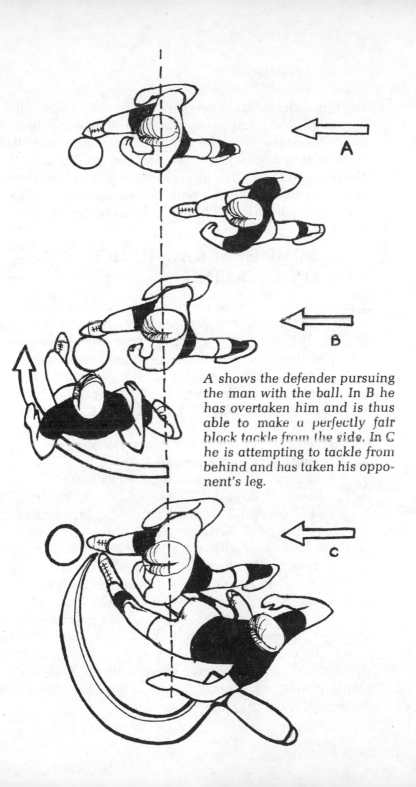

A shows the defender pursuing the man with the ball. In B he has overtaken him and is thus able to make a perfectly fair block tackle from the side. In C he is attempting to tackle from behind and has taken his opponent's leg.

mistimed the tackle. They thus succeed in stopping their opponent, and often in injuring him. It is to be hoped that as soccer develops in the United States this sort of tackle will be very firmly penalized by referees. Tackling from the rear permits the talented player to be stopped by unfair tactics—and there is no point in learning to play well if you can be arbitrarily chopped down by unskilled opponents.

SOME GENERAL ADVICE ON TACKLING

One of the great arts in tackling is knowing *when* to go in and make the tackle. If you could be sure that you would win the ball every time you went into a tackle, you would have nothing to worry about. Opponents, however, as you will have read in the section which deals with "two on one" situations, constantly try to tempt a defender to commit timing errors. When this happens, the attacker, by fooling the defender and taking the ball around him, has taken the defender out of the game. Defenders must learn to prevent this from happening to them.

Attackers will use all sorts of tricks to fool you. They will "show you the ball." This means that when dribbling, an attacker will push the ball a little bit farther from his foot than is normal. Seeing this, you think he's lost control of the ball, when, really, the attacker still has the ball well within reach of his foot. As you come into the tackle he pulls the ball away, leaving you tackling nothing.

Sometimes, players will run at less than top speed while dribbling. You watch, judge, and carefully choose the spot where your foot will meet and capture the ball, and then go into the tackle. As you do so, the attacker will suddenly change pace and move at top speed—or suddenly stop as you come into the tackle. The result is the same—you are left to tackle nothing!

To protect himself the defender (or tackler) should keep several key points in mind.

1. Keep goalside of the attacker. "Goalside" means between the attacker and the goal he is attacking (and which you are defending). If you are between the attacker and the goal, there is not much chance that he will be able to score a goal. If the attacker wants to try to score, he has got to get the ball around you and then beat the goalie with his shot. If you keep goalside of him, forcing him to take the ball outward (toward the touchline), there is not much chance that he will be able to cause danger to your goal. What that attacker would like to do is to pass you by, on the inside (getting between you and the goal with the ball). If he can do that, your goal is in very great danger.

2. Make the attacker go where you want him to go. A good defender, by keeping close (but not too close) to the attacker, and positioning himself correctly, can "shepherd" the attacker into quite harmless positions. If a defender can force an attacker into a position on the field where the latter can neither pass nor threaten the goal, then the defender has won that particular duel without ever attempting to make a tackle.

3. Choose the right moment to make your tackle. Shepherd the attacker—crowd him by getting in close to him. If you crowd him it will worry him and he will probably drop his head to watch the ball (fig. 43) because he dare not let it stray half an inch too far from his foot. If you can make him drop his head and watch the ball you've done one good thing—you've made sure that he will not get a good pass off to a teammate, because he is playing blindly. Now watch his hips and legs. If he is going to try to fool you by changing his pace or direction, that is where you will see the first signs.

4. Try to steal the ball before the attacker gets it fully under control. Many a tackle would not have to be made if

Fig. 43 *The defender, in the lighter sleeves and socks, is defending so closely and aggressively that he has forced the attacker, in the darker socks, to drop his head to watch the ball. The defender has "made the attacker blind."*

the defender did not allow the attacker to get the ball in the first place. When the other team has the ball, the good defender is close to the attacker that he has been told to mark. He is watching to see if someone is going to try to pass the ball to *his* attacker, and if someone does so, he is in there, fast, cutting off the pass before it ever gets to the attacker, or, if he cannot do that, making his tackle while the attacker is still trying to bring the ball under control. It is very, very difficult for any player to trap a ball and avoid a tackle at the same time.

PRACTICE DRILLS FOR TACKLING

Opposed Number Passing

This is exactly the same as Number Passing, which is one of the earliest passing practices, the only difference being that there are two teams with three, four, or five in each. If we call the teams Red and Blue, then Red 1 marks Blue 1, while Red 2 marks Blue 2, and so on. If Reds start with the ball, Red 1 keeps it until Red 2 calls his number. When Red 1 passes to Red 2, Red 3 calls Red 2's number, and so on through the team. However, each of the Reds is marked by his opposite number on the Blue team, so that when Red 2 calls for the ball, Blue 2 knows that he must try to intercept the pass before it gets to Red 2—or tackle him when he has got it. Each marker is keeping close to his man, trying to stop him from receiving a pass, trying to take the ball from him by tackling when he gets it, and generally making life difficult for him. The attackers, on the other hand, are trying to get away from their markers, and are not calling for the ball until they are certain they can safely receive the pass.

This game, which in the early stages should be limited to three players on each team, is great for developing accurate passing—passes delivered with the right "weight" on them, quick, neat ball control, good running off the ball, and sensible calling for the ball. For the defenders it promotes good marking, shepherding, decisive interception of passes, and firm, well-timed tackling.

Goalkeeping

The problem with training to be a good goalkeeper is that your function is unique. While there are ten other players who must practice using their feet, heads, chests, and knees, but not their hands, you alone as a goalie must practice *handling* the ball in all sorts of different situations.

Basically, the goalie is there to defend the goal—to stop the ball going into the goal—and there are three ways that this is done. The ball may be caught, or otherwise smothered; it may be knocked clear of the goal; or, if the goalie is unable to apply any force, it may be deflected off its course. There are, therefore, two important skills that the young goalie must learn and they are handling and positioning. Of the two, positioning is the more important because good handling is a fairly natural skill to most people, while positioning has to be studied and learned. Unless a goalie is in the right position to reach the ball, the best handling in the world will not save a goal. So, let us think first about positioning.

According to the rules of soccer, a goal is twenty-four feet long and eight feet high. For young players this is usually reduced to twenty-one feet by seven feet. If you look at a goal with a goalkeeper standing in the center of it, the area the goalie is unable to cover is much greater than the area that he *can* cover. This is the view that your opponent, who is about to shoot for goal, has of the situation. Even if you allow for the additional area that the goalie can cover by jumping upward or diving sideways, there is still a large area on either side of him that he cannot possibly get to from his central position on the goal line. Thus, the opponent can choose the spot to aim at, knowing in advance that the goalie is probably not going to be able to stop the ball.

This, figure 44, is how a player who is taking a penalty kick sees the goalie in his goal and this is why nearly

Fig. 44

all penalty kicks (taken from a spot twelve yards in front of the goal) result in a scored goal. The goalie, who is forced by the rules to stand still on the goal line until the ball has been kicked, cannot cover enough of the face of the goal to give himself any chance of stopping a well-directed shot. A penalty kick is a free shot at goal. A good kicker will make every penalty kick into a free goal, and so the first lesson the young goalie must learn is not to give the shooter a similar advantage during the normal course of the game. If the shooter is more or less in front of goal, the goalie must move forward, toward him, for perhaps two yards. This immediately "closes up" the goal to the shooter, because the goalie is now covering more of it (fig. 45). The closer the goalie gets to the shooter, the more of the goal he closes off, until he gets to a point where he has almost closed it off altogether (fig. 46).

This does not mean that the goalie must go rushing forward every time it looks as if someone might shoot at goal. The farther out of the goal the goalie moves, the easier it is for a shooter to lob or chip the ball over the goalie's head and into the goal. When, however, an attack on goal is developing, the goalie should be nearer to the six-yard line than to his goal line. By doing this he is closing a large part of the goal off to all the attackers, and is putting himself in the best position to deal with a shot. If a goal looks well defended and closed up by the goalie, the attacker will probably try to make a pass rather than a shot—which is exactly what you want him to do. If, on the other hand, the goalie is on the goal line, the goal looks big and inviting, and the attacker is liable to take a shot. A good goalkeeper will *save* a shot, but a better goalie will, by good position-ing, *prevent the shot from being made!* Remember this: The team that doesn't shoot doesn't score, and the team that doesn't score cannot win.

Exactly the same thing applies when the attacker is somewhere to the side, rather than in front of goal. If you

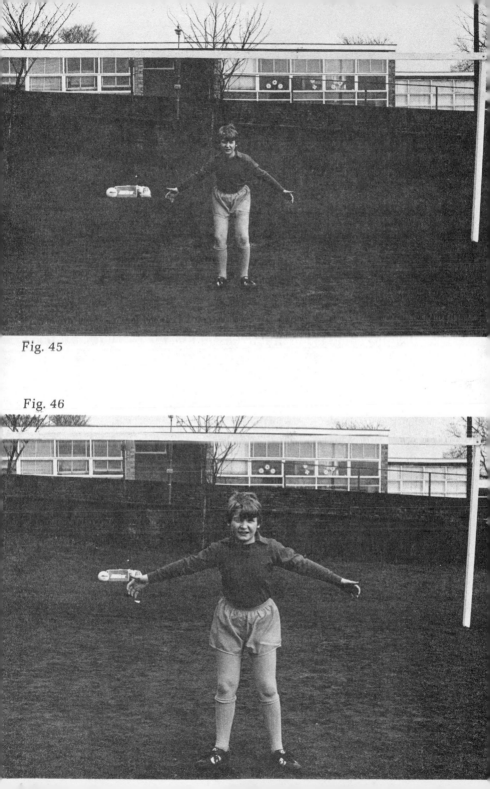

Fig. 45

Fig. 46

get into the wrong position, you give him a big, inviting goal area to shoot at and score in.

If, however, you move to the side of the goal where the shot is coming from, and then move forward toward the shooter, you can completely block out the goal from his sight. There is not much danger that the ball will be lobbed

over the goalie's head from the side, because the angle is too fine. The danger here lies in having the ball pushed across the front of you, in the form of a pass to another attacker who is running in on goal from the other side. By going to one side of your goal you have left the other side completely open. Every goalie should have an understanding with his backs so that whenever the goalie goes across his goal to cover one side, a back will cover the other side of the goal.

When you need to cover the possibility of a shot from the side, move to the near goalpost and then move forward (out of goal), until you cannot quite touch the post with your outstretched hand (fig. 47), and your position will be approximately correct. You would then make minor adjustments in your position depending on where the man with the ball is.

Fig. 47

What you have is a sort of flat arc across the front of the goal, around which the goalie will move when his goal is threatened. He will be constantly placing himself between the ball and his goal, blocking off as much of his goal as possible from the attacker.

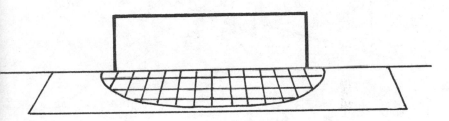

This will put the goalie in the best position to deal with any shots which are fired at his goal. Now and again, however, an attacker will break through the defense and come racing in on the goal with the ball at his feet, and there will be no one to stop him except the goalie. In this situation the goalie knows that there are only two things the attacker can do. He can either try to *shoot* the ball past the goalie into the goal, or he can try to dribble it round the goalie and *push* it into the goal. Whichever the attacker wants to do, the goalie must, at least, make it difficult for him—and in the end try to stop him from doing either. The goalie must come out of his goal and go straight at the attacker, and he must do it quickly. If the goalie comes out first, he forces the attacker to act quickly, and this alone will often force a mistake. As the goalie goes forward toward the attacker, every step he takes blocks off the goal a bit more. Eventually he might close off the goal so completely that the attacker no longer has the choice of shooting or dribbling—he has got to dribble and the goalie knows this. When you know what your opponent is going to do, the situation becomes that much easier to deal with.

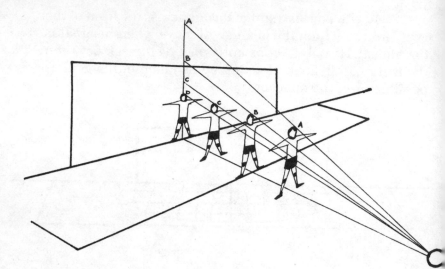

As the goalkeeper moves forward he eventually gets to a point where any ball going over his head will also go over the cross bar. (See Lines A and B) The same applies to either side of him. He gets to a point that any ball passing to the side of him will miss the goal. (See 1 and 2) It should be remembered however that the further out of his goal the goalkeeper comes the more vulnerable he is to the ball which is chipped or lobbed over his head.

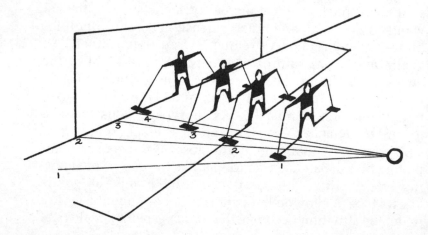

Once you know he is going to try to dribble the ball around you, just throw yourself down on the ball and clutch it to you. This might sound dangerous, but if you go in hard, without hesitating, and try to get your back into the attacker's legs as you go down, you will not come to much harm. Watch the ball as you go in and down to secure it. Pull it into your body as soon as you have got your hands on it (fig. 48).

Fig. 48

The actual handling skills come more naturally than the kicking skills. Most shots will come in at you in one of four ways.

1. Low—along the ground
2. Higher—up to shoulder height
3. Higher still—so that you have to jump to get the ball
4. Out of reach to the side—requiring a diving grasp at the ball

THE LOW SHOT

A ball coming at you along the ground, or close to it, should always be gathered from a kneeling position. In this position (fig. 49) the hands are the first line of defense, but if, by chance, the ball beats the hands, the legs form a

Fig. 49

second line of defense to stop its going past you and into the goal. The goalkeeper drops onto one knee and watches the ball come right into his hands. He allows the ball to come to his hands rather than reaching out and grabbing it, and as soon as he has his hands around the ball he pulls it into his stomach. His whole body forms a curve into which the ball is cradled.

THE HIGHER SHOT

It is always important in goalkeeping to get some part of your body right behind your hands, to act as a second line of defense. When the ball is coming at you at waist, chest, or shoulder height, it is reasonably easy to get your trunk behind your hands and pull the ball into the cradle of the chest and stomach. If the ball is slightly below waist height, the goalie will have to bend his knees enough to allow the ball to come into hands which are held in front of the stomach. If the ball is at chest or shoulder height, the goalie will have to get up onto his toes or even jump in order to clutch the ball in against his stomach. As with the low shot, you should allow the ball to come to your hands, not reach out to catch it with extended arms. Let the ball come into the cradle formed by the chest and stomach and then wrap the hands around it (fig. 50). With the ball firmly cradled in your arms and protected by your body, it is not likely to jump out if an attacker jostles you as you catch it.

DEALING WITH THE HIGH BALL

This is necessary when the ball comes in high—at well over head height. This means that you've got to jump to catch it. It can happen in two ways—first, when a rising shot is coming in and, second, when a high ball is coming across or onto the goal and the goalie must get it before

Fig. 50

someone else does! Whichever way it happens, the technique is the same. Watch the ball, time your jump, and stretch the arms up as far as possible so that you get your hands to the side and back of the ball. The thumbs should be almost touching at the back of the ball. The ball should be caught while it is still in front of the head, and thus well within the field of vision (fig. 51). In other words, the goalie should never lose sight of the ball; he should be able to watch it right into his hands. As soon as he has the ball in his hands he should pull it down to his stomach and cradle it. It is important to pull the ball down quickly because while the arms are extended there is no second line of defense behind the hands. Without this, accidental contact with another player—either while the goalie is up in the air, or as he lands—could cause the goalie to lose the ball.

Sometimes it is wiser not to attempt to catch the high ball, but to either deflect it over the crossbar or to knock it away, usually by punching it. This will occur when the goalie has to jump for a ball with a group of other players, some of whom are attackers. In this situation, although he might get his hands around the ball, he would not be certain of being able to hold it. Also, he doesn't know how he will land—another possible threat to ball control. If the ball is coming in on goal at a considerable speed, he can, by putting one or both hands under the ball, push it upward so that it passes safely over the crossbar. He has given away a corner kick to his opponents, but he has made his goal safe.

If, however, the approaching shot is a dropping ball or one which is coming *across* the goal rather than *in* on goal, then it is very difficult to push the ball over the crossbar. In such cases, the goalie would be better advised to punch the ball away from the immediate danger area in front of his goal. Goalkeepers should try, when punching, to make the contact with the knuckles of both fists together, and to punch right through the center of the ball (fig. 52). If it is impossible to get both hands to the ball, then contact

Fig. 51

Fig. 52

should be made with the knuckles of one hand. Some goalies are able to punch a ball twenty yards or more this way, and that, for a punched ball, is a good clearance. The kind of contact the goalie is able to make with the ball depends largely on how many players are going up together for it, and how well or badly the goalie was placed when he went into his jump. If the goalie is able to jump right underneath the ball, he can choose what he wants to do, because he has the length of his arms as an advantage over all the other players, who are not allowed to touch the ball with their hands (fig. 53). If, however, there are two other players between him and the ball, the goalkeeper will be pleased if he is able to get a good one-handed punch at it. In such circumstances, the goalie will often have to punch with the side of his fist and be content with knocking the ball away sideways, merely to get it away from the immediate danger area in front of his goal. This is a fairly desperate measure because the goalie can neither clear the ball away far enough to give his team time to reorganize their defense before another attack comes in, nor can he be certain where or to whom the ball will go—it might go straight to another attacker who will shoot it back at goal almost before the goalie has got his feet back on the ground! Whatever happens however, it is better than missing it altogether in the most dangerous area of the field— right in front of your own goal!

DIVING FOR THE BALL

It is an old soccer saying that "A good goalie doesn't have to throw himself about; he gets into the right position before the shot is made and can catch the ball with both his feet on the ground." Like a lot of old sayings, there is some truth in this: many of the diving saves seen in soccer matches would not have been necessary if the goalie had been where he should have been when the shot was made.

Fig. 53

But, again, like a lot of old sayings, it is only true up to a point. You can be an expert positioning goalie and still have to make diving saves. What else can you do when you are unsighted and don't see the shot being made—your first sight of the ball might occur when it is on its way toward the corner of your goal! Or when you have positioned yourself perfectly to take a shot, which is then deflected off another player and changes course on its way to goal! The only way to deal with situations like these is to dive for the ball. Of course, goalies are human, too, and a misjudgment or a mistake might also necessitate diving for the ball.

When making a diving save, try to catch the ball while you are in midair; otherwise you have to be satisfied with getting one hand to the ball and keeping it out of the goal by pushing it away. In another kind of diving save the goalie throws himself sideways in order to get down and smother the ball. This is normally more of a falling than a diving action. The goalie knows that he can get to the ball, so, watching it all the time, he pushes himself into a sideways fall, and as he reaches the ground he stretches out and grasps the ball with both hands, pulling it in to his chest and stomach (fig. 54). This is the type of diving save that a goalie would normally choose to make rather than trying to jump sideways and then drop onto one knee to gather the ball—which would take much longer to do. The two important points are, first, to go down on your side rather than on the chest and stomach, and, then, to get your hands behind the ball and pull it into your body quickly. In the true diving save the goalie throws himself sideways through the air to try to catch a ball or to push it sideways to keep it out of the goal (fig. 55). When you have to do this, if you are able you should get your hands around the ball while you are still in the air, and pull it into your chest quickly, so that you have got it firmly against the front of your body when you hit the ground. The impact, as you land, could easily cause the ball to jump out of your hands

Fig. 54

Fig. 55

if they are still outstretched. Try to land on your side because landings on the chest and stomach are painful and likely to knock all the breath out of you—especially if you've pulled the ball in, and then land on it. If you are unable to catch the ball but are able to get a hand to it and push it away, you should—even as you are falling to the ground—watch where it has gone. If it is still in play, bounce up onto your feet as soon as you hit the ground, and be ready, because it will probably be on its way back to goal by then.

In addition to handling practice, goalkeepers should also practice ball distribution. When a goalie gets the ball in his hands, he has ten players on his own team in front of him, and he has to get the ball safely to one of them. He might need to give a short, quick pass to a defender, or he might need to send the ball half the length of the field to an attacker, but whatever he does, it must be done accurately and, when necessary, quickly. The goalie must be able to throw a ball to a teammate, to roll it, or to kick it. Some goalies can throw a ball almost as far as they can kick it, and this is a very useful skill to have, because a throw can be delivered much faster than the types of kick that goalkeepers tend to use, and with much more accuracy over a long distance.

The two types of kick mainly used by goalies are the punt and the placekick. The placekicking technique is described in the "Kicking" chapter.

THE PUNT

This is, historically, the oldest form of kicking in football games of all kinds; it is the only form of kicking which is still used in all forms of football—American, Rugby, Soccer, Australian Rules, Gaelic, and so on. If you've played any football and you can punt a football, you can punt a soccer ball, because the technique is exactly the same.

The ball is held in both hands with the arms extended downward. The head is down watching the ball. As the kicking leg starts to swing forward, the ball is released, and the kicking leg straightens with a fast, powerful action as contact is made with the ball (fig. 56). The head is kept down after the ball has been kicked and a full follow-through of the kicking leg is permitted. Almost anyone can punt a ball a long distance, given a little practice, but it takes a lot of practice to kick the ball over the required distances with the necessary accuracy to ensure that the ball always goes to a teammate, and never to an opponent.

Fig. 56

THE GOAL KICK

It is very important for every goalkeeper to be able to kick a "dead" ball well, because during the course of a game he will have to take several goal kicks: the ball is placed on a spot within the goal area, and from there it is kicked into play. The goalie normally takes these kicks, so it is necessary for him to be able to hit a good long ball from the spot—to the halfway line, or farther—with a fair degree of accuracy. A goal kick should be a long pass to a teammate. We have already dealt with this type of kick in the section that deals with kicking, but, briefly, the nonkicking foot is slightly behind the ball, and the ball is hit with the laces of the boot (the instep) at a point slightly below the midline of the ball, so that the ball will rise. Use a full follow-through with the kicking leg after contact with the ball.

PRACTICE DRILLS
FOR GOALKEEPING

As we have said before, the practice drills which are good for the rest of the team are not really suitable for the goalie. By far the best practice is obtained by having three or four players stand around the edge of the penalty area (or about eighteen–twenty yards from your goal), firing shots at you, one at a time.

At first, it is better for both you and the shooters to pay more attention to *where* the ball is kicked than to how hard. Tell them what sort of ball you want, for instance, "Keep it low and to my right," or, "Put them all in to my left." This will allow you to concentrate on gathering low balls, or to get some jumping and diving practice. You can also ask teammates to throw high balls into goal to allow you to practice catching and turning them over the crossbar. It is, however, almost impossible for your teammates to kick accurately enough to put every ball exactly where you need it to receive the right practice.

Another very useful drill for sharpening your movements and making you more agile requires two or three teammates standing level with the penalty spot. Let them throw (underarm) balls into the goal at various heights and to the left or right of you. As you save each ball, or as it goes over the goal line, the next one is thrown, so that you, in the goal, are on the move all the time, dealing with ball after ball in quick succession.

Do join in the kicking practices with the rest of the team—you need to be a good kicker. Practice placekicking and punting for distance and accuracy. Give yourself a target to aim at—another player (who can kick the ball back to you), or a circle marked on the ground—and try to hit it ten times out of ten.

Another good game to play requires that two of you stand at an equal distance from a center line. One kicks the ball and the other catches it. Having caught it, the second man can then kick it from the place where he caught it. If he fails to catch it, he must kick it from five yards behind the place where the ball hit the ground. What each player is trying to do is to drive the other back until he goes across the end line. A soccer field is ideal for this game.

Glossary of Common Soccer Terms

Back: a player whose role is mainly defensive

Bend (the ball): to kick the ball so that it swerves in flight

Center (the ball): to make a pass from a wide position to the center of the field, near to goal (This is also called "crossing" the ball.)

Clearance: usually a kick, but sometimes a header which sends the ball clear of your own goal area

Corner Kick: When a player plays the ball and it goes out of play over his own goal line, but outside the goal, the other team restarts the game by taking a free kick from the small arc at the corner flag, on whichever side of the goal the ball went over the goal line.

Dead ball: the ball when stationary—as it would be preceding a free kick

Far post: The goalpost farther away from the player with the ball

FIFA: initials of Fédération Internationale de Football Association, the world governing body of soccer

First time: playing the ball as it comes to you without first attempting to control it (This usually refers to passing or shooting at goal.)

Follow-through: when kicking the ball, allowing the kicking leg to continue with the kicking action after contact with the ball has ceased

Forward: a front-line attacking player—a striker or a winger.

Free kick: a dead-ball kick awarded to a team on account of an infringement of the rules by their opponents, who are not permitted to be closer than ten yards from the ball when the kick is taken. A free kick can be direct, which means that a goal may be scored with the kick, or indirect, when a goal may not be scored directly from the kick.

Goal area: sometimes called "the six-yard box" (see plan of pitch)

Goal kick: a dead-ball kick taken from within the goal area to restart play after the attacking team has played the ball over the goal line without scoring a goal (The kick is normally taken by the goalkeeper.)

Goalside: between an attacker and the goal you are defending, or, if you are the attacker, between the defender and his goal

Half: a team's half of the field is the half which contains the goal which that team is defending. The other half of the field is their opponents' half.

Inswinger: a center, or a corner kick executed in a way which bends it inward, toward the goal

Kickoff: a kick from the center spot that either starts a game, or restarts it after a goal or halftime

Lob: a short, high kick, usually made to send the ball over the head of an opponent

Mark (an opponent): to stay close to an opponent when you

are in defense, to try to ensure that he does not get the
ball, or if he does, that he is prevented from doing
anything useful with it

Midfield (player, sometimes called "Link"): a player
whose function can be both defensive and offensive,
but is primarily to set up attacks for his own forwards
and to prevent the other team's midfield from doing
the same for their forwards (The team that controls
the middle of the field should win the match.)

NASL: initials of the North American Soccer League, the
nationwide professional league

Near post: the goalpost nearer to the player with the ball

Offside: a technical type of foul which occurs when a
player who is in his opponents' half of the field has
less than two opponents between him and the goal he
is attacking when a teammate plays the ball

Outswinger (see Inswinger): in this case, the ball bends
outward, away from the goal

Penalty area: the eighteen-yard by forty-four-yard area in
front of the goal (Any foul on the person which is
committed inside this box is punished by the award of
a penalty kick, which may be taken by any member of
the offended team.)

Penalty kick: a direct free kick awarded as a result of a foul
on the person of an attacker inside the penalty area
(The kick is taken from the penalty spot.)

Penalty spot: a spot marked twelve yards in front of the
goal, from which penalty kicks are taken

Return pass: a pass which is made directly back to the
player who originally passed it (This type of pass is
used in the wall pass situation.)

Running off the ball: running without the ball to get into a
position to receive a pass, or to support a teammate, or
to distract your opponents by running as a decoy

Shepherd: to make an attacker go in a specific direction
(This is sometimes called "jockeying.")

Shielding or Screening (the ball): keeping one's body between a defender and the ball to prevent him from making a tackle or other attempt to take the ball away

Square ball: a pass which goes across the field

Stand off: in defense, to refuse to be tempted into a tackle, but rather to keep goalside of the attacker, backing away in front of him, keeping him contained (This is sometimes known as "containing" an attacker.)

Striker: a forward whose main role is to score goals or to act as a target man

Support (a teammate): running close by a teammate who has the ball so that he may pass to you if he wishes (In defense, you support by being near a teammate as he goes into the tackle, in case he is unsuccessful, in which case you will have his man covered.)

Sweeper: a specialist back who operates behind the main line of defense to gather up balls that come through the main line (He "sweeps up" behind the other backs.)

Target man: a striker, normally a big man, at whom long passes, mostly through the air, are directed (The target man is expected to pass the ball off very quickly to a teammate, probably using a header. A mobile target man can make life very difficult for any defense, and other players will score many goals from his passes.)

Through ball: a pass that is hit more or less straight forward, in an attempt to get a ball through the main line of backs, with a striker chasing it

Throw-in: the method of bringing the ball back into play when it has passed over the touchline (A player from the team which did not play the ball over the touchline throws the ball back into the playing area, using a two-handed throw, releasing the ball when it is over his head—figure 57.)

Touchline: see field diagram (p.4)

Unsighted: when a player, particularly a goalie, cannot see

the ball as it is played, or loses sight of it as it travels

Wall: a line of players, positioned ten yards in front of the ball at a free kick to block the goal

Weight (of a pass): the amount of force with which the ball arrives. (The greater the weight on the ball, the more difficult it is to control. Getting the right weight on a pass is almost as important as its accuracy.)

Winger: an attacking player who usually operates near the touchline.

Fig. 57